100 Hikes / Travel Guide

OREGON COAST
& COAST RANGE

THIRD EDITION

William L. Sullivan

Navillus Press

Above: Simpson Cove in Shore Acres State Park (Hike #71).

Below: Harts Cove at Cascade Head (Hike #31).

Published by the Navillus Press   *www.oregonhiking.com*
1958 Onyx Street   ISBN 0981570119
Eugene, Oregon 97403   Printed in USA

Cover: Whaleshead Beach (Hike #90) Inset: Pisaster ochraceus starfish. Spine: North
Head Lighthouse (Hike #3). Back cover: Stout Grove. Page 1: Sunset at Newport with
pelicans. This page: Frankport Beach from Sisters Rocks (Hike #81).

SAFETY CONSIDERATIONS: Many of the trails in this book pass through Wilderness and remote country where hikers are exposed to unavoidable risks. On any
hike, the weather may change suddenly. The fact that a hike is included in this book,
or that it may be rated as easy, does not necessarily mean it will be safe or easy for
you. Prepare yourself with proper equipment and outdoor skills, and you will be
able to enjoy these hikes with confidence.
Every effort has been made to insure the accuracy of the information in this book. The
author has hiked all 100 of the featured trails, and the trails' administrative agencies
have reviewed the maps and text. The book is updated every year. Nonetheless, construction, logging, and storm damage may cause changes. Corrections and updates are
welcome, and often rewarded. They may be sent to the publisher or *sullivan@efn.org.*

Easy Moderate Difficult

Contents

Great for kids Open all year Backpackable

🌼 - Oregon Coast Trail segment   🚲 - Bicycles OK   🐎 - Horses OK
🌼 - Wildflowers (count petals for peak month)   🐕 - Dogs on leash   🚫 - No pets
*Parking fee   C - Crowded or restricted backpacking area   🚙 - Rough access road

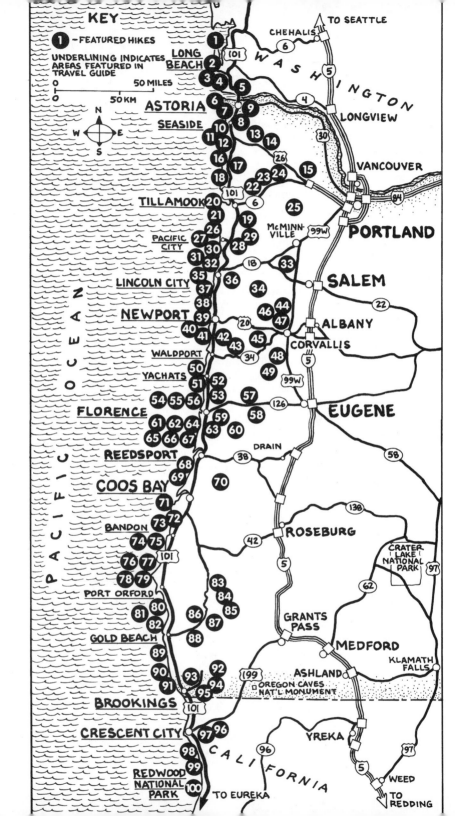

KEY

1 – FEATURED HIKES

UNDERLINING INDICATES AREAS FEATURED IN TRAVEL GUIDE

0 — 50 MILES
0 — 50 KM

N
W — E
S

PACIFIC OCEAN

TO SEATTLE

CHEHALIS
6

WASHINGTON
101
5

LONGVIEW
4
30

VANCOUVER
84

LONG BEACH

ASTORIA

SEASIDE

TILLAMOOK

PACIFIC CITY

LINCOLN CITY

NEWPORT

WALDPORT

YACHATS

FLORENCE

REEDSPORT

COOS BAY

BANDON

PORT ORFORD

GOLD BEACH

BROOKINGS

CRESCENT CITY

REDWOOD NATIONAL PARK

McMINN-VILLE
99W

PORTLAND

SALEM
22

ALBANY

CORVALLIS
5
99W

EUGENE
58

DRAIN
38

ROSEBURG
42
138

CRATER LAKE NATIONAL PARK
97

GRANTS PASS
62

MEDFORD

KLAMATH FALLS

ASHLAND
199

OREGON CAVES NAT'L MONUMENT

YREKA
96

CALIFORNIA

TO EUREKA

WEED

TO REDDING
97
5

⊛ - Oregon Coast Trail segment   bike - Bicycles OK   horse - Horses OK
wildflower - Wildflowers (count petals for peak month)   dog - Dogs on leash   no pets - No pets
*Parking fee   C - Crowded or restricted backpacking area   rough road - Rough access road

⊛ - Oregon Coast Trail segment   ☏ - Bicycles OK   🐴 - Horses OK
✿ - Wildflowers (count petals for peak month)   🐕- Dogs on leash   🐕- No pets
*Parking fee   C - Crowded or restricted backpacking area   🚗- Rough access road

Introduction

Welcome to the Oregon Coast—363 miles of cliff-edged capes, public beaches, wild rivers, sand dunes, rainforest, and coastal mountains. Many of the top attractions are within easy reach of Highway 101, but others are accessible only by trail. To help you explore both the civilized and the wild parts of Oregon's spectacular shore, this book blends two kinds of guides—a detailed **Travel Guide** for touring by car and a complete **Trail Guide** for planning adventures on foot.

HOW TO USE THIS BOOK

The Travel Guide

The book is divided into 18 sections, from Washington's Long Beach in the north to California's Redwood National Park in the south. Each section begins with a Travel Guide that includes an overview map and a description of the area's car-accessible attractions. Both the map and the text are annotated with symbols (described below), identifying campgrounds, lighthouses, museums, and other popular destinations. Here too are tips for bicycling, birdwatching, kayaking, canoeing, and horseback riding.

The overview maps show major Highway 101 mileposts, so it's easy to use the Travel Guide as a highway logbook. As you drive from one area to the next, simply flip forward or backward through the book to the next Travel Guide map.

The Trail Guide

Following each Travel Guide section are descriptions of that area's hiking trails. To help you choose a hike, symbols in the upper right-hand corner of each hike's heading identify trail features. For example, 67 of the hikes have symbols recommending them as best trails for hikers with children.

A hike's difficulty is rated in the boldface listing at the start of each entry. **Easy** hikes are generally less than 3 miles round trip and gain less than 500 feet of elevation. These short hikes usually only require a couple of hours to complete.

Trips rated as **Moderate** range from about 3 to 5 miles round trip and may gain 1000 feet of elevation. Some moderate hikes require a bit of route-finding —for example, following posts through sand dunes.

Difficult hikes vary from 4 to 8 miles round trip and may gain 2000 feet of elevation. Hikers need to be in good condition and will need to take several

---

KEY TO SYMBOLS:

🐾 Good hike with kids	❶ Featured hike	📖 Viewpoint
🐾 Backpacking	♿ Barrier-free trail (pp244-6)	🦜 Birdwatching
🧗 Crowded backpacking	⑩ Other trail (see pp247-250)	☆ Tidepooling
❄ Closed in winter	🌲 Old-growth forest	🛶 Canoeing/kayaking
🐴 Horses permitted	🗼 Lighthouse	🚤 Boat ramp
🚲 Bicycles permitted	🏔 Picnic Area	🏕 Campground
	🏛 Information center	🏛 Museum

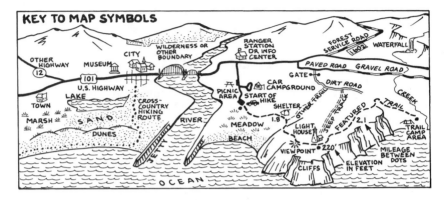

rest stops. **Very Difficult** hikes demand top physical condition, with a strong heart and strong knees. These challenging hikes are 8 to 15 miles round trip and may gain 3000 feet or more. Backpackers can break these hikes into easier two- or three-day trips.

In general, the trails of Oregon's Coast and Coast Range are less demanding than trails in more mountainous parts of the state. As a result, this book uses a slightly easier rating scale than other volumes of the Oregon 100 Hikes series.

Distances are given in round-trip mileage, except for those trails where a car shuttle is recommended. Then the hike's mileage is listed as one way only.

Elevation gains tell much about the difficulty of a hike. Those who puff climbing a few flights of stairs may consider even 500 feet of elevation a strenuous climb, and should watch this listing carefully. Note that the figures are for each hike's *cumulative* elevation gain, adding all the uphill portions, even those on the return trip.

Only a few trails are **closed seasonally** by snow or to protect wildlife. Identified by a snowflake symbol, these hikes include a boldface listing with the approximate dates the trail remains open. Note, however, that winter storms may temporarily close any of the trails in this book, or may cause icy or muddy conditions that make trails unsafe even when they are technically open. Hikers must rely on their own caution and good judgment.

TIPS FOR TRAVELERS

Climate

Marine air keeps Oregon's coastal climate mild, with generally snowless winters and cool summers. Summertime visitors are often puzzled to find a strip of **fog** hugging the beach while skies are sunny just a few miles inland. As a rule, expect fog on the Coast when high temperatures in Portland and Eugene hit the 90s. One way to avoid the problem is to visit the beach in spring or fall. The crowds are thinner then and there are a surprising number of warm, sunny days — especially in March, April, and May.

Summers also bring **north winds**, which is why cagey hikers and bicyclists trek from north to south, keeping the wind at their backs. Even if you're just planning a picnic on the beach, it's often wise to choose a spot on the south side of a headland's cliff, where you'll be sheltered from the north wind. In summer, north winds generally bring good weather while south winds presage a storm.

Winters are less predictable. Storms come from all angles, pounding 20- and 30-foot waves against the shore. Snow is truly rare, but much of the Coast's 60 to 100 inches of annual rainfall hit in winter — at times, almost horizontally. High surf strips the beaches of most of their sand. The sand is then washed offshore by wave action and returned neatly in the spring like a batch of fresh laundry. Despite winter's wet and wild ways, the season has its charms. Beachcombing and wave watching, for example, are at their peak after a winter storm.

Beach Rules

Oregon's 260 miles of beaches are entirely open to the public. Visitors should keep in mind a number of rules, some of which are simply good advice:

- Never turn your back on the ocean. Unusually large "sneaker waves" can sweep up the beach at any time.
- Don't swim. The Alaska Current chills the water year-round to a numbing, goosebump-and-blue-fingernail temperature. The more serious hazard, however, is the undertow — the pull of withdrawing waves. Only wade on shallow beaches, and then only if the tide is coming in. Never wade on the north side of headlands, where the southbound current is deflected to sea.
- Pick up a free tide table at a visitor center or check *www.saltwatertides.com*. Oregon's share of the Pacific Ocean rises and falls about 8 feet twice a day, so high and low tides are about 6 hours apart.

Several other beach rules have the force of law:

- Fires are banned in driftwood piles or against large logs.
- Climbing on most offshore rocks is banned to protect sea birds.
- Harassing seals, sea lions, and other marine mammals is forbidden. Do not approach a cute, "abandoned" seal pup. It is resting while its mother hunts for food, and human contact may simply scare the mother away.
- Collecting tidepool life is banned in most places, even for educational or food purposes. Do not pry starfish or other living animals from the rocks. Do not poke sea anemones or walk on top of living mussel beds. Do not leave rocks overturned, because the animals on both the top and the bottom are adapted to their positions and will die if left in a new habitat.
- Cars are banned on 67% of the state's beaches and are restricted seasonally on another 7%. Where driving is allowed, the speed limit is 30 miles per hour and all the usual highway regulations apply.
- Shooting firearms on the beach is illegal.

Campgrounds on the Oregon Coast

More than 70 public campgrounds along the Coast and in the Coast Range make camping an attractive option. In general, the 19 state park campgrounds here are somewhat larger, more popular, and more expensive, but they offer hot showers when other public camps generally do not. Some of the smaller public campgrounds do not even have running water, and in this case are usually free. While most coastal county parks are also fairly primitive, three exceptions are not only large but have hot showers: Barview (north of Tillamook), Windy Cove (at Winchester Bay, south of Reedsport), and Bastendorff Beach (west of Coos Bay). All three are near major river mouths.

Virtually all Forest Service, county, BLM, and state forest campgrounds are open only in summer. By contrast, state park campgrounds stay open from April through October, and a few stay **open year-round** (Fort Stevens, Nehalem Bay, Cape Lookout, Devils Lake, South Beach, Beverly Beach, Washburne, Honeyman, Tugman, Umpqua Lighthouse, Sunset Bay, Bullards Beach, Cape Blanco, Humbug, Harris Beach, and Loeb). At 14 of these state parks, tenters can escape rain by renting a yurt, a circular, framed tent with a wooden floor and bunks.

State park **campsite reservations** for the summer season from the Memorial Day weekend to the Labor Day weekend are accepted for fourteen of the most popular parks (Cape Disappointment, Fort Stevens, Cape Lookout, Nehalem Bay, Devils Lake, Beverly Beach, South Beach, Beachside, Honeyman, Tugman, Umpqua Lighthouse, Sunset Bay, Bullards Beach, and Harris Beach). To place a state park reservation, call 800-452-5687 during business hours (or go to *www. reserveamerica.com*) at least two days in advance, but not more than 9 months in advance. Expect a nonrefundable $8 service charge in addition to the campsite fee (about $13-21 for a tent, $22 for a full RV hook-up, and $36-41 for a yurt). For instant confirmation, pay by VISA or Mastercard. When paying by check, book at least 21 days in advance.

The Coast's many private campgrounds cater primarily to RVs and typically offer less secluded sites. However, private campgrounds provide hot showers and other services.

Bicycling the Oregon Coast
The 367-mile Oregon Coast Bike Route from the Washington border to California is one of the most scenic bicycling tours anywhere. Although most of the route follows Highway 101, where car and truck traffic is a serious distraction, the highway shoulder has been widened to 3 feet in most places. Detours on backroads avoid six of the least scenic parts of Highway 101. The route is not flat, gaining a cumulative total of 16,000 feet—mostly in climbs across coastal headlands. Bicyclists typically complete the tour in 6 to 8 days. Virtually all pedalers travel from north to south, both to catch the prevailing north winds of summer and to see the much better views on the ocean side of the road.

Hiker/biker campsites are available at major state parks (Fort Stevens, Nehalem Bay, Cape Lookout, Devils Lake, Beverly Beach, South Beach, Washburne, Honeyman, Tugman, Sunset Bay, Bullards Beach, Cape Blanco, Humbug Mountain, and Harris Beach). For about $6 a night, these grassy, shared areas are a great way to meet other non-motorized travelers and get hot showers. For a free Oregon Coast Bike Route map with touring tips, contact the Oregon Department of Transportation, Transportation Building, Salem, OR 97310 *(www.oregon.gov/ODOT/HWY/ BIKEPED/docs/)*, or call 503-986-3556.

TIPS FOR HIKERS

Safety on the Trail
Hikers on the Oregon Coast are rarely more than an hour's walk from civilization. On these trails you're more likely to worry about running out of camera memory than running into wilderness hazards. In fact, the biggest danger is leaving the trail to explore coastal cliffs. Each year slippery rocks and unpredictable waves claim an amateur rock scrambler or two.

Drinking Water. Day hikers should bring all the water they will need—roughly a quart per person. A microscopic parasite, *Giardia*, has forever changed the old

Cabins at L. L. "Stub" Stewart State Park (Hike #15).

custom of dipping a drink from every brook. The symptoms of "beaver fever," debilitating nausea and diarrhea, commence a week or two after ingesting *Giardia*. If you're backpacking, bring an approved water filtration pump or boil your water 5 minutes.

Proper Equipment. Even on the tamest hike a surprise storm or a wrong turn can suddenly make the gear you carry very important. Bring a pack with the ten essentials: a warm, water-repellent coat, drinking water, extra food, a knife, sun screen, a fire starter, a first aid kit, a flashlight, a map, and a compass.

Parking Permits

Hikers should expect to pay a day-use parking fee of $5 per car at about a third of the featured trails in this book, including every trail in the Oregon Dunes National Recreation Area (Hikes#62-67 and 69). Details are in the text or at the trailhead. Two different types of one-year passes are available for $35 per car. The Oregon Coast Passport is valid at most coastal trailheads. The Recreation Fee Pass is valid at national forests and BLM sites nationwide.

Rules on the Trail

As our trails become more heavily used, rules of trail etiquette become stricter. Please pick no flowers, leave no litter, and do not shortcut switchbacks.

For backpackers, low-impact camping was once merely a courtesy, but is on the verge of becoming a requirement, both to protect the landscape and to preserve a sense of solitude for others. The most important rules:

- Camp out of sight of trails, at least 100 feet from lakes or streams.
- Build no campfire. Cook on a backpacking stove.
- Wash 100 feet from any lake or stream.
- Camp on duff, rock, or sand—never on meadow vegetation.
- Pack out garbage—don't burn or bury it.

Seven of the featured hikes pass through designated Wilderness Areas. Additional restrictions apply only to these areas, with violations subject to fines:

Blacklock Point (Hike #77).

- Mechanized equipment (including bicycles) is prohibited.
- Groups in Wilderness Areas must be no larger than 12.

The Oregon Coast Trail

The Coast's ultimate hiking challenge, the Oregon Coast Trail (OCT) follows beaches, trails, and highways for over 360 miles from the Washington border to California. Construction of this ambitious route began in 1972, but large gaps remain. Only about 75 miles of the route consist of actual trail. Another 200 miles of the OCT simply follow public beaches. About 85 miles still follow the shoulder of Highway 101 and other roads.

To plan a trip on the OCT, look in the table of contents for symbols marking hikes that follow completed portions of the route. Then flip to the specific hike descriptions, where you'll find ⊛ OCT symbols in the margin highlighting instructions for through hikers.

Many long-range OCT hikers simply stop for the night in motels. Others tent in campgrounds. Camping on the beach itself is banned in state parks and within most city limits, but it's an acceptable option elsewhere, as long as you pitch your tent out of sight of houses, and well above the flotsam that marks the night's high tide limit. Bring a good pad, because sand is rock hard.

Free OCT maps showing the entire 360-mile route in ten sections can be downloaded from *www.oregon.gov/oprd/parks*, or you can get them from the Oregon Parks and Recreation Department, 725 Summer St. NE, Suite C, Salem, OR 97301.

FOR MORE INFORMATION

Visitor Bureaus

Many of the best things to do and see on the Oregon Coast are free — or nearly free — so this book focuses on noncommercial tourist destinations. Local visitor bureaus are glad to provide information about restaurants, motels, and commercial attractions. Here are the telephone numbers and websites for this free service.

Astoria — 800-875-6807, *www.oldoregon.com*
Bandon — 541-347-9616, *www.bandon.com*
Brookings — 800-535-9469, *www.brookingsharborchamber.com*
Cannon Beach — 503-436-2623, *www.cannonbeach.org*
Coos Bay — 800-824-8486, *www.oregonsbayarea.org*
Crescent City — 800-343-8300, *http://exploredelnorte.com*
Depoe Bay — 877-485-8348, *www.depoebaychamber.org*
Florence — 541-997-3128, *www.florencechamber.com*
Garibaldi — 503-322-0301, *www.visitgaribaldi.com*
Gold Beach — 541-247-0923, *www.goldbeachchamber.com*
Lincoln City — 541-994-3070, *www.lcchamber.com*
Long Beach — 800-451-2542, *http://funbeach.com*
Nehalem Bay — 503-812-5510, *visittheoregoncoast.com/cities/nehalem*
Newport — 800-262-7844, *www.newportchamber.org*
Pacific City — 503-392-4340, *http://pacificcity.org*
Port Orford — 541-332-8055, *www.portorfordoregon.com*
Reedsport — 800-247-2155, *www.el.com/to/reedsport*
Rockaway Beach — 503-355-8108, *www.rockawaybeach.net*
Seaside — 503-738-6391, *www.seasidechamber.com*
Tillamook — 503-842-7525, *www.gotillamook.org*
Waldport — 541-563-2133, *www.waldport-chamber.com*
Yachats — 800-929-0477, *www.yachats.org*

Trail Management Agencies

If you'd like to check trail conditions, call directly to the trails' administrative agencies, listed below along with the hikes for which they manage trails.

Hike	Managing Agency
9	Astoria Parks — 800-875-6807
45	Benton County Parks — 541-766-6871
42, 43, 51, 52	Central Coast District/Waldport — 541-563-8400
76, 77	Coos Bay District BLM — 541-756-0100
58	Eugene District BLM — 541-683-6600
33, 48	Finley Wildlife Refuge — 541-757-7236
85-88, 92-95	Gold Beach Ranger District — 541-247-3600
28, 29, 31, 32, 36	Hebo Ranger District — 503-392-5100
8	Lewis & Clark Nat'l Historic Park — 503-861-2471
32	The Nature Conservancy — 503-802-8100
62-67, 69	Oregon Dunes Nat'l Rec Area — 541-271-6000
6-8, 10-13, 16-21, 26, 27, 30-32, 35, 37, 38, 40, 41, 50, 53, 54, 61, 68, 70, 72-75, 77-82, 89-91, 93	Oregon State Parks — 800-551-6949
46-47	Oregon State College Forests — 541-737-4452
83-84	Powers Ranger District — 541-439-6200
96-100	Redwood Parks — 707-465-7335
34, 39, 49	Salem District BLM — 503-375-5646
44, 54-57, 59, 60	Siuslaw National Forest — 541-750-7000
71	South Slough Estuarine Reserve — 541-888-5558
14, 22-24	Tillamook State Forest — 503-842-2545
25	Washington County Parks — 503-846-8715
1-5	Washington State Parks — 360-902-8844

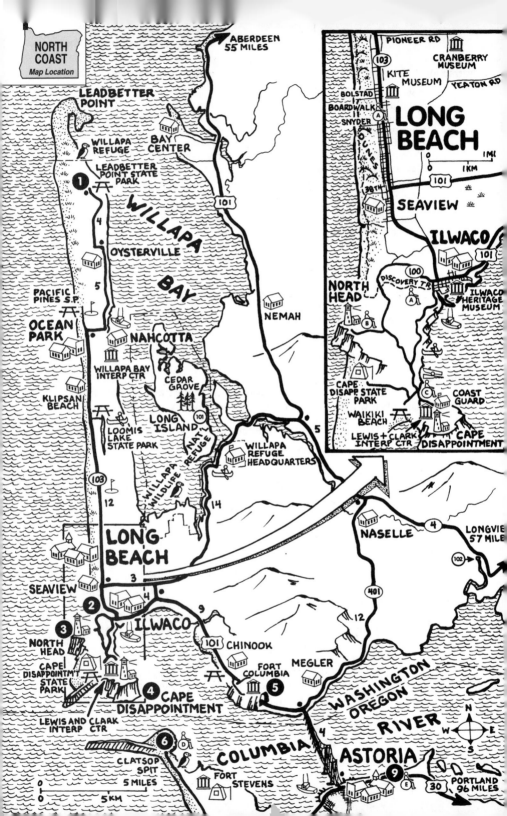

Poster from the early 1900s promoting the Long Beach area.

LONG BEACH

One of the world's longest beaches lines this southern Washington peninsula. The 28-mile beach backed with low, grassy dunes has drawn summer visitors since the 1880s. But the beach is just one of the area's charms. Inland is vast Willapa Bay, teeming with bird life. To the south is Cape Disappointment, with two scenic lighthouses. And the peninsula is dotted with quaint villages of Victorian vintage.

Boardwalk

The city of **Long Beach** bustles with a carnival atmosphere in summer. The best place to see and be seen is on the **Boardwalk**, a 0.4-mile promenade along the grassy beachfront dunes (see Hike #2). The beach itself is tops for kite-flying, volleyball, and sand castling. Cars are allowed on most of the area beaches (with a 25 mph limit), but are banned April 15 to Labor Day from the Boardwalk south to the 38th Street beach access in Seaview and north of Surfside Estates for 2.7 miles.

The entire town turns out for the week-long **International Kite Festival** in August. If you miss it, stop by the **World Kite Museum** at 303 Snyder Drive to see some prize winners. Open 11-5 daily in summer (otherwise 11-5 Friday-Tuesday), the museum charges $5 for adults, $4 for seniors, and $3 for kids.

Cape Disappointment State Park

At the mouth of the Columbia River, Fort Canby's erstwhile artillery base is now part of the Lewis and Clark National and State Historical Park. Short trails lead to picturesque lighthouses on the headlands at North Head (Hike #3) and Cape Disappointment (Hike #4). The year-round campground has 220 sites, 3 cabins, and 14 yurts (reservations: *www.parks.wa.gov* or 888-226-7688). For a picnic, try Waikiki Beach, set in a scenic cove beside Cape Disappointment's cliffs. Or drive 1.5 miles past the picnic area to the North Jetty to watch waves roll through the Columbia River bar.

Lewis and Clark Interpretive Center

Also at Cape Disappointment, this museum is perched atop the bluff where Lewis and Clark planted a flag by the Pacific Ocean. Exhibits feature the explorers, as well as the history of Cape Disappointment's lighthouse, artillery bunkers, and

Coast Guard station. Admission ($5 for adults, $2.50 for kids age 7-17) includes a 10-minute movie. Open daily in summer 10-5 (winters Wed-Sun 10-5).

Ilwaco

This fishing village is rich with history, boasting Victorian houses and historic murals on downtown buildings. The **Columbia Pacific Heritage Museum**, a block off Highway 101 on 115 Lake Street SE, features displays of Native American culture, a pioneer village complete with trading post, and a restored railway depot housing a 50-foot model of the Long Beach peninsula's "Clamshell Railroad" as it looked in 1920. Winter hours are Tue-Sat 10-4 and Sun 12-4; summer hours are Tue-Sat 9-5 and Sun 12-4. Admission is $5 for adults, but Thursdays are free. Other top attractions in town include a **waterfront promenade** with shops and restaurants, and the **Discovery Trail** (see Hike #2).

Nahcotta and Oysterville

Discovery of rich oyster beds in Willapa Bay made **Oysterville** a boomtown in 1854 and county seat from 1855 to 1893. Today the community is on the National Register of Historic Places, with a schoolhouse, cemetery, and restored church worth a visit. The Long Beach peninsula's "Clamshell Railroad" never reached Oysterville, instead stopping at Nahcotta, 4 miles to the south. **Nahcotta** is a livelier burg, and a good place to buy oysters or stroll the harbor's dock. A replica oysterhouse on Nahcotta's bayfront houses the **Willapa Bay Interpretive Center,** with exhibits of the bay's historic oyster industry, open 10-4 Fri-Sun from Memorial Day through Labor Day. Admission is free.

Pacific Coast Cranberry Research Museum

By a cranberry bog, this museum features the history, machinery, and products of the local cranberry industry. At the north end of Long Beach turn right on Pioneer Road. Open daily 10-5 from April 1 to December 15 and by appointment.

Fort Columbia State Park

This restored 1896 fort overlooking the Columbia River includes a museum, artillery bunkers, trails (see Hike #5), and two rentable historic buildings. The interpretive center in the former barracks (open 11-4 daily from July 1 through early September) features exhibits on the area's early exploration, coastal artillery, and Chinook tribal culture. To rent the two-bedroom Steward's House ($143-191) or the four-bedroom Scarborough House ($233-311) call 888-226-7688 or check *https://washington.goingtocamp.com.*

Willapa National Wildlife Refuge

The huge estuaries of Willapa Bay draw thousands of geese, ducks, and shorebirds during the fall and spring migrations. The refuge protects several areas of the bay, open to hikers and birdwatchers. The Leadbetter Point area is described in Hike #1. Long Island, with its old-growth cedar grove, is accessible only by boat; launch at the refuge headquarters on Highway 101. The freshwater marshes at the southern end of the bay have some of the best birding. Parking areas are located at the end of Yeaton Road (east from Long Beach) and Jeldness Road (off Highway 101, 6 miles south of the refuge headquarters). Unleashed dogs are banned, hunting and clamming are restricted, and camping and fires are only permitted in five primitive campgrounds on Long Island.

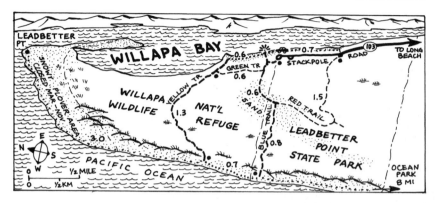

1   Leadbetter Point

Easy
4-mile loop
No elevation gain

Right: Willapa Bay Viewpoint

Most visitors to this park near the sandy tip of the Long Beach Peninsula simply take the shortest possible path to the ocean beach. It's true that the beach is a gem, so quiet that you can usually find unbroken sand dollars, but if you hike there on a slightly longer loop through the Willapa Wildlife Refuge you'll also see the vast tidal mudflats of Willapa Bay and have a better chance at spotting some of the refuge's 202 bird species.

The trails are open all year, but from October to May (when the birding is best) you'll need rubber boots to wade the puddles that block both paths to the beach. Camping, fires, and unleashed dogs are not allowed in the refuge.

To find the park from Long Beach, drive 12 miles north on Highway 103 to Ocean Park. Turn right at a blinking red light and follow "Highway 103 North" signs for 9 more miles, zigzagging through Nahcotta and Oysterville to the end of Stackpole Road. Expect to pay $10 to park if you don't have a Discover Pass.

The trail forks 30 yards beyond the parking area. The left path heads directly for the ocean, but if you're interested in the slightly longer loop, keep right instead, following yellow trail markers. This path leads 100 yards to a viewpoint deck at Willapa Bay's beach. Turn left along the sandy shore 0.4 mile to a signpost marking the resumption of the trail. Then keep straight for more than a mile, following the trail across the peninsula through shore pine woods to a broad, windswept ocean beach. Walk left along this beach 0.7 mile until you spot a trail signpost atop the grassy foredune. Head inland here on a 1.4-mile path to complete the loop back to the north parking lot.

2   Long Beach

Easy (3 short hikes)
2.8 miles round trip
No elevation gain

Moderate (from Ilwaco to beach)
4.4 miles round trip
200 feet elevation gain

Difficult (entire trail, with shuttle)
7.2 miles one way
100 feet elevation gain

William Clark of the Lewis and Clark expedition hiked north along the shore of Long Beach on November 19, 1805. Before turning back, he carved his name on a tree to claim the territory for the United States.

Today the community of Long Beach is a strip of tourist shops and vacation homes, but a 7.2-mile path follows Clark's route through a quiet landscape of forests and dunes. The wide, mostly paved Discovery Trail is popular with beachcombers, strollers, and families on bicycles.

If you're short on time, sample the route with three short walks at beach access points. For a longer sample, hike from the harbor village of Ilwaco to a scenic ocean cove at Beards Hollow.

To drive here from Astoria, take the Columbia River bridge and follow Highway 101 west 11 miles to Ilwaco. (To pronounce this town's name like a local, rhyme it with *taco*.) Where Highway 101 turns right at Ilwaco's traffic light, go straight on Highway 100 toward Cape Disappointment. After 1.9 miles, turn right at a sign for Beards Hollow. Expect to pay $10 to park if you don't have a Discover Pass.

From the far end of the parking area, take the paved path straight ahead 0.5 mile through an alder forest to the beach. When Clark visited in 1805, the ocean extended all the way to what is now the parking lot. Beards Hollow won its name in 1853 when the body of Captain Edward Beard washed ashore in this cove after his ship, the *Vendalia,* had wrecked nearby. Construction of the Columbia River jetties made shipping safer but also sanded in the cove, which has become a marsh and a forest. When you reach the sandy beachgrass of the current shore

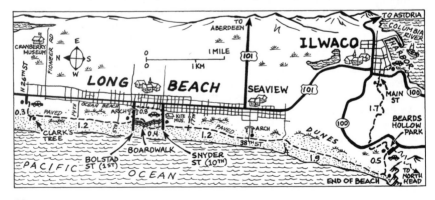

The boardwalk and paved Discovery Trail at Long Beach.   Opposite: Beards Hollow.

the Discovery Trail turns sharply right. For a short walk leave the paved path here, walk straight through the sand to the beach, and stroll left a few hundred yards to the base of North Head's basalt cliff. At all but high tide you can skirt the cliff to a hidden beach protected from the wind.

For the second of the three short hikes, drive back to Ilwaco's traffic light, turn left on Highway 101, and continue straight 3 miles to Long Beach. At a traffic light between 9th and 11th Streets, turn left on Sid Snyder Drive for 0.4 mile.

Park in a gravel lot just before the beach and hike north (to the right) on a large, raised boardwalk through the dunes. If you're bicycling, take the paved Discovery Trail beside the boardwalk.

When the boardwalk ends after 0.4 mile you could simply return the way you came. To make a loop through town, however, turn right on a sidewalk along Bolstad Avenue. After 0.2 mile turn right on Ocean Beach Boulevard for 9 blocks back to Snyder Drive and your car.

For the third short walk, drive the main highway another 1.4 miles north through Long Beach, turn left on 26th Street for two blocks, and hike the paved Discovery Trail 0.3 mile through the dunes to the Clarks Tree Monument. Although the location and design of Clark's original tree carving are unknown, this bronze tree statue overlooking the beach captures the spirit of that day in 1805.

If you'd prefer a more substantial hike on the Discovery Trail, start in Ilwaco. Turn off Highway 101 in downtown, drive three blocks south and park near the harbor. Here you can stroll a waterfront walkway to look at shops and boats.

Then walk two blocks inland to Main Street and turn left. Follow the street a few blocks up to its end at a private driveway and veer right on the Discovery Trail. The wide path is gravel here, but paving is planned. You'll cross a board-walk, skirt a swamp, cross a paved road at the 1.3-mile mark, and then descend to another boardwalk at the Beards Hollow parking lot. Turn right on the paved path half a mile to the beach. This makes a good turnaround point if you decide you don't need to retrace Clark's entire route north through the oceanfront dunes of Long Beach.

The North Head lighthouse.   *Below: The rentable lighthouse keeper's residence.*

3 North Head

Easy (to North Head)
0.6-mile loop
30 feet elevation gain

Moderate (from Beards Hollow)
2.6 miles round trip
400 feet elevation gain

Difficult (to McKenzie Head)
6.4 miles round trip
800 feet elevation gain

Three trails connect near the picturesque lighthouse atop the surf-pounded cliffs of North Head. For a quick visit, take the 0.6-mile loop to the lighthouse itself. If you have more time, start instead at Beards Hollow and hike to the lighthouse through the headland's ancient spruce forest. If you're still going strong, continue 1.7 miles to the historic artillery bunker at McKenzie Head.

From Astoria, take the bridge to Washington and follow Highway 101 west 11 miles to Ilwaco. At the stoplight in the center of town continue straight toward Cape Disappointment on Loop 100. After 2.3 miles turn right on North Head Lighthouse Road for 0.5 mile. At the sign "Park Hours 6:30am to Dusk" pull into a gravel lot on the left. If you don't have a Discover Pass, expect to pay $10 to park.

The lighthouse trail is the leftmost road, closed by a post. This path soon emerges from spruce woods to a headland meadow of big white cow parsnip blooms, pink wild roses, curly wild cucumber vines, and blue salal berries. At the lighthouse itself, views extend from the Columbia River jetties to Long Beach. Volunteers offer tours of the tower for a $2.50 donation from 10am-4pm in summer, and occasionally in winter. Kids are free, but are not allowed below age 7. The tower was built in 1898 when the nearby Cape Disappointment lighthouse proved insufficient to prevent a rash of shipwrecks near the Columbia River mouth. Since 1937 the

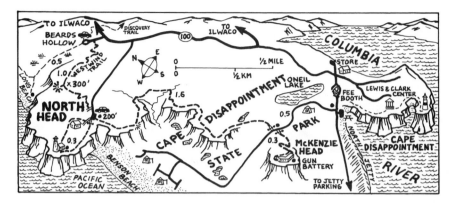

tower's light comes from an electric beacon. Mounted 192 feet above sea level, the light is visible 16 miles to sea.

To return on a loop, look behind the lighthouse outbuildings to find the Light Keeper's Trail, a concrete walkway to the house where the keeper once lived. These days the quaint three-bedroom house has been restored as a vacation rental. Expect to pay over $800 for a summer weekend, or a bit less to stay in a neighboring duplex. For reservations call 888-226-7688 or check *https://washington.goingtocamp.com.*

For a more substantial hike at North Head, start instead at Beards Hollow. To find it from the stoplight in Ilwaco, drive straight on Highway 100 toward Cape Disappointment 1.9 miles and turn right to a parking area. Look for a "Westwind Trail" sign on the left, before the restrooms. This path switchbacks uphill amid Sitka spruces 6 feet in diameter with gangly, wind-twisted limbs.

After a mile the Westwind Trail descends to the North Head parking area. Of course you can detour 0.3 mile over to the lighthouse at this point, but if you're going strong, you might also want to continue onward to McKenzie Head. On the left side of the parking area, look for a brown hiker-symbol sign beside a set of wooden steps leading downhill. Follow this path across a meadow and into another stand of ancient Sitka spruce. Soon you'll reach a clifftop viewpoint overlooking the state park campground on the forested plain below. Incredibly, the entire plain did not exist in Lewis and Clark's day. Their 1805 sketches show the ocean extending all the way to this cliff. Construction of the Columbia River North Jetty backed up a square mile of sand flats that have since sprouted forest.

The trail has a few muddy spots where it dips through a rainforest glen. After 1.6 miles the path drops to an alder forest on the flatlands and reaches the paved entrance road to the campground. Across the road and 50 yards to the left is a big gravel pullout marking the trail up McKenzie Head itself. This broad path climbs 0.3 mile to a huge concrete terrace with a circular pit—all that remains of the artillery that kept watch over the mouth of the Columbia until the end of World War II. Follow a tunnel-like hallway 100 yards through a monstrous concrete bunker to find a second, matching artillery terrace on the other side of McKenzie Head. Then return as you came.

Other Options

If you're camped at Cape Disappointment—or if you want a shortcut to McKenzie Head—you can start this hike from the campground entrance road. Look for a brown hiker-symbol sign by the roadside 0.5 mile past the park's entrance booth.

4   Cape Disappointment

Easy (to lighthouse)
1.2 miles round trip
200 feet elevation gain

Easy (Coastal Forest Trail)
1.4-mile loop
100 feet elevation gain

Members of the Lewis and Clark expedition reached this dramatic coastal headland after trekking nearly 3000 miles. Today the hike is shorter and features several added attractions — a lighthouse, an artillery bunker, and a museum.

For the easiest route to the views at "Cape D" (as the locals call this headland), start at the Lewis and Clark Interpretive Center. To get there from Astoria, take Highway 101 north across the bridge and west 11 miles to Ilwaco. At the traffic light in the center of town go straight on Loop 100, following signs for Cape Disappointment for 3.4 miles. At the crossroads for the park's boat launch go straight another half mile to the Interpretive Center's parking turnaround. Expect to pay $10 if you don't yet have a Discover Pass.

At the far right end of the parking lot, climb the paved trail 300 yards to the Interpretive Center. On the way you'll pass the concrete ruins of Battery Harvey Allen, a bunker that housed three 6-inch guns from 1906 until after World War II. Explorable passageways and storage rooms remain. The Interpretive Center itself features walk-through exhibits of photographs, artifacts, and journal entries from the Lewis and Clark expedition. Hours are 9am to 5pm daily in summer (winters Wed-Sun 10-5). It's $5 for adults, and kids age 7-17 are $2.50.

When you leave the museum, walk to the ocean viewpoint and turn left along the bluff's rim to find the trail to the Cape Disappointment lighthouse. After 0.3 mile you'll pass a viewpoint of Dead Man's Cove, a picturesque chasm in the cape's cliffs where a shipwreck casualty once washed ashore. The hidden beach here has been closed by the Coast Guard, so continue straight until you can turn right

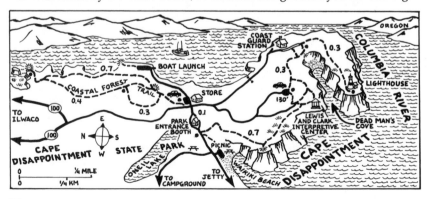

Cape Disappointment lighthouse. Opposite: Lewis & Clark Interpretive Center.

on a concrete pathway that skirts the cove's clifftops for 0.3 mile to the lighthouse.

The oldest lighthouse still in use on the West Coast, this 53-foot brick tower was built in 1856 to cut the appalling frequency of shipwrecks on the Columbia River bar, the "Graveyard of the Pacific." In fact, the ship that originally tried to bring materials for a lighthouse here in 1853 sank with its cargo 2 miles offshore on Peacock Spit.

When you return to your car you'll only have logged 1.2 miles. If this sounds short for a day's outing, you might prefer starting the hike at a trailhead that's slightly farther away, where you'll also be able to add a loop through old-growth woods on the Coastal Forest Trail.

To find this alternate trailhead, drive as to the Lewis and Clark Interpretive Center, but when you reach the crossroads in Cape Disappointment State Park turn left toward the boat launch and immediately park in the shuttle bus parking area on the left, opposite the Fort Canby Store. From here the lighthouse is a 1.4-mile hike away. Simply cross the road, walk along the campground entrance road past the fee booth, and turn left at a sign for the Cape Disappointment Trail. This path climbs steeply to fabulous headland meadows full of browsing deer and viewpoints before delivering you to the usual route to the lighthouse.

If you still have energy after your lighthouse hike, spend it on a 1.4-mile loop along the Coastal Forest Trail. This path begins at the northwest corner of the shuttle bus parking lot where you parked your car, marked with a sign by the paved road. Keep right at all junctions to explore this jungly rainforest's trail network. Along the way, 10-foot-thick spruces twist contorted branches above a carpet of wild lily-of-the-valley. Viewpoints overlook tidal flats, craggy islets, and the Ilwaco boat channel.

5　Fort Columbia

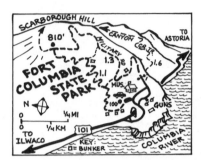

Easy (historic walk)
0.3-mile loop
80 feet elevation gain

Moderate (to Scarborough Hill)
2.4-mile loop
710 feet elevation gain

Below: Fort Columbia.

The Lewis and Clark expedition camped at Station Camp on the north shore of the Columbia River near this headland for ten days in November, 1805, while they scouted the river mouth. It was an eerie camp among the 36 longhouses of a deserted Chinook village where many people had died of disease. In a historic, democratic decision that tallied the votes of a young woman (Sacagawea) and a black slave (York), they decided to spend the winter on the far side of the river.

The US Army built Fort Columbia a mile west of Station Camp in 1896-1904 to aid Fort Canby and Fort Stevens in defending the river. Converted to a state park in 1950, the well-preserved fort includes a trail through the ancient Sitka spruce forest to viewpoints on Scarborough Hill. Two of the historic buildings are even available as vacation rentals: the two-bedroom Steward's House and the four-bedroom Scarborough House. Prices and reservation information are on page 18.

From Astoria, take the bridge to Washington and turn left on Highway 101 for 2.5 miles. After a tunnel, turn left into the park entrance and keep left for 0.2 mile to a large parking lot on the left. Expect to pay $10 to park if you don't yet have a Discover Pass for Washington state parks.

Facing the parking lot is a 1902 barracks that serves as the park's interpretive center. Open 11am-4pm daily from July 1 to early September, this museum has machine guns, native basketry, and a flier describing buildings and bunkers at the fort. Stroll up the street to the Commanding Officer's Quarters and turn

downhill to the right across the parade grounds to explore bunkers and a pair of 6-inch artillery guns.

For a more energetic hike through the woods, return to your car and look for a "Scarborough Hill Trail" sign at the far left end of the parking lot. If you keep left at all junctions on this path for 1.1 mile you'll pass four observation bunkers and switchback up to the forested crest of Scarborough Hill. Then turn right on the old Military Road (a wide trail) to return 1.3 miles to your car.

The Flavel House Museum in downtown Astoria.

ASTORIA

Astoria clings like a barnacle to the Oregon shore of the Columbia River. Wars, boomtimes, and countless winter storms have overswept this tenacious town since 1811, when fur traders built it as the first permanent United States settlement west of the Mississippi. Today the Astoria area not only has its share of beach diversions, but it's also rich with historic forts, Victorian mansions, and the lore of seafarers. An old-fashioned trolley offers rides along the town's riverfront, a promenade that connects with a walking tour of the historic district (Hike #9).

Commercial Street

To explore downtown Astoria, start at **Godfather's Books & Espresso** (Commercial and 11th Street). Check out Astoria's Scandinavian heritage next door at **Finn Ware** and window shop to the **Liberty Theater**, a restored 1925 vaudeville and movie hall at the corner of 12th Street (*www.liberty-theater.org*). A **Farmer's Market** sets up a block away at 12th and Marine Drive on summer Sundays 10am to 3pm. Another draw is a microbrewery overlooking the harbor — the **Wet Dog Cafe & Astoria Brewing Company** a block north on the promenade at Eleventh. The best coffee, however, is at the **Astoria Coffeehouse** at 243 Eleventh.

Columbia River Maritime Museum

In this first-rate interpretive center on Astoria's waterfront at 17th Street you can spin the wheel of a steamboat pilothouse, walk the bridge of a World War II destroyer, or watch the rotating prisms of a lighthouse lens. Other exhibits feature shipwrecks, fishing, and early exploration. Hours are 9:30-5 daily. Admission ($12 for adults, $10 for seniors, $5 for kids) includes a visit to the adjacent lightship *Columbia* that served as a floating lighthouse at the river's entrance until 1979.

Fort Clatsop

Centerpiece of the Lewis and Clark National Historical Park, this interpretive center includes a replica of the log stockade where explorers Lewis and Clark spent the rainy winter of 1805-06. Take Highway 101 south of Astoria 4 miles and follow signs. Open 9-5 daily (9-6 in summer) for $3; kids are free. See Hike #8.

Fort Stevens State Park

This former military reservation at the mouth of the Columbia River is home to the largest campground in the Oregon park system with 476 sites, 11 cabins, and 15 yurts (for reservations call 800-452-5687). There's lots to do for day visitors too: swim at Coffenbury Lake, hike 5 miles of trails, ride 7 miles of paved bike paths, lounge on a broad beach beside the rusting remains of the 1906 *Peter Iredale* shipwreck, watch for birds on Clatsop Spit, or climb on the Columbia River's south jetty. Expect a $5 day-use fee. See Hikes #6 and #7 for details.

Military Museum

Also in Fort Stevens State Park, a historic area includes concrete bunkers and gun batteries dating to the Civil War. A Japanese submarine fired 17 shells nearby in World War II. Today a military museum displays uniforms, armaments, and photos of the fort's history. Hours are 10-6 daily from June through September and 10-4 daily the rest of the year. Civil War reenactments, blacksmithing demonstrations, walking tours of underground bunkers, and tours of the park from the back of a 1950s Army truck are available in summer. Drive Highway 101 south of Astoria 7 miles and follow signs to Fort Stevens Historic Area. Expect a $5 parking fee. For information call 800-861-3170 x21.

Flavel House

Captain George Flavel built this Queen Anne-style mansion in 1885, having profited handsomely from the dangers of river navigation as a Columbia River bar pilot. Elegantly restored and furnished with period antiques, the house at 441 8th Street is open daily 10-5 from May through September and 11-4 from October through April. Adults are $6, seniors and students $5, and kids age 6-17 are $2.

To sample the mansion lifestyle, book a room at **Clementine's Bed &**

The Columbia River bridge from Astoria's waterfront.

Breakfast, kitty corner from the Flavel House at 847 Exchange Street. The inn combines Astoria's oldest building and an 1888 Italianate mansion. Rooms run $99-149. For reservations, check *www.clementines-bb.com* or 503-325-2005.

Astoria Column
The best viewpoint of Astoria is atop this 125-foot tower on Astoria's Coxcomb Hill. Look for Cape Disappointment (Hike #4) to the northwest and Saddle Mountain (Hike #13) to the southeast. Built by the Great Northern Railroad in 1926 to promote travel, the tower is patterned after Trajan's Column in Rome, but is painted with scenes from Astoria's history. Turn off Highway 30 at 16th Street and follow signs. Open dawn to dusk. Expect a $1 annual parking fee.

Fort Astoria
Fur tycoon John Jacob Astor sent a crew to build Astoria's original trading outpost in 1811. The British bought the site and renamed it Fort George in 1813. A free display and a replica of one tower are on the site at 15th and Exchange. Next door, a red brick warehouse with the **Fort George Brewery and Public House** toasts the fort's checkered past with Vortex IPA and rock fish tacos.

Heritage Museum
A block east of Fort Astoria, the 1904 City Hall now houses exhibits of Astoria's native tribal culture, ethnic immigrants, shipwrecks, and art. The museum at 1615 Exchange is open daily 10-5 May-September and Tuesday-Saturday 11-4 the rest of the year. Admission is $4 for adults, $2 for seniors, and $1 for kids.

Hanthorn Cannery
Dating to 1875, the oldest cannery building on the lower Columbia now houses a free Bumble Bee Seafoods interpretive center, open daily 9-6. Ride Astoria's riverfront trolley to its eastern end (or drive to 39th Street), and walk out Pier 39.

Youngs River Falls
A short trail in a woodsy county park leads to the base of the Youngs River's 50-foot cascade, noted by Lewis and Clark. Drive 8 miles south of Astoria on Highway 202 toward Jewell and turn right at a sign for Youngs River Falls for 3.7 miles to a large, unmarked parking area at a hairpin curve.

The South Jetty at Clatsop Spit.

6   Clatsop Spit

Easy (jetty exploration)
1.2 miles round trip
No elevation gain

Moderate (around Clatsop Spit)
4.5-mile loop
No elevation gain

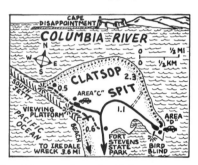

Huge waves explode against the boulders of the South Jetty, where the Columbia River meets the ocean. Freighters steam nearby. Brown pelicans circle offshore, then suddenly dive beak-first in the hopes of scooping up fish.

To find the jetty, drive Highway 101 south of Astoria 4 miles (or north of Seaside 9 miles), and turn west at a sign for Fort Stevens State Park. Follow park signs 4.9 miles, turn left at the day-use entrance (just past the camping entrance), and drive past Battery Russell a total of 3.9 miles to a fork. To the left is parking area C at the jetty. The 360-mile Oregon Coast Trail begins here and follows the beach 16 miles south to Gearhart.

For a quick hike, park at area C and walk to a 20-foot viewing platform overlooking the South Jetty. From here you can either explore left along the jetty a few hundred yards to the broad ocean beach, or hike right 0.5 mile along the sandy margin of the jetty to the Columbia River's calmer beach. On the way watch for the tracks of large brown California ground squirrels.

For a more strenuous 4.5-mile loop—and the best birdwatching—it's best to drive 1.4 miles past area C and park at area D instead. A short boardwalk here leads to a bird blind overlooking the tidal flats of Trestle Bay.

Start the loop at the far left corner of parking area D, where a trail leads through the dunes to the Columbia River beach. Walk left along the beach 2.3 miles to the jetty, turn left along the jetty's sandy margin half a mile to the viewing platform, and continue 0.3 mile along the jetty's top to an X-crossing of abandoned roads—now big, sandy trails. Turn left 0.3 mile to the paved road. Then follow the road's shoulder left 1.1 miles back to parking area D.

7   Fort Stevens

Easy (around Coffenbury Lake)
2.4-mile loop
No elevation gain

Moderate (from Battery Russell)
5-mile loop
100 feet elevation gain

This 11-square-mile state park between the Columbia River and the Pacific has lots of attractions: the largest campground in Oregon, a popular picnic area at swimmable Coffenbury Lake, a collection of old artillery gun emplacements, and a broad beach with the rusting remains of the *Peter Iredale* shipwreck. The Oregon Coast Trail follows the beach for the length of the park.

All of Fort Stevens' main features are connected by a well-maintained trail network through the flat coastal forest. About half the paths are paved for cyclists. Described here are two hikes on quieter footpaths.

If you're bringing kids, head for the 2.4-mile loop around Coffenbury Lake. Drive Highway 101 south of Astoria 4 miles (or north of Seaside 9 miles) turn west at a sign for Fort Stevens State Park, and follow park signs 4.6 miles. Opposite a KOA campground, turn into the park's campground entrance. Then go straight 0.3 mile (ignoring a right-hand fork to a fee station) and park at Coffenbury Lake's picnic area A.

Here you can buy the required $5 parking permit from a machine. You'll also find a dock, a boat ramp, and a sandy beach where the swimming is much less cold and windy than in the ocean. Cross the beach to the right to find the lakeshore trail, a path lined with alder, spruce, sword ferns, and elderberry.

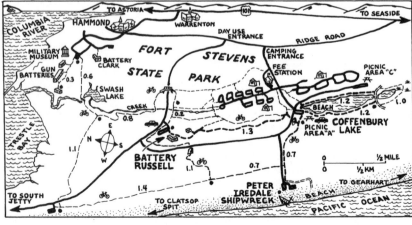

The wreck of the Peter Iredale. *Opposite: Gun near military museum.*

After 1.2 miles, turn left for 150 yards on an old road that dikes the marshy end of the lake. Then keep left again on the continuation of the trail around the lake to your car.

If you wish the hike were a little longer — or if you want to avoid Coffenbury Lake's parking fee — start at historic Battery Russell instead. To find this trailhead, drive straight past the park's campground entrance 0.3 mile to the day use entrance and turn left for a mile to a big parking loop on the left.

Drive around the loop to an exhibit board describing the history of Battery Russell, which guarded the Columbia River entrance from 1904 to 1944. Climb a staircase and walk the length of the enormous concrete bunker to a wide sandy trail. Then keep right at all junctions. The trail follows the crest of an ancient sand dune overgrown with a forest of spruce, shore pines, Scotch broom, and wild lily-of-the-valley.

When you reach a paved bike path, duck right through a tunnel under a road and turn left to picnic area A at the start of the Coffenbury Lake loop trail. After hiking around the lake, return the way you came.

Other Hiking Options

Paved paths extend to the *Iredale* wreck and the Military Museum (see map), but these are more fun on a bike than on foot. For a bit of adventure, explore the 1-mile loop trail around a marsh at the far south end of Coffenbury Lake.

8   Fort Clatsop

Easy (tour of the fort)
0.4-mile loop
No elevation gain

Moderate (3 walks)
4.4 miles round trip
50 feet elevation gain

Difficult (Fort-To-Sea Trail, with shuttle)
6.9 miles one way
340 feet elevation gain

Lewis and Clark's band of explorers built Fort Clatsop in a mere two weeks, just in time to spend the Christmas of 1805 indoors. For the next three months they waited out the cold, rainy winter on a river south of present-day Astoria

In 2006 the National Park Service rebuilt a replica of the log stockade at what is thought to be the original site. For a one-hour visit, stroll a 0.4-mile loop path from a visitor center to the fort. If you have a couple of hours, explore the park on three short walks. For a longer visit, hike the entire Fort-To-Sea Trail, a route blazed by the explorers through the rainforest to Sunset Beach on their way to boil saltwater to restock their salt supply.

Drive Highway 101 south of Astoria 3 miles (or north of Seaside 10 miles) and follow signs for Lewis and Clark National Park east 3 miles to the entrance road of Fort Clatsop's visitor center, where a $3 admission gains you access to two movies and a hall of exhibits. Then take a 100-yard path that leads from a side door of the visitor center to the fort itself. Clark sketched the fort's layout in his journal, showing that enlisted men had bunks in the rooms to the left while officers had beds and a real fireplace in rooms to the right.

After touring the fort, go out the front gate and veer left on a paved path 200 yards to the expedition's canoe landing, where a boardwalk now overlooks the Lewis and Clark River. You could turn back here, but if you have time, continue a mile along the riverbank on a gravel path to Netul Landing, where you'll find a kiosk with displays.

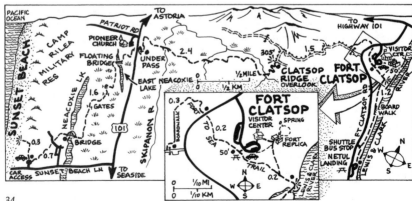

The next two recommended walks begin at the Sunset Beach Trailhead. You may want to arrange a car shuttle between Sunset Beach and Fort Clatsop so you can hike the trail between them one way. To drive to Sunset Beach, go back to Highway 101 and turn left for 4 miles. Between mileposts 14 and 15, turn right on Sunset Beach Lane for 0.9 mile to the trailhead parking area on the right.

First take a broad, level path from the far end of the trailhead turnaround for 0.3 mile to a viewpoint deck on a grassy dune overlooking the broad beach. Cars are allowed on the beach itself, so most hikers turn back here. If you hear artillery, it's the National Guard practicing at a military camp to the north.

Then walk back to the trailhead and take the Fort-To-Sea Trail that starts behind the restroom and climbs through the woods toward Fort Clatsop, 6.2 miles away. For a short sample of this route, turn back after 0.7 mile when you reach an 80-foot arched footbridge across Neacoxie Lake, a long narrow lake with lilypads.

If you're tackling the entire Fort-To-Sea Trail, a shuttle comes in handy. The first 0.7 mile of this "sea-to-fort" route will take you to the Neacoxie Lake bridge described above. Then the trail zigzags through cow pastures and crosses a floating footbridge over East Neacoxie Lake. At the 1.6-mile mark you'll duck through a tunnel beneath Highway 101.

After that the path crosses the sluggish Skipanon River and climbs through scenic, mossy rainforest for 2.4 miles to a viewpoint atop Clatsop Ridge. The final 1.5-mile section of the route to Fort Clatsop follows old gravel roads through a conifer forest thinned by a windstorm in 2007.

Fort Clatsop.   Opposite: Statue of Sacagawea outside the visitor center.

9   Astoria   👫 🚲

Easy
2.6-mile loop
150 feet elevation gain

Left: The Liberty Theatre.
Below: Riverfront trolley.

Refer to map on page 30.

From the barnacled piers of cannery docks to the painted gingerbread of Victorian mansions, this picturesque city on the Columbia River wears its history with a salty pride. A 2.6-mile walking tour samples the old town's sights.

Start at the Columbia River Maritime Museum, on Highway 30 at 17th Street, 1.5 miles west of the Highway 101 bridge across the Columbia River. The museum itself has first-rate displays of lighthouses, ships, and Astoria history. Admission includes a pass to board the lightship *Columbia* anchored nearby.

In front of the museum you'll pass a trolley stop for "Old 300," a restored 1913 San Antonio streetcar that passes every 45 minutes in summer (daily from noon to 6pm), and on non-stormy weekends in the off season. Fares on the 2.8-mile track along Astoria's waterfront are $1 per trip or $2 per day.

A promenade also follows the trolley route, so you can either walk or ride the first 0.7 mile of the recommended loop tour, heading west past docks, shops, offices, restaurants, and former fish-packing plants to Sixth Street. Here detour to the right to climb a viewing platform by the river's main shipping channel.

Then head inland a block on 6th Street, turn left beside busy Highway 30, and keep straight on quiet Astor Street 3 blocks. At 10th Street turn right 2 blocks to Astoria's business district, turn right on Commercial two blocks to the county courthouse, and turn left on 8th Street to the Flavel House, a museum in a sumptuous Queen Anne-style mansion built by a Columbia River bar pilot.

Then follow the zigzagging route mapped on page 30, admiring the elegant churches and ornate homes, several of which have been converted to bed & breakfast inns. A few blocks before returning to your car at the riverfront museum you'll pass a replica stockade tower built on the site of the original 1811 Fort Astoria.

The Turnaround on Seaside's Promenade.

SEASIDE

Founded as a tourist goal in 1873 by railroad king Ben Holladay, Seaside today revels in its carnival mood. Arcades and snack shops line the "Million-Dollar Walk," the section of Broadway between Highway 101 and the beach.

But this part of the Oregon Coast is not all glitz. Just south of Seaside lies the upscale village of Cannon Beach and some of the state's most beautiful natural scenery—cliff-edged islands and quiet, forest-draped capes.

Seaside Museum and Historical Society

Indian artifacts and the history of Seaside's beach tourism are featured in this museum at 570 Necanicum Drive. Hours are 10am-3pm from October to April and 10am-4pm in summer. Closed Sundays. The $3 admission ($2 seniors, $1 students) includes a visit next door to one of Seaside's original beach cottages.

Quatat Marine Park

Explore the Necanicum River from this downtown Seaside park on four blocks of riverfront between First and A Avenues, with picnic tables, paved paths, and a boat dock. Canoe, kayak, paddleboat, and "bumper boat" rentals are nearby.

Ecola State Park

Postcards of the Oregon Coast often wear photos of this park on the cliff-edged capes of Tillamook Head, where waves roll in against craggy islands and secluded beaches. An 8-mile trail extends the length of the park, but the best viewpoints are at the Ecola and Indian Beach picnic areas. Expect a $5-per-car fee. See Hike #11.

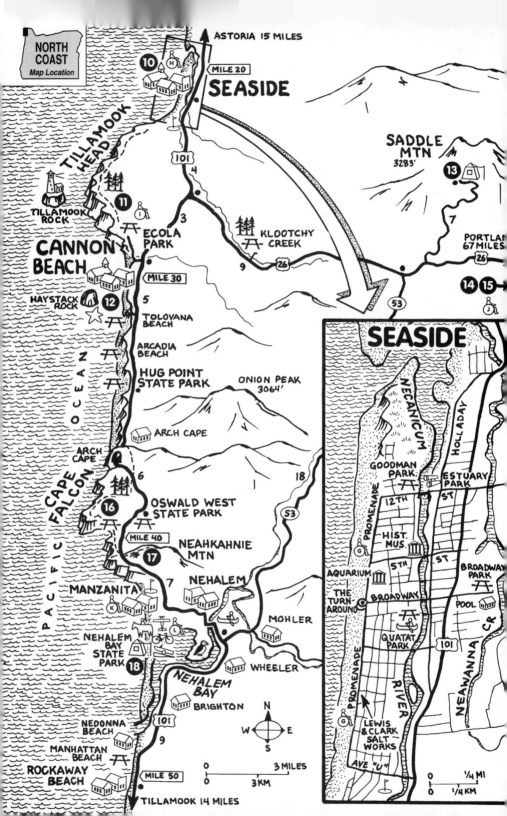

Cannon Beach

Seaside's sophisticated cousin, this coastal village has an artistic flair. The area was named for a cannon that washed ashore in 1846 from a shipwrecked US Navy sloop. You can see the original cannon (and learn about two more discovered in 2008) at the **Cannon Beach History Center**, a free museum open Thursday through Monday 1-5pm at Sunset and Spruce Streets, near the town's south entrance off Highway 101.

Today Cannon Beach is packed with coffee houses, bungalows, art galleries, and shops. **Hemlock Street** is window-shopping central. Start at the **Cannon Beach Book Company** (130 Hemlock), keeping an eye out for cute shops hidden in courtyards. See Hike #12.

Sandcastle Day draws crowds to watch spectacular sand sculptures being built—and swallowed by the tide—each year on a Saturday in early June. The community **Coaster Theatre**, downtown at 108 N. Hemlock Street, stages plays Fri-Sat at 8pm (schedule at *www.coastertheatre.com* or 503-436-1242).

Hug Point State Recreation Site

A 100-yard path descends from this picnic area south of Cannon Beach to three scenic sandy coves protected from the wind. A lacy 12-foot waterfall spills into the northernmost cove beside two explorable caves. Nearby, an early 20th-century wagon road around the cliffs is accessible at low tide. See Hike #10.

Oswald West State Park

In the wildest and most spectacular part of the northern Oregon Coast, surfers and picnickers hike a quarter mile from Highway 101 down through an old-growth rainforest to Short Sand Beach's dramatic cove. Trails from here lead to the tip of Cape Falcon and the viewpoint atop Neahkahnie Mountain (Hikes #16 and #17). The park is named for the clever Oregon governor who, in 1913, had the state's beaches declared public highways to help assure that the beaches would never fall into private developers' hands.

Manzanita

Like a small, Oregon-flavored version of California's Carmel, this seaside village in the shadow of Neahkahnie Mountain (Hike #17) features art galleries and an upscale ambience. Start your stroll at the town's heart, a coffee shop a block from the ocean on Laneda Avenue, the village's main street.

Nehalem Bay State Park

On the sandy peninsula below Neahkahnie Mountain's rugged shoulder, this park has a 265-site campground (summer reservations accepted), 18 yurts, a separate 17-site equestrian camp with corrals and horse trails, a 2400-foot airstrip, and a 1.5-mile paved bike loop. See Hike #16.

L.L. "Stub" Stewart State Park

This large state park in the Coast Range forest is crossed by the Banks-Vernonia railroad trail (Hike #15). In addition to campsites for tenters, RVs, equestrians, and backpackers, the park offers 15 cabins and a disc golf course. Reserve a spot at *www.oregonstateparks.org* or 800-452-5687. Drive Highway 26 east of Seaside 50 miles (or west of Portland 28 miles) and turn north 4 miles on Highway 47.

10 Seaside Promenade

Easy
3-mile loop
No elevation gain

As a beach resort, Seaside might be said to date to the winter of 1805-06, when explorers Lewis and Clark established a salt-making camp on the beach here, perhaps partly to escape the inland gloom of Fort Clatsop, where it rained all but twelve days of their 106-day stay.

Later Seaside became known as the end of the railroad. In the 1920s Portland families would board at 6:30am, bring breakfast to eat on the train, pile out for a few hours on the beach, and return in the evening—all for a 25-cent fare.

Today tourists crowd the strip of arcades, fast-food joints, and gift shops lining Broadway. Away from the neon lights, however, Seaside's old-fashioned charm and picturesque natural setting have survived. The 3-mile walking loop described here visits the best of old Seaside: the beachfront Promenade, the Necanicum River estuary, and the cottage-lined back streets.

From Highway 101, follow "Seaside Downtown" signs to Broadway and turn west 6 crowded blocks to the Turnaround, a small circular plaza overlooking the beach. City parking lots are a block away from the beach and one block to either side of Broadway.

In the middle of the Turnaround a statue of Lewis and Clark portrays Lewis solemnly surveying the volleyball courts, kites, and lifeguard chairs on the busy beach. Clark looks aside to the 1000-foot cliffs of Tillamook Head (Hike #11), at the southern end of the beach.

Turn right at the statue and head north along the Promenade, a 15-foot-wide paved walkway between the grassy foredunes and downtown's hotels. After two

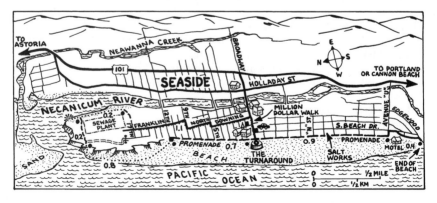

Seaside's Promenade.   Opposite: Cottages in Seaside.

blocks you'll pass the Seaside Aquarium, a vintage 1937 tourist draw boasting an octopus. Soon after, the hotels give way to cottages from the 1910s and 20s.

When the Promenade ends at 12th Avenue, walk left through the dunes and continue north along an increasingly quiet stretch of beach. From here you can see the lighthouse on Tillamook Rock, an island off the tip of Tillamook Head. After 0.8 mile the beach peters out beside an eroded riverbank at the mouth of the Necanicum River. Scramble up a 20-foot bluff and continue inland between the eroded bank and a sewage treatment plant for 0.2 mile to an estuary shore. Here you can explore left 100 yards to find a viewpoint at the tip of a rocky spit. Then turn around and follow the riverbank upstream 0.2 mile. Turn inland to the right at the far end of the sewage treatment plant, follow the fenceline to gravel 17th Street for a block, and turn left on paved Franklin Avenue.

Follow Franklin Avenue past cute beach bungalows back toward town. On the way you'll have to jog half a block to the right at Ninth and Fifth Streets, so you'll end up on North Downing when you reach a big public parking lot just before the Million-Dollar Walk. On your left at Broadway is Seaside Town Center, an indoor collection of 20 shops with a carousel where rides cost $2.

Other Options

The Promenade also extends south of the Turnaround 0.9 mile to a blocky motel just a few blocks from the Necanicum riverbank site of railroad czar Ben Holladay's original Seaside House (1873-1882). On this part of the Promenade you'll pass a sign pointing half a block left to a miniature park with a replica of the stone oven Lewis and Clark built in 1806 to boil buckets of seawater for salt.

If you're hiking the Oregon Coast Trail south along the beach from Fort Stevens, you'll have to detour inland through Gearhart, follow Highway 101 south half a mile, turn right on Holladay Drive to 12th Avenue, and take the beach south past Seaside to Sunset Boulevard and Tillamook Head (Hike #11).

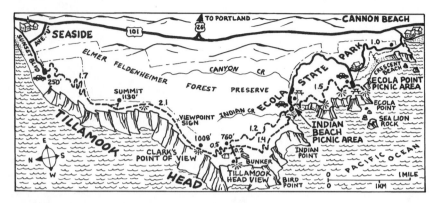

11   Tillamook Head

Easy (to Indian Beach)
3 miles round trip
400 feet elevation gain

Moderate (to WW II bunker)
3-mile loop
900 feet elevation gain

Difficult (shuttle across headland)
6.1 miles one way
1350 feet elevation gain

Tillamook Head rises 1000 feet from the ocean, with jagged capes and rocky islands. The Lewis and Clark expedition crossed this formidable headland in 1806 to buy the blubber of a stranded whale from Indians at Cannon Beach. At a viewpoint along the way Clark marveled, "I behold the grandest and most pleasing prospect which my eyes ever surveyed."

 Today the Oregon Coast Trail traces Clark's route across the headland from Seaside to Cannon Beach. The headland itself is a tilted remnant of a massive, 15-million-year-old Columbia River basalt flow. Incredibly, the lava welled up near Idaho and flooded down the Columbia River to the seashore here.

From Highway 101, take the north exit for Cannon Beach and follow Ecola State Park signs 2 miles to the park's entrance booth. A day-use fee of $5 per car is collected here. Dogs must be on leash.

For a quick sample of the park's scenery, turn left at the booth, park at the Ecola Point picnic area, and walk 200 yards out a paved path from the far left-hand end of the parking lot. You'll find a railed viewpoint on a headland with a spectacular panorama from Cannon Beach to Tillamook Rock's island lighthouse.

For a 3-mile hike, walk back to the parking lot and take an unpaved trail north 1.5 miles to Indian Beach. This route climbs around scenic bluffs past three of the best viewpoints in the park. Then a left-hand spur drops to Indian Beach, a good turnaround point. Ahead, the main trail bridges Canyon Creek to the Indian Beach picnic area parking lot.

For the longer hikes at Tillamook Head it's best to start at the Indian Beach picnic area. Drive there by turning right at the park's fee booth for 1.5 miles.

The trail starts behind the restroom on the right. After 200 feet ignore a footbridge to the left and keep straight on the main trail, an old roadbed that climbs relentlessly through an ancient spruce and alder rainforest. After 1.2 miles you'll reach a trail crossing at a camping area for backpackers. Three open-sided shelters here have four bunks apiece, but no water and no stoves. The bunks are available for free on a first-come-first-served basis, although you'll need a parking permit for your car for every day of your visit.

Hike straight past the camping area 0.2 mile to find the concrete bunker that housed a radar installation in World War II. Just beyond is a cliff-edge viewpoint, breathtakingly high above a rugged rock beach.

A mile to sea is Tillamook Rock, a bleak island with a lighthouse that operated from 1881 to 1957. Nicknamed "Terrible Tilly," the light was repeatedly overswept by winter storms that dashed water, rocks, and fish into the lantern room 150 feet above normal sea level. The island was finally bought by funeral entrepreneurs who brought in urns of cremated remains by helicopter.

If you're ready to return on the loop to your car, walk back to the camp shelters and turn right on a path 1.4 miles downhill to the Indian Beach parking lot.

If you'd prefer to continue across Tillamook Head, walk behind the camp shelters to find a trail that climbs and dips for 2.6 miles, passing some excellent views north (including the one Clark liked), before switchbacking down through the forest 1.7 miles to a parking area at the end of Sunset Boulevard. Boardwalks cross muddy spots along the way. To find this northern trailhead, drive Highway 101 to Seaside's southernmost traffic signal, turn west on Avenue U for two blocks and turn left on Edgewood (which becomes Sunset) for 1.2 miles to road's end.

The view south from Ecola Point.   Opposite: Camp shelters atop Tillamook Head.

12   Cannon Beach

Easy (to Haystack Rock)
2.2-mile loop
No elevation gain

Moderate (shuttle to Hug Point)
5.1 miles one way
No elevation gain
Open except at high tide

This arts-oriented village on one of Oregon's most beautiful beaches is grappling with its own popularity—and seems to be winning. Clusters of tasteful shops and boutiques fill the small, busy downtown. Strolling lovers, sandcastling kids, and kite fliers dot the white sand beach. Puffins, cormorants, and murres watch from scenic, protected islands.

When William Clark, Sacagawea, and others from the Lewis and Clark expedition hiked here in 1806 they found Indians using hot stones in wooden troughs to render blubber from a 105-foot beached whale. Clark bought as much blubber as the tribe would sell—300 pounds—to supplement the expedition's lean diet, and named nearby Ecola Creek after the Indians' word for whale, *ekoli*.

The name Cannon Beach dates to 1846, when the Navy schooner *Shark* broke up while crossing the Columbia River bar. A chunk of the deck, complete with capstan and cannon, washed ashore south of Hug Point. Two more cannons surfaced there in 2008.

If you're coming from Portland or Seaside, take the first Cannon Beach exit (also signed for Ecola State Park) and keep left for 0.7 mile to a city parking lot by the information center on 2nd Street. (If this lot's full, you may have to drive another 11 blocks to the Haystack Rock parking area on Hemlock Street.)

From the info center, walk down 2nd Street to the beach. This is the route of the Oregon Coast Trail on its way from Tillamook Head (Hike #11) for 6.8 miles to Arch Cape (Hike #16).

Once you're on the beach, head left for 1.1 mile to Haystack Rock, a massive,

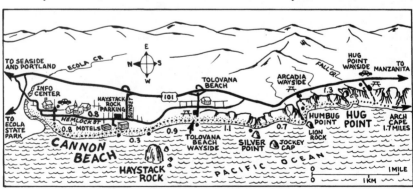

Haystack Rock from Cannon Beach.   Opposite: Shops on Hemlock Street.

235-foot-tall sea stack dominating the beachscape. The spires of the Needles rise from the surf nearby. Low tides reveal pools of anemones and starfish on the reefs here. Feel free to look, but don't disturb these animals by touching them, and avoid walking on the mussels. Climbing on Haystack Rock is banned to protect seabird habitat.

If you're ready to return on the short loop through town, walk 0.3 mile back to a beach access where a huge pipe emits a creek beside blocky motels. Walk up this access a block and turn left on Hemlock Street for 0.8 mile, passing quaint cottages on your way back to downtown.

If you choose instead to continue along the beach, a good goal is Hug Point Wayside—especially if you can arrange a 5-mile car shuttle so you only have to walk one way. Or you could catch the free shuttle bus that runs the length of Hemlock Street hourly from 11am to 5:30pm in summer.

The beach near Hug Point is actually a historic wagon route. Before the coast highway was built, settlers reached the community of Arch Cape by driving south along this beach. The most dangerous narrows was Hug Point, named because drivers had to hug the headland to pass even at the lowest tide. Nearby Humbug Point won its name when travelers mistook it for the tricky headland and rounded it easily, only to see the real Hug Point ahead. About 1920, frustrated locals blasted a narrow roadbed around Hug Point just above the waves. Today the ledge gives hikers dry passage except at high tide, when waves block the route altogether.

If you make it around Hug Point you'll find a hidden cove where Fall Creek cascades into a pool beside two short, sandy caves. A few hundred yards beyond is the railed trail up to Hug Point Wayside's parking lot. To drive here, simply take Highway 101 south of Cannon Beach 5 miles.

Saddle Mountain. Opposite: Antique logging machinery on Sunset Rest Area sign.

13   Saddle Mountain

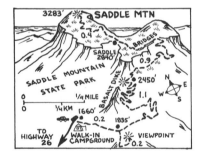

Difficult
5.2 miles round trip
1620 feet elevation gain

Highest point in northwest Oregon, this saddle-shaped peak commands a panorama from the ocean to the truncated cone of Mt. St. Helens. The climb is especially popular in May and June, when wildflowers fill the mountain's meadows with the richest floral display in the entire Coast Range. Avoid the steep path after mid-winter ice storms.

The Columbia River basalt forming Saddle Mountain erupted 15 million years ago near Idaho, poured down the Columbia's channel, and fanned out to the sea. Here the lava puddled up in a deep bay. When the Coast Range later rose, erosion stripped away the surrounding soft rock, turning the erstwhile bay into a mountain. The summit still has a lumpy, pillow-shaped surface typical of lava cooled quickly by water.

Start by driving Highway 26 west of Portland 66 miles (or east of Seaside 10 miles). Turn at a state park sign near milepost 10. Follow a winding, one-lane paved road uphill 7 miles to its end at a picnic area and 10-site campground.

The path starts in a forest of alder and salmonberry. Flowers line the trail in spring: 5-petaled white candyflower, pink bleeding hearts, green stalks of fringecup, 3-petaled white trilliums, wild lily-of-the-valley, and pairs of white fairy bells. Old 8-foot stumps recall 1920s logging and 1930s fires.

After 0.2 mile a large unmarked side trail to the right leads 0.2 mile to a bare-topped rock outcrop with the park's best view of Saddle Mountain itself.

Continuing on the main trail, you'll switchback steeply up 1.1 mile to a spine of rock running up the mountain like a stone wall. This basalt dike is part of the same lava flow that formed the rest of the mountain. Here, however, the weight of the flow extruded molten lava down into cracks in the ground, where the lava developed the hexagonal fractures typical of slow-cooled basalt. Exposed by erosion, the dike now resembles a stack of cordwood.

Another half mile's climb brings you to the wildflower meadows on the peak's upper slopes. Several rare flower species, including Saddle Mountain bittercress (a pink, 4-petaled mustard) are found almost exclusively here. This unglaciated summit served as a refuge for alpine species in the Ice Age, when the Cascade Range was buried in ice. Blooms you're likely to spot include red paintbrush, blue iris, purple larkspur, and cushions of bluish phlox. Flower picking is prohibited.

At the 2.2-mile mark you'll cross the mountain's saddle, with a dizzying view down to your car. Cables anchored along the final 0.4-mile pitch help you climb the steep slope to the top's railed viewpoint. The coastal panorama extends from Nehalem Bay in the south to Astoria's bridge in the north. On clear days, Cascade snowpeaks from Mt. Jefferson to Mt. Rainier shimmer to the east.

14   Highway 26 Waysides

Easy (Four-County Point)
1.6 miles round trip
100 feet elevation gain

Easy (Sunset Rest Area)
0.8-mile loop
150 feet elevation gain

Most travelers on busy Highway 26 overlook these short, woodsy trails, but why not stop to stretch your legs on the trip to the coast? The two paths here are easy enough that you can hike both in an afternoon.

The first trail leads to the only spot in Oregon where can you stand in four counties at once. A granite slab marks this geographical vortex, where the corners of Clatsop, Columbia, Tillamook, and Washington counties meet.

Drive Highway 26 west of Portland 39 miles (or east of Seaside 41 miles) to a brown hiker-symbol sign with a parking pullout on the north between mileposts 34 and 35.

Start at a sign for the "Four County Points Trail," a path that heads into a grove of 5-foot-thick Douglas fir with vine maple and sword fern. After 100 yards the trail turns up to the left for 0.8 mile to the monument, but a well-traveled spur

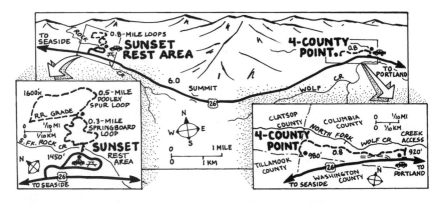

also continues straight a few yards to the pebbled shore of North Fork Wolf Creek, a closer goal that's popular with children.

The second hike starts 6 miles west on Highway 26 at the Sunset Rest Area (45 miles west of Portland or 35 miles east of Seaside, between mileposts 28 and 29). Drive all the way around the parking loop to a big signboard describing the Sunset Infantry Division to whom the rest area is dedicated.

The trail starts behind the signboard, crosses a broad creek on a 100-foot bridge, and promptly forks. Turn right on the Springboard Loop, a nature trail through a pleasant alder forest; a few blackened, 7-foot stumps recall the logging and fires that once ravaged this area. If you keep left at junctions after this, you'll return to your car on a very easy 0.3-mile loop through a pleasant alder forest. If you keep right at junctions instead, you'll add the 0.5-mile Dooley Spur Loop.

15   Banks-Vernonia Railroad

Easy (to Buxton trestle)
0.5-mile loop
100 feet elevation gain

Difficult (to L. L. Stewart Park)
9.9-mile loop
1000 feet elevation gain

Left: The Buxton trestle, converted to a trail.

The wide, well-graded Banks-Vernonia State Trail traces an abandoned railroad grade 20 miles through the forested Coast Range foothills. Good goals along the way include a colossal timbered trestle and a network of loop trails in the new L.L. "Stub" Stewart State Park. All routes are open to hikers, bicyclists, and equestrians. Dogs must be on leash.

The railroad line was built 1919-1922 to haul logs to the Columbia River and to transport lumber to Portland from the Oregon-American mill in Vernonia. After the mill closed in 1957, a steam excursion train ran here for five years. The rails were removed in 1973 and the state parks department bought the line in 1974.

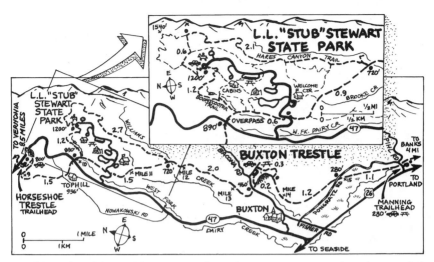

All 20 miles of the trail between Banks and Vernonia are paved, with a parallel bark dust path for horses. The path detours around the closed, partly dismantled the Horseshoe trestle.

A picnic area beside the huge, intact Buxton trestle is a good place to start your visit. Find it by driving Highway 26 west of Portland 28 miles. Near milepost 46, turn north off Highway 26 onto Fisher Road for 0.8 mile. Then curve right on Bacona Road for 0.6 mile to the trailhead parking area on the right.

Walk to a brown metal gate at the far end of the parking lot and turn sharply right down a wide paved path marked "walk bicycles". This path descends to a bridge over Mendenhall Creek and then climbs to the paved railroad route. Turn right across the trestle, a bridge that has been planked and railed for safety. On the far side, a paved path to the right leads back to your car for a short loop.

If you'd like a longer hike, continue straight on the railroad after crossing the Buxton trestle. The path crosses Bacona Road and launches into a forest of second-growth Douglas fir, bigleaf maple, and bracken. Wild iris flags the route with blue in spring. Mileposts mark quarter-mile intervals.

After 2 miles you'll cross Williams Creek and reach a sign for the Hares Canyon Trail on the right. This is the start of an unpaved loop around a large state park that opened in 2007. Named for timber baron L. L. "Stub" Stewart, the park features 80 car campsites, 12 walk-in tent sites, 23 hike-in campsites, 16 equestrian campsites, and 15 rental cabins, all set in a relatively young Douglas fir forest.

For the loop around the park, turn uphill to the right on the Hares Canyon Trail. After 100 feet a spur down to the right deadends at the creekbank, a possible lunch spot. Otherwise follow signs to stay on the Hares Canyon Trail for 2.7 uphill miles (keeping right at most junctions) to the Clayhill Horse Staging Area. Walk directly across this huge gravel parking lot to find a wide gravel trail. Then follow signs for the Boomscooter Trail downhill for 1.2 miles. When you reach the paved Banks-Vernonia railroad trail, detour 300 yards to the right to see the railroad's highway overpass. Then turn around and follow the paved trail 3.5 miles back down to your car.

Other Options

If you're bicycling, you might park at the Manning Trailhead (between mileposts 47 and 48 on Highway 26) and ride the paved path 2.3 miles to the Buxton trestle as a warm-up.

16   Cape Falcon

Easy (to Short Sand Beach)
1.2-mile loop
100 feet elevation gain

Moderate (to Cape Falcon)
5 miles round trip
300 feet elevation gain

Difficult (shuttle to Arch Cape)
8 miles one way
1200 feet elevation gain

For more than 12 miles, the Oregon Coast Trail traverses the old-growth rainforests and craggy capes of Oswald West State Park. Here are three options for day hikers: a short stroll to a secluded beach, a moderate hike to Cape Falcon's vista, and an 8-mile trek through the forests to the community of Arch Cape.

Start by driving Highway 101 south of Seaside 18 miles (or north of Tillamook 30 miles) to Oswald West State Park. At a large "Beach Access" sign a bit south of milepost 39, turn into a large parking lot on the east side of the highway. The trail starts by the restroom at the far left end of the lot and ducks under the highway bridge.

The path follows Short Sand Creek through an old-growth rainforest of mossy alder, hemlock, red cedar, and spruce. Douglas squirrels scold from the 6-foot-thick trunks. Salal, salmonberry, and three varieties of ferns line the route.

Keep right at junctions for 0.4 mile to follow the creek down to a picnic area in the trees overlooking Smuggler Cove, where pirates once brought contraband ashore. At a big signboard, a 50-foot path descends to Short Sand Beach, a favorite spot with surfers.

For a short loop, go down to the beach and wade an ankle-deep creek to the left. Beyond the creek 200 feet, climb up across the driftwood to find a trail into the woods. Keep left for 0.2 mile, crossing a suspension footbridge over Necarney Creek. At a trail junction with a large post, turn right to return to your car.

If Cape Falcon's your goal, go back to the picnic area overlooking Smuggler Cove. Instead of going down to the beach, follow a "Cape Falcon" pointer to a

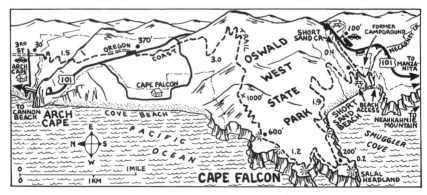

Cape Falcon.   Opposite: Surfers at Short Sand Beach.

smaller trail into the woods to the north. Wear boots because this path has roots and muddy spots. As you head out the cape you'll gain views of Neahkahnie Mountain (Hike #17). Finally you'll reach a junction beside a field of wind-trimmed salal bushes. For the Cape Falcon viewpoint, turn left on a 0.2-mile spur trail that becomes increasingly panoramic and rugged before petering out near the tip of the salal-covered headland.

If you're not ready to turn back yet, continue north on the Oregon Coast Trail. The next 1.2 miles pass three cliff-edge viewpoints framed by twisted old-growth spruce. After this the trail climbs steeply inland through viewless woods.

If your goal is Arch Cape, hike onward and upward. The path climbs over a broad, 1000-foot ridge and then drops to a crossing of Highway 101. On the far side, the trail briefly follows an abandoned road before climbing to a broad pass and switchbacking down to Arch Cape Creek and the trailhead.

To leave a shuttle car here, drive 3.8 miles north of the Os West parking lot to the far end of a tunnel, turn right on East Beach Road for 0.4 mile, and park on the shoulder at Third Road. The trail begins on the right.

Other Options

Oregon Coast Trail trekkers usually hike this 12-mile section from north to south instead. To find the trail from Cannon Beach (Hike #12), hike south past Hug Point 1.7 miles and turn left under the highway bridge at Arch Cape Creek.

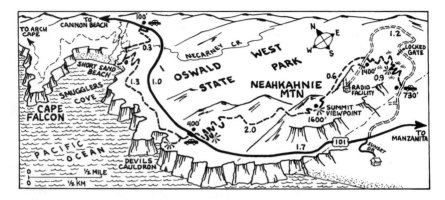

17 Neahkahnie Mountain

Moderate (to summit viewpoint)
3 miles round trip
900 feet elevation gain

Difficult (shuttle to beach parking lot)
5.1 miles one way
1000 feet elevation gain

Left: Neahkahnie Mountain from Cape Falcon.

Neahkahnie Mountain juts 1600 feet above the beach. Indians thought it a viewpoint fit for gods, and named it with the words *Ne* ("place of") and *Ekahni* ("supreme deity"). White men shroud the peak with legend as well. Treasure seekers sift the beach at the mountain's base, spurred by tales of gold buried by sailors from a shipwrecked Spanish galleon. The discovery here of a strangely inscribed block of beeswax, possibly of Spanish origin, adds to the speculation.

Drive Highway 101 south of Seaside 20 miles (or north of Tillamook 28 miles) to a brown hiker-symbol sign opposite Sunset Drive, between mileposts 41 and 42. Turn east on a gravel road for 0.4 mile and park at a wide spot.

At the far end of this small pullout, look for a tiny trail sign on the left where the trail begins. Steep switchbacks lead up through meadows 0.9 mile to a ridgetop junction. Continue straight on a path that contours 0.6 mile around the wooded back of the mountain to an unmarked opening — the summit meadow viewpoint.

Most hikers return as they came. But if you can arrange a car shuttle, it's worth continuing down the far side of the mountain. This portion of the Oregon Coast Trail, muddy in spots, descends 2 miles through forest to a crossing of Highway 101. If you want to park a shuttle car here, look for a gray post at a viewpoint pullout 0.2 mile south of milepost 40. But as long as you're shuttling a car, you should take it another mile to the first big Oswald West parking lot. Then you can hike the very scenic 1.3-mile stretch of the Oregon Coast Trail to Short Sand Beach. From there, keep right at junctions for 0.3 mile to the parking lot.

18 Nehalem Bay

Moderate
5.2-mile loop
No elevation gain

Right: Nehalem Bay from Neahkahnie Mtn.

Shorebirds and seals outnumber people on the beach rimming Nehalem Bay's dune-covered peninsula. Drive Highway 101 south of Seaside 22 miles (or north of Tillamook 26 miles) to milepost 44, just south of Manzanita. Follow signs a mile to Nehalem Bay State Park's entrance and then follow "Beach Access" pointers another 1.7 miles to a picnic area at road's end. Expect a $5 parking fee.

A sandy path behind the restroom leads through a grassy foredune to the broad beach. Neahkahnie Mountain's cliffs loom to the right. A drunk captain and inexperienced crew sailed the British 3-masted *Glenesslin* into those cliffs on a calm, sunny day in 1913; rusted iron parts remain. Legends say a 16th-century Spanish galleon also foundered nearby and that the survivors buried a treasure.

Walk left along the beach 2.3 miles to Nehalem Bay's jetty. A 1990 archeological dig here unearthed a Salish salmon-fishing camp from 1300-1600 AD. Walk inland along the jetty's edge 0.5 mile to a broad bayshore beach where 50 harbor seals often lounge. It is illegal to harass these marine mammals. Even approaching within 100 yards will set them galumphing toward the bay.

On a low bluff to the left, a "Restroom" sign marks an outhouse and picnic table at the end of the spit's inland horse trail, a 4-wheel-drive track overgrown with Scotch broom. This is a possible return route, although all the trails beyond this point are faint, rough, and confusing. The scenery and birdwatching are best if you simply continue along the soft bayshore beach 2.2 miles to a boat ramp and follow the paved road 0.2 mile left to your car.

Oregon Coast Trail hikers coming from Neahkahnie Mountain (Hike #17) simply follow Highway 101 to the park and hike out the spit. For a boat shuttle across the mouth of Nehalem Bay, call Jetty Fishery at 503-368-5746.

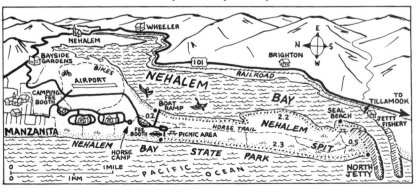

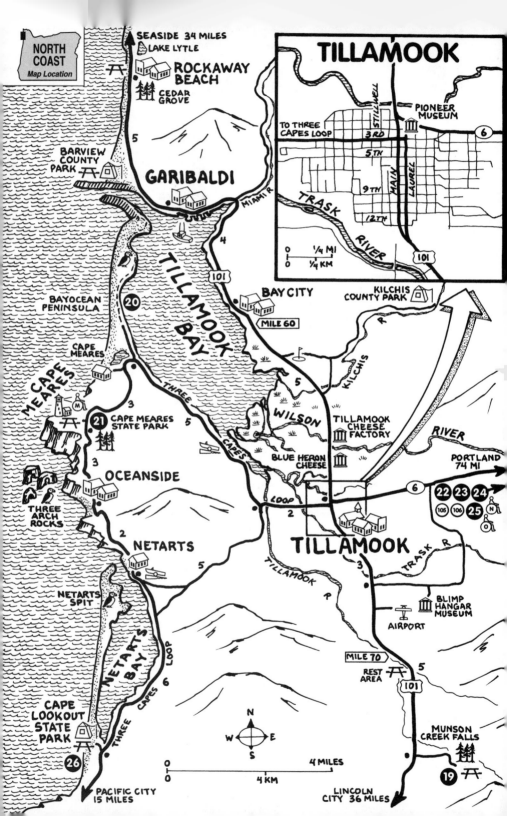

Sea stacks at Oceanside.

TILLAMOOK

Five rivers meander across dairy pastureland to Tillamook Bay in this coastal county touted as the "land of cheese, trees, and ocean breeze." To the south, Highway 101 takes an inland shortcut, but the Three Capes Scenic Route provides a coastal loop past Cape Meares, Cape Lookout, and Cape Kiwanda.

Cheese Factories

When local dairymen in the 1880s tired of having their butter spoil before it reached Portland and San Francisco on unreliable ships, they built their own sailing ship and started making cheddar cheese. Today the **Tillamook Cheese Factory**, 2 miles north of Tillamook on Highway 101, is one of Oregon's most popular tourist stops, with a self-guiding tour, a restaurant, and a gift shop. Daily hours are 8-8 in summer, 8-6 in winter. The **Blue Heron French Cheese Company**, a mile farther south on Highway 101, is open 8-8 in summer and 9-6 in winter, featuring camembert and brie.

Tillamook Air Museum

This museum's enormous hangar once housed four Navy blimps that prowled the coast for Japanese submarines during World War II. Twenty stories tall, the 1942 hangar remains the largest clear-span wooden building in the world. The museum's collection of World War II aircraft, including barrage balloons and fighter planes, will be moved to an Eastern Oregon site in Madras in 2016 to prevent rust. Until then, daily hours are 9-5. Adults are $12, seniors $11, and kids 6-17 $8.

Cape Meares State Scenic Viewpoint

A lighthouse, a bluff-top picnic area, and the odd-limbed Octopus Tree are the top attractions in this park on the Three Capes Loop west of Tillamook. The base of the 1890 lighthouse is open to visitors 11am-4pm daily from April through October. See Hike #21.

Cape Lookout State Park

This picturesque park on the Three Capes Loop stretches from a massive, cliff-edged headland to the tip of the 5-mile-long Netarts sand spit. In the middle is a beachside picnic area and a popular 212-site campground with 6 rentable cabins and 13 yurts (summer camping reservations accepted). See Hike #26.

Tillamook Forest Center

On Hwy 6 between Hillsboro and Tillamook, this free interpretive center features a climbable 40-foot lookout tower, a 250-foot suspension footbridge across the Wilson River to nearby Jones Creek Campground, trails along the Wilson River, and exhibits on forestry. Open in spring Wed-Sun 10-4, in summer daily 10-5, and in fall Wed-Sun 10-4. Closed in winter. See Hike #22.

Pioneer Museum

Displays at this restored 1905 Tillamook County courthouse include quilts, Indian artifacts, a stagecoach, a blacksmith shop, a pioneer house, and a steam-powered donkey logging engine. A cut above average, the museum at 2106 Second Street is open Tuesday through Sunday 10am-4pm. Adults are $4, seniors $3.

Three Arch Rocks

Half a mile to sea from Oceanside, 220,000 birds of 13 species nest on these wave-carved islands. Murres crowd the ledges. Sea lions loll nearby. Protected as a national wildlife refuge in 1907, the area's 17 acres of islands are an official wilderness. Because boats, kayaks, jet skis, and airplanes can scare away the birds, venturing closer than 1000 feet is banned. Bring binoculars or a spotting scope to watch from Oceanside, a cute village with a tunnel to a hidden beach.

Oregon Coast Scenic Railroad

Ride a train pulled by a 1910 steam locomotive on the scenic 5-mile route between Garibaldi and Rockaway Beach. Trains leave Garibaldi at 10am, noon, and 2pm and Rockaway Beach at 11am and 1pm daily in July and August (in June and September, only on weekends). Fares for the 1 ½ -hour round trip run $18 for adults and $10 for children age 2-10. Call 503-842-7972 or check *www.ocsr.net*.

Rockaway Beach

The broad, breezy beach in this tourist village keeps kite shops hopping. Most popular beach access is the state park picnic area at First Avenue in mid-town. On 12th at the north edge of town is a boat ramp for freshwater Lake Lytle (powerboats permitted). On the south edge of town on 6th is a 25-acre old-growth cedar grove protected by the Nature Conservancy.

Museum in downtown Tillamook.

Munson Falls.

19   Munson Falls   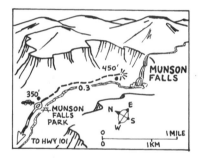

Easy
0.6 miles round trip
100 feet elevation gain

The Coast Range's tallest waterfall plunges 266 feet into an old-growth forest canyon. It's just off Highway 101, but surprisingly few travelers discover this small state park and the easy trail along rushing Munson Creek to the base of the slender, 5-tiered cataract. The falls are named for Goran Munson, who came from Michigan to settle near here in 1889.

Drive Highway 101 south of Tillamook 8 miles. Just before milepost 73, turn left at a sign for Munson Falls Natural Site. After 0.7 mile the narrow road turns to gravel. Follow signs another 0.9 mile to a small turnaround with a few picnic tables.

The large trail at the end of the turnaround ambles along the creek amidst 5-foot-thick red cedars, huge alders, and bigleaf maples with moss-draped branches. Watch for yellow monkeyflower, graceful lady ferns, red elderberries, and pink salmonberries.

After 0.3 mile the trail ends at a picnic table with a view of the top third of Munson Creek's waterfall. It's no use trying to see the rest of the falls by scrambling up through brush, either. A non-profit organization (funded by Microsoft billionaire Paul Allen) helped purchase this property in the late 1990s, however, so an expanded trail system to other viewpoints is a future possibility.

Bayocean Spit

Moderate (to sandy draw)
3.9-mile loop
100 feet elevation gain

Difficult (to jetty)
8.1-mile loop
No elevation gain

The scenic, sandy peninsula sheltering Tillamook Bay not only has some of the coast's best birdwatching, but it's also the site of one of Oregon's strangest ghost towns. Sample the sights on a 3.9-mile loop that's easy enough for hikers with children. Or plan a longer, 8.1-mile loop to the jetty at the spit's tip.

The ghost town story begins in 1907, when a Kansas City realtor named T. B. Potter platted the "Queen of Oregon Resorts" on the sandy spit. The city of Bayocean soon boasted a hotel, grocery, bowling alley, and the largest indoor saltwater swimming pool on the West Coast. Visitors were ferried from Portland by ship. Hundreds of lots were sold. Then one night Mrs. Potter reported that her husband had gone violently insane. He was never seen again. Development ceased.

In 1917, when construction of Tillamook Bay's north jetty changed ocean currents, street after street of the town began eroding into the sea. A 1932 jetty extension sped the process. By 1952 Bayocean Spit was an island, wiped clean of its city. A dike built in 1956 to protect the bay caused the spit to regrow, creating Cape Meares Lake.

From Highway 101 in downtown Tillamook, follow "Three Capes Scenic Route" signs west of town. After 2 miles you'll turn right on Bayocean Road. After another 5 miles look for a big signboard on the right describing the Bayocean Spit. Turn right on a gravel road along a dike for 0.9 mile to a big parking area.

The trail starts as an old gated road through the Scotch broom along the

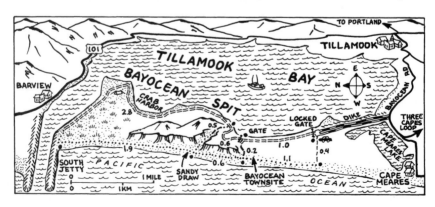

Cape Meares from the Beayocean Spit.   Opposite: Bayocean Spit from Cape Meares.

bayshore. If you bring a bicycle you can ride this flat road out the spit to the jetty, but hikers see more birds and can take the loop along the beach.

So walk the road for a mile. Along the way, watch the bay for ducks and long-necked loons. Great blue herons stand like sticks in the mudflats. Curlews stride along the shore, probing the sand with long thin bills.

After a mile you'll reach a road gate at the base of a forested hill. Turn left here on a sandy path that ducks through salal and shore pine 0.2 mile to the beach. (If you try to hike the loop in reverse, this trail at the edge of the forested hill will be hard to find.) Head right along the beach 0.6 mile to a big sandy gap in the forested bluff on the right.

If you're ready to head back on the shorter loop, turn inland through the grassy dunes in this draw. After 0.3 mile the sandy opening narrows to a trail that descends into the forest. The path dives through dense salal before emerging at the bayshore road. Your car is 1.6 miles to the right.

If you'd prefer the long loop, continue along the ocean beach 1.9 miles to the jetty. Loons, tufted puffins, and brown pelicans often fish in the bay mouth. Turn right for a few hundred yards to find the start of the bayshore road. While you're following it 4.4 miles back to your car, scan across the bay to spot Garibaldi's docks to the left and the distant roof of the huge Tillamook blimp hangar to the right.

21 Cape Meares

Easy (to light and Octopus Tree)
0.6 mile round trip
100 feet elevation gain

Moderate (from beach to Big Spruce)
3.6 miles round trip
500 feet elevation gain

An 1890 lighthouse and an ancient spruce forest top this dramatic bluff. The headland's name honors British Captain John Meares, who built a fur-trading fort in Nootka, Alaska and sailed south in 1788 questing for the great river of the Northwest. He overlooked the Columbia and turned back here.

For a short stroll to the lighthouse, drive west from downtown Tillamook 10 miles (or north from Pacific City 26 miles) following "Three Capes Scenic Route" signs, and take the Cape Meares State Park entrance road 0.6 mile to a turnaround. A wide paved path straight ahead leads 0.2 mile to the short white lighthouse, built of cast iron by a Lake Oswego foundry. Its spectacularly prismed, 1-ton lens was hand-ground in Paris in 1887, shipped around Cape Horn, and hoisted ashore by a derrick built of spruce logs. You can visit the gift shop in the tower's base 11am-4pm daily from April through October.

To the south, the view extends past Three Arch Rocks to Cape Lookout. To the north, the view includes Pyramid Rock and (closer to shore) Pillar Rock, crowded with hundreds of black-and-white nesting murres in May and June.

Return to your car and cross the parking lot to find the short, wide path to the Octopus Tree, a 12-foot-thick spruce with big, odd limbs. For a longer stroll, walk halfway around the tree to find a smaller path that continues half a mile to the highway, passing several viewpoints.

So far you'll have walked less than an hour. For a more substantial hike, drive back to the Three Capes Loop highway, turn left toward Tillamook for 2 miles,

The view south from Cape Meares.   Above: The Cape Meares lighthouse.

Vandals' bullets damaged the lighthouse's Fresnel lens in 2010.

turn left on Bayocean Road 0.6 mile into the community of Cape Meares, and go straight on gravel 100 feet to a beach access parking area. Two hiking routes climb from here to the cape itself: a scenic low-tide route along the beach and a longer high-tide path through brushy backwoods.

If the tide's at all low, walk left along the beach 0.4 mile to its end at a promontory. At low tide, you can round this headland to a gravel beach in a secluded cove. A rope here helps you scramble up this beach's bank. Then a trail climbs 0.9 mile to the start of the lighthouse road. The route passes through a large, slow-moving landslide area, so you may have to scramble over rough spots. Keep right at the trail junction beside the road to continue 0.2 mile to trail's end at Big Spruce, a 16-foot-thick, 144-foot-tall giant 750 to 800 years old that is Oregon's largest spruce. Make this tree your turnaround point.

If the tide's high you'll have to start this hike differently. From the beach access in the town of Cape Meares, walk along 4th Street 0.3 mile, turn left on Pacific Street to Fifth Street, turn right on this gravel road for 200 yards, and continue straight on a gated, grassy lane marked by an Oregon Coast Trail post. A "Trail Closed" sign here in 2013 referred to the landslide area more than a mile ahead. If you continue anyway, you'll find the path too muddy for tennis shoes and too brushy for shorts. The trail meanders 0.8 mile through scrub to join the low-tide route above the gravel beach.

Long-distance Oregon Coast Trail trekkers will find that Cape Meares has the only developed stretch of path for miles. To the north, the hiking route follows roads around Tillamook Bay and then traces the beach to Nehalem Bay (Hike #18). South of Cape Meares, the route follows roads to Cape Lookout (Hike #26).

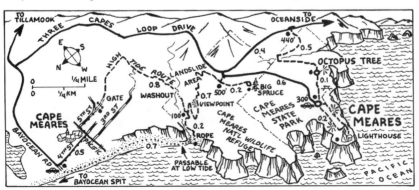

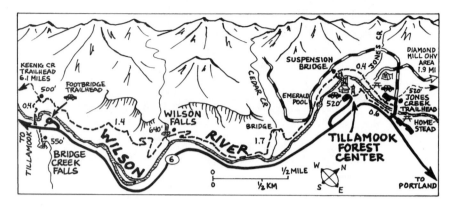

22 Wilson River

Easy (to Tillamook Forest Center)
1-mile loop
50 feet elevation gain

Difficult (to Bridge Creek Falls)
7.8 miles round trip
450 feet elevation gain

The Tillamook State Forest's free interpretive center beside the Wilson River has lots of attractions—a suspension footbridge, a climbable fire lookout tower, and displays describing the rainforest's regrowth since the 1933 Tillamook Burn. But the river itself is the star of the show. An easy one-mile loop crosses the bridge to give you a taste of the scenery. A longer hike takes you downriver to two small waterfalls and a high footbridge where you can watch salmon loll in green pools.

Although you could park right next to the Tillamook Forest Center, you might want to start half a mile upriver and stretch your legs a bit on the Wilson River Trail first. This also allows you to plan your trip whenever you want, because the Forest Center's parking lot is open only when the center is open, 10am-4pm daily in summer, otherwise Wednesday through Sunday.

Drive Highway 6 east of Tillamook 22 miles (or west of Portland 52 miles). At a sign for the Jones Creek Campground between mileposts 22 and 23, turn north on North Fork Road, cross a river bridge, and promptly turn left into the gravel Jones Creek Day Use Area parking lot.

Start by a big signboard and take the trail downstream to the right through a picnic area in a mossy riverside rainforest of Douglas firs, bigleaf maples, and alders. After 0.4 mile you'll reach the 250-foot suspension footbridge. Cross it to tour the free interpretive center, where you'll find exhibits, a gift shop, and a movie. Go out the far (front) door to see the 40-foot lookout tower.

To return on a short loop, take a trail near the base of the lookout tower, following

Wilson River gorge at Footbridge Trailhead.   Opposite: Tillamook Forest Center.

signs for the Smith Homestead Day Use Area. After hiking a half mile upstream along the riverbank you'll reach North Fork Road. Take a sidewalk left across the Wilson River bridge and turn left on a short trail left through the woods to your car.

For a longer hike from the interpretive center, recross the suspension footbridge over the Wilson River and turn left on the Wilson River Trail. After a quarter mile you'll pass an emerald pool that's fine for summer swimming. Next the path briefly joins the Cedar Creek Road. Then it ducks under a powerline, crosses Cedar Creek on a lovely little footbridge, ambles another mile, and switchbacks up to dainty Wilson Falls. Delicate maidenhair ferns surround this 60-foot, fan-shaped cascade.

For the next 1.4 miles the trail wends away from the river. At a T-shaped junction, turn left at a sign for the Footbridge Trailhead. When the path grows faint under powerlines, veer a little to the right to find the footbridge, a railed 100-foot span high above a spectacular basalt gorge.

On the far side of the bridge, turn left along the shoulder of Highway 6 for 200 feet to the end of a guardrail. Then carefully cross the highway to a "Waterfall" sign. Here, stone steps from the 1930s lead 0.2 mile up a canyon to Bridge Creek Falls, a 40-foot chute in a mossy rock face.

If you've had the foresight to leave a shuttle car at the Footbridge Trailhead, a parking area on Highway 6 at milepost 20, you're good to go. If not, don't be tempted to walk back to the visitor center along the busy, narrow highway. Retrace your steps on the Wilson River Trail, a route that's nice enough to see twice.

Other Options

Buses from Tillamook and Portland stop at the Tillamook Forest Center once a day on Sunday and twice every other day. Call 503-815-8283 for schedules.

The Wilson River Trail extends 20.6 miles in all. Below the Footbridge Trailhead, the path climbs away from the river to avoid private land and then switchbacks down to end at Keenig Creek's picnic area, near milepost 18 of Highway 6. Upstream from the Tillamook Forest Center, the trail passes a noisy off-highway vehicle area, crosses the North Fork Wilson River on a lovely arched footbridge, and climbs on its way to the Kings Mountain Trailhead (see Hike #23).

23 Kings Mountain

Difficult (to Kings Mountain)
5 miles round trip
2530 feet elevation gain

Difficult (to Elk Mountain)
3.2 miles round trip
2000 feet elevation gain

Very Difficult (both peaks)
10.9-mile loop
3850 feet elevation gain

Steep, rugged trails climb to sweeping Coast Range viewpoints atop Kings Mountain and neighboring Elk Mountain. In May and June, wildflowers brighten the upper ridges. Below, ancient snags and regrowing forests recall the Tillamook Burn fires of the 1930s and 1940s. For an athletic challenge, connect the two summits via a ridgecrest hiking route, partly on abandoned roads.

To find the Kings Mountain trailhead, drive Highway 6 west of Portland 49 miles (or east of Tillamook 25 miles) to a brown hiker-symbol sign at a gravel parking area just east of milepost 25. The trail leads up into a mossy alder forest with sword ferns and tiny, 5-petaled candyflower. After a mile the trail steepens sharply and the forest shifts to drier Douglas fir woods. At the 2.2-mile mark the path climbs into a glorious ridgecrest meadow of red Indian paintbrush, blue larkspur, wild strawberry, purple penstemon, cushions of bluish phlox, and the huge white plumes of beargrass. Summit views extend from Mt. Hood to the ocean beyond Tillamook Bay. Hikers can sign a register kept in a blue plastic tube. The trail continues toward Elk Mountain, but if you're planning to tackle this difficult traverse, it's best to start at the other end.

To find the Elk Mountain trailhead, drive Highway 6 to milepost 28 and turn north at a sign for Elk Creek Campground. After 0.3 mile, drive past the campground pullout, continuing straight across a bridge to a trailhead parking area at road's end. Two trails begin here. Mountain bikers use the barricaded old road (the Elk Creek Trail) at the far end of the lot, but hikers generally take the much shorter Elk Mountain Trail on the left.

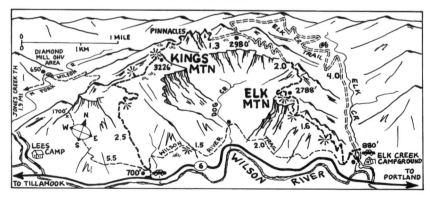

View from Kings Mountain.   Opposite: Devils club.   Below : Gales Creek.

This path scrambles up a steep, rocky crest with all the subtlety of a bobsled run. Loose scree makes the route especially treacherous. As consolation, there are lots of orange Indian paintbrush and viewpoints. After dipping across four saddles, reach the summit meadow of beargrass and Cascade lilies.

If you're continuing on the still more difficult traverse, take the path that dives off the far side of Elk Mountain's summit. For the next mile you'll often have to use your hands to follow the scrambly ridgecrest route, at times atop a narrow rock hogback. Then continue on an old road 1.5 miles to a junction in a pass and turn left for 1.3 miles to Kings Mountain's summit and the start of a long descent. Just before reaching Highway 6, turn left on the Wilson River Trail for 3.5 miles to complete the loop back to your car.

24   Gales Creek

Difficult
7.2-mile loop
1200 feet elevation gain

(Refer to map on following page)

At the crest of the Coast Range, where the devastating Tillamook Burn fires of 1933, 1939, and 1945 began, the regrown Tillamook State Forest has become such a popular destination that it is now divided into two recreation zones. South of Highway 6, motorcycles and all-terrain vehicles whine through the woods. North of the highway, however, non-motorized recreation reigns. Sample this quieter area on a new network of trails at Gales Creek.

Drive Highway 6 to the Coast Range west of Portland 39 miles (or east of Tillamook 35 miles). At a "Gales Creek CG" sign near milepost 35, turn north through a yellow gate onto a gravel road. If the gate is locked (usually November to mid-May), park near it and walk. After 0.7 mile, just beyond a picnic area, turn left into a large trailhead parking lot.

Two trails start here, both open to hikers and bicycles, but not horses. Take the path to the right, which traverses a slope above Gales Creek. The forest of Douglas fir and mossy bigleaf maple has a jungly understory of ferns, thimbleberry, and oxalis. A few black snags and stumps remain from the old fires.

After 0.8 mile you'll cross a footbridge to a T-shaped trail junction. To the right is the trail up Gales Creek, but storm damage closed this route in 2008. When it reopens it will again amble to the canyon's head at Bell Camp Road; day-hikers generally find a creekside lunch spot along the way where they can declare victory and turn back.

For the loop hike, however, turn left onto the Storey Burn Trail when you reach the T-shaped junction. This route climbs a side canyon, passes a 15-foot waterfall, and meets gravel Storey Burn Road. Cross the road and walk 200 yards on a dirt spur to a parking lot to find the continuation of the trail. In another 1.6 miles the path ducks under a gigantic Highway 6 bridge and then crosses a wide dirt trail used by off-highway vehicles. Continue 0.3 mile, keeping left at forks, climb to a gravel road, and turn left up this road 0.3 mile. Then skirt to the right around a highway equipment yard to Highway 6.

To complete the loop, you'll have to walk to the right along the noisy shoulder of the busy highway 0.3 mile. At a hiker-symbol sign, carefully cross the highway to a trail sign at the far end of a huge parking pullout for the Summit Trailhead. This path descends along Low Divide Creek 2 miles, following portions of a historic railroad grade. A spur trail to the left offers a shortcut back to the parking area with your car — or you can simply go straight to the gravel road and follow it left 300 yards to your car.

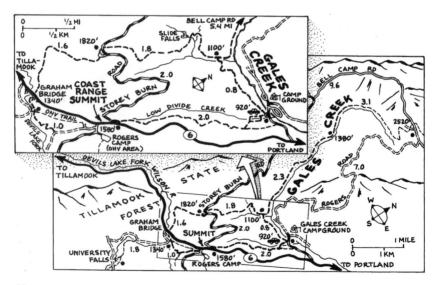

25 Hagg Lake

Easy (south shore)
3.2 miles round trip
50 feet elevation gain

Easy (north shore)
3.6 miles round trip
30 feet elevation gain

Difficult (around lake)
13.1-mile loop
200 feet elevation gain

Right: Trillium.

Fishermen and waterskiers have long since found Hagg Lake, the reservoir created in this rural Coast Range valley near Forest Grove in 1975. But relatively few hikers have discovered the charms of the 13.1-mile footpath around the lake, even though it's just a half hour's drive from Portland.

Short walks along either the north or south shore lead through old-growth forests and grassy fields with lake vistas. Visit March to June for the best woodland wildflowers. Skip summer weekends if you're bothered by the whine of powerboats.

From Freeway 217 in Beaverton, turn west for 12 miles on Highway 8 through Hillsboro to Forest Grove. Then turn left for 5 miles on Highway 47 (toward McMinnville) and turn right at a "Hagg Lake" pointer for 3 miles to the park's fee booth. Expect to pay $6 per car here from early March to late November.

For a short hike on the quiet, south shore of the lake, drive past the fee booth 0.3 mile and turn left across the dam (toward Boat Ramp C) for 0.8 mile to a small pullout on the right with a red post inscribed "Trail."

The path hugs the shore amid young alder and Douglas fir. In spring expect big, 3-petaled white trilliums and droopy, 6-petaled fawn lilies. Ignore left-hand side trails; they lead to the road. In 0.6 mile you'll cross an arm of the reservoir

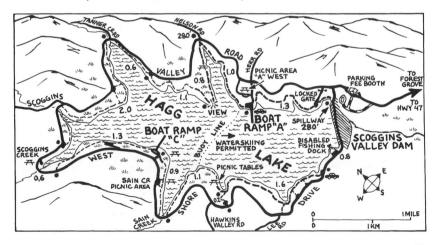

on a huge log and a footbridge. After another mile, cross the end of a second reservoir arm on a zigzagging 90-foot bridge and reach an X-shaped junction. The lakeshore trail turns right to several picnic tables amidst scenic lakeside firs — a good lunch spot and turnaround point.

If you'd prefer a slightly longer hike from the park's main picnic area on the busier, north shore of the lake, drive straight past the fee both for a mile, and then turn left at a sign for Boat Ramp "A". The parking lot for Picnic Area "A" West is to one side of this entrance road. The easiest way to find the trail around the lake, however, is to drive straight to the boat ramp and start walking to the right along the lakeshore.

From Boat Ramp "A" the trail sets out through an old-growth Douglas fir forest. Wear boots to cross a few muddy spots, and remember to stay on the trail, because the woods do have some poison oak. After hiking a mile counter-clockwise around the lake you'll briefly join the highway, opposite Nelson Road. Keep left past a red trail post to continue on the path, which passes four picnic tables in the woods before entering a broad, grassy field. In another 0.4 mile, the tip of a grassy promontory offers perhaps the best view of the lake anywhere. This makes a nice turnaround point, especially if you're hiking with children.

If you're confident you can manage the 13.1 miles around the lake, press onward. Note, however, that the lakeshore path crosses abandoned farm fields (now maintained as elk pasture) for much of the next 6 miles. In a few spots the trail parallels the road closely, and 1.4 miles of the loop follows the road itself.

The west shore of Hagg Lake.

NORTH HEAD LIGHTHOUSE (Hike #3) helps the nearby Cape Disappointment light to mark the Columbia River entrance.

THE LIGHTHOUSES

CAPE DISAPPOINTMENT (Hike #4) in Washington has a light from 1856, the West's oldest still in use.

TILLAMOOK ROCK'S lighthouse (pp42-43) won the nickname "Terrible Tilly" because of winter storms.

Oregon has no natural harbors along its rocky coast, so navigation has always been treacherous, plagued by shipwrecks. Congress authorized two lighthouses in the 1850s, and another nine between 1868 and 1896. The lights that remain on this wildly beautiful, rugged shore are scenic goals for hikers and tourists.

The strangest and least visitable of these lighthouses stands atop Tillamook Rock, an island crag one mile off the shore of Tillamook Head (Hike #11). Engineers had originally wanted to build the light on the mainland, but because Tillamook

YAQUINA BAY LIGHTHOUSE (Hike #39), in Newport, is now a museum with a gift shop and a ghost story.

CAPE MEARES (Hike #21), with its red-prismed light, is a popular stop on the Three Capes Scenic Loop.

HECETA HEAD (Hike #53) has the state's most photographed lighthouse. The keeper's house is a bed & breakfast inn.

...ead is 1000 feet high and often hidden
...y fog, they decided in 1878 to mount
...he beacon on this 121-foot island
...nstead.

It proved to be a difficult place to
...uild anything. The first surveyor
...ho landed was swept away by
...wave and drowned. The next
...uilder ferried workers to the
...sland by suspending them from
...ulleys and zinging them across the sea on
...cable strung from a ship.

It took seven months to dynamite a flat
...pot, and another seven months to build
...he tower. When it was done, gigantic
...orms off the North Pacific routinely
broke lantern windows 144 feet above
sea level. In 1935
the Coast Guard
replaced the

CAPE BLANCO
(Hike #78)

light with a whistling buoy, and in
1954 they sold the island at auction.
Eventually it was bought by Eternity
At Sea, a funeral business that heli-
coptered urns to the island, carrying
the cremated remains of people who
want to be buried in a lighthouse
when they die.

BANDON'S COQUILLE RIVER LIGHTHOUSE (Hike
#74) was built right on the rock ships needed to miss.

YAQUINA HEAD
LIGHTHOUSE
(Hike #39), atop a
93-foot tower, is
Oregon's tallest.
Legend has it that a
worker died when
he fell between the
tower's brick walls,
and his ghost still
moans.

SEASIDE'S PROMENADE (Hike #10) separates this old-time resort town from the grassy dunes and a busy beach.

THE LIGHTSHIP COLUMBIA is a permanent exhibit at Astoria's Columbia River Maritime Museum (Hike #9).

THE DEVILS CAULDRON ((Hike #17) has no guardrails, so take care if you approach this viewpoint.

A FOOTBRIDGE SPANS NECARNEY CREEK along the Oregon Coast Trail in Os West State Park (Hike #16).

A statue at Seaside's Turnaround (see p38) honors explorers William Clark and Meriwether Lewis.

CLARK'S POINT OF VIEW on Tillamook Head (Hike #11) marks the route the explorers took to Cannon Beach.

Sent by President Jefferson to scout and claim the Oregon Country, Lewis and Clark's Corps of Discovery canoed down the Columbia River in late 1805. They camped for ten days across the river from present-day Astoria to reconnoiter. Clark led a group to plant an American flag at the mouth of the river atop Cape Disappointment. Back in camp, the corps voted to build winter quarters on a slough 6 miles south of Astoria where the hunting was better.

Their journals include complaints that rain fell on all but twelve of the 106 dreary days they spent in Fort Clatsop's 50-foot-square log stockade.

Clark also grumbled that their diet lacked salt and fat. He led a trip to Seaside's beach and boiled seawater to obtain a quart of salt a day. Then he hiked to Cannon Beach to get blubber from a stranded whale. With these provisions, the explorers left Fort Clatsop early in 1806 and returned east.

FORT CLATSOP (see p34) is a reconstruction of the explorers' winter quarters near present-day Astoria.

AT CAPE DISAPPOINTMENT (Hike #4) the explorers planted a flag. Today you can visit a museum and lighthouse.

NEAHKAHNIE MOUNTAIN (Hike #17) rises 1600 feet.

THE FLAVEL HOUSE (Hike #9), now a museum, was built by a wealthy Columbia River bar pilot in 1885.

NEWPORT (Hikes #39 and 40) has two lighthouses, two excellent aquariums, and the lovely Yaquina Bay Bridge.

IS THAT MUSHROOM EDIBLE?

Western Oregon's rainforests sprout each fall with hundreds of varieties of mushrooms—so many, in fact, that the Forest Service has begun regulating professional mushroom hunters. Several communities hold annual mushroom festivals.

Unfortunately there are no simple rules to separate the few edible species from those that are poisonous or simply unsavory. Sample wild fungi only if you're with an expert with a detailed guide.

◁ Edible but strange-looking, morels sprout in spring, particularly after a fire.

GOLDEN CHANTERELLE (*Cantharellus cibarius*) is common and delicious—peppery when raw and firm when cooked. Orange ribs run down onto its stem.

PANTHER AMANITA (*Amanita pantherina*) is deadly poisonous and very common. Note that the papery white gills under its cap are not attached to the stem.

TSUNAMIS IN OREGON

Never in written history has the Oregon Coast suffered a major earthquake or a devastating tsunami (tidal wave). So why do so many beaches have warning signs?

In the late 1980s scientists realized that earthquake pressure gradually builds up off Oregon's coast as the North American continent slowly arches westward across the Pacific seafloor. Then the ground suddenly drops, causing a massive quake and tsunami every 300 to 600 years.

Excavators found one clue to this violent past: repeated layers of tsunami debris in estuary soils many miles inland. Another tipoff was the stumps of a drowned forest exposed at low tide at many Northwest beaches. Ring counts of the trees show they all died at once in 1700.

The earthquakes are about 30 times

more powerful than the 1906 San Francisco temblor, and launch a tsunami surge that raises sea levels by as much as 20 feet.

Although it has been more than 300 years since the last great coastal earthquake, the next one might not occur for centuries. On any given day the risk posed by snoozing on the beach is statistically no greater than the risk of driving a car.

SALISHAN SPIT (Hike #37) has many homes that are vulnerable to tsunamis.

CASCADE HEAD (Hikes #31 and 32) earned its name for a waterfall that spills into the ocean at Harts Cove.

AT CAPE LOOKOUT (Hike #26), hang gliders sometimes sail over the long beach toward Netarts Spit.

NEWPORT'S NYE BEACH (Hike #39), one of the state's oldest resort beaches, still catches sunsets.

THE TRAIL TO HARTS COVE (Hike #31) is closed for six
months each year to protect rare headland butterflies.

Cape Kiwanda and Haystack Rock at Pacific City (Hike #27).

PACIFIC CITY

The shore between Tillamook and Lincoln City is the quietest stretch of coastline within a 2-hour drive of Portland. Long beaches and headlands here remain delightfully pristine. Highway 101 detours inland, approaching the beach only at the posh cottages of Neskowin, where the downtown consists of a single general store, a restaurant, and two golf courses.

Three Capes Loop
A coastal alternative to the inland portion of Highway 101, this scenic route south of Tillamook passes sandy Cape Kiwanda, cliff-edged Cape Lookout, and lighthouse-topped Cape Meares. The route also skirts three estuaries (Nestucca Bay, Sand Lake, and Netarts Bay), and visits three villages (Pacific City, Netarts, and Oceanside).

Sand Lake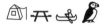
Sand Lake resembles a coastal river bay without a river. It's best known for the dune landscape to its north, where off-highway vehicles roar out from their staging area at the Forest Service's Sand Beach Campground. But the estuary itself is actually a quiet haven for coastal wildlife. To explore a small area of grassy, motor-free dunes on the spit between Sand Lake and the ocean, head for the picnic area beside the Forest Service campground.

Whalen Island
A 1.4-mile trail circles this wooded island in Sand Lake. With a small Tillamook County park and the Clay Myers State Natural Area, the scenic island is a great place to canoe, kayak, or watch birds in Sand Lake's estuary. Access is by a bridge from the Three Capes Loop Drive 6 miles north of Pacific City. The park includes a small campground, picnic area, and boat ramp.

Harts Cove (Hike #31).

Pacific City and Cape Kiwanda

Scenic Cape Kiwanda shelters Pacific City's busy beach. With the morning's outgoing tide, fishermen back boat trailers across the sand to launch dories dramatically through the waves. Surfers in wet suits paddle nearby. Hikers explore the cape's wave-sculpted tip (see Hike #27) Hang gliders soar from sand dunes atop the cape's neck. People watch the show from the patio of the Pelican Pub and Brewery beside the main beach access parking lot. To find it, drive a mile north of Pacific City on the Three Capes Loop.

Nestucca Bay

Canoeing and kayaking on this relatively undeveloped, many-armed estuary are best when winds are low. Start at any of three launch sites: at Straub State Park (see Hike #27), on the road between Pacific City and Highway 101, and where Highway 101 crosses the Little Nestucca River.

Mount Hebo

Once a radar base scanned the skies from this 3176-foot, flat-topped mountain. The base is gone, but the panorama from the summit meadows remains. Either hike there from the campground at Hebo Lake (Hike #28), or drive to the view. The paved road to the top starts beside the Hebo Ranger Station, just off Highway 101 on Highway 22.

Cascade Head

The meadowed capes at Cascade Head can be reached only on foot (see Hikes #31 and #32), but non-hikers have other options. The Salmon River estuary at the foot of the cape is a labyrinth of winding waterways, perfect for canoe or kayak exploration. Launch at the Knight Park boat ramp on Savage Road. For a scenic drive through the Cascade Head Experimental Forest, take Slab Creek Road (an old, 11-mile section of Highway 101) from Otis to Neskowin.

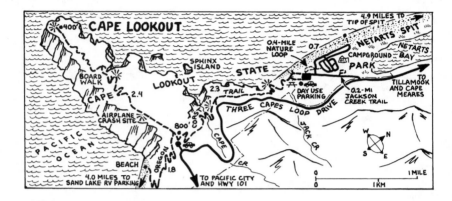

26   Cape Lookout

Moderate (to tip of cape)
4.8 miles round trip
400 feet elevation gain

Moderate (to south beach)
3.6 miles round trip
800 feet elevation gain

Easy (shuttle to picnic area)
2.3 miles one way
800 feet elevation **loss**

Like an unfinished dike to Hawaii, this narrow, cliff-edged cape juts 2 miles straight out into the Pacific Ocean. At the trailhead atop the cape, hikers have three choices: walk out to the viewpoint at the cape's tip, descend to a secluded beach at the southern base of the cape, or amble north along the bluffs to the state park's popular picnic area and campground. The trails have muddy spots unsuitable for tennis shoes.

The cape itself dates back 15 million years, when lava flows from Eastern Oregon poured down the Columbia River and fanned out. All along the northern Oregon Coast, tough remnants of that massive basalt flood have survived to form headlands and islands.

From downtown Tillamook, head west on 3rd Street and follow signs for Cape Lookout State Park 13 miles. Continue past the campground turnoff 2.6 miles to the signed trailhead turnoff on the right. (If you're driving here from the south, take the Pacific City exit of Highway 101 and follow the Three Capes Loop 16 miles north to the top of a pass and the trailhead sign.)

To hike to the tip of the cape, take the left-hand trail at the end of the parking lot and keep straight at a junction 100 yards beyond. The dense forest of gnarled old spruce and hemlock trees shelters ferns, salal, salmonberry, and candyflower, an edible little 5-petaled white bloom with delicate pink stripes.

The first view south, after 0.6 mile, is just above the site where a B-17 bomber crashed into the cape's 800-foot cliffs on a foggy day in 1943. If the weather's clear, you can spot Haystack Rock off Cape Kiwanda, as well as Cascade Head and distant Cape Foulweather.

Another 0.6 mile brings you to a railed overlook with your first view north. Note Three Arch Rocks off Cape Meares and the blue silhouette of Neahkahnie Mountain. Next the trail detours above a cove where the old path slid into the sea in 1992. A boardwalk helps hikers cross mudpits on the new route.

At the tip of the cape, red paintbrush, white yarrow, and scarlet fireweed brighten a clifftop meadow 400 feet above the waves. A red buoy moans offshore. Bring binoculars to watch for gray whales here from December to June. Up to 20,000 migrate from Alaska to Mexico each year. Sometimes as many as 30 per hour round this prominent cape. Remember to save some energy for the return hike uphill to the trailhead.

If you'd rather try a less heavily used path from this trailhead, take the Oregon Coast Trail either south or north. To the south the path switchbacks 1.8 miles down to a beach that stretches to the Forest Service campground at Sand Lake. The first 2 miles of this beach are quiet, but the last 2 miles are open to cars.

To the north of Cape Lookout, the Oregon Coast Trail descends gradually through an old-growth spruce forest with views of Sphinx Island, to the picnic grounds at the state park's day-use parking area. For an easy hike, leave a shuttle car here (a parking fee is charged) and hike this 2.3-mile trail all downhill.

Other Hiking Options

For a difficult trek from the campground, walk the beach 4.9 miles to the tip of Netarts Spit, where seals and shorebirds often hang out. The spit has views of Netarts, Oceanside, and Three Arch Rocks. It's not easy to return on a loop because the muddy shores of Netarts Bay are largely unhikable.

View from Cape Lookout Trail.   Opposite: Trail to southern beach.

27 Pacific City

Easy (to Cape Kiwanda)
1 mile round trip
100 feet elevation gain

Difficult (around Nestucca Spit)
5.7-mile loop
100 feet elevation gain

Best known for its dory fishing fleet, Pacific City's beach offers a number of attractions for hikers. Start with a short stroll at the beach's busy north end by Cape Kiwanda. The tidepools, clifftop viewpoints, and sand dunes here are especially popular for hikers with children. For a quieter loop, head for Bob Straub State Park at the south end of the beach, where a network of sandy trails allows hikers and equestrians to explore Nestucca Spit.

Drive Highway 101 north of Lincoln City 18 miles (or south of Tillamook 25 miles) and turn west on the Three Capes Scenic Route for 2.7 miles. In the center of Pacific City, turn left for 2 blocks across a river bridge, and then turn right for a mile to the huge Cape Kiwanda parking lot on the left, beside the Pelican Pub.

Fishermen here launch dories directly through the waves, taking advantage of the natural breakwater created by Cape Kiwanda and massive Haystack Rock, a mile offshore. Summer mornings you can watch fishermen back their trailered boats into the shallows, slide them off, and then race to jump aboard. The tricky procedure is reversed when the fleet returns in mid-day.

A short walk takes you to the foot of the wave-sculpted yellow sandstone cape. At low tide you can explore the tide pools and shallow caves along its base. For a viewpoint, climb past a signboard on a sand slope to a junction atop the bluff. Both forks of the trail deadend in 200 yards at views of surf-smashed cliffs. Do not leave the trail or venture beyond the viewpoints; every few years self-styled adventurers slip to their deaths here.

If you want to cross the headland, return to the beach and hike up through the

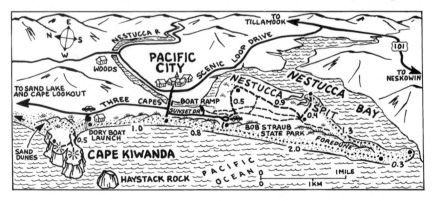

Haystack Rock from Nestucca Spit.   Opposite: Haystack Rock from the Pelican Pub.

dunes farther inland. Here you'll reach a windy, sandy pass where hang gliders launch to sail down the far slope to cars waiting on the beach below.

For the longer hike around the Nestucca Spit, return to your car and drive a mile back toward Pacific City. At the junction by the bridge, jog right onto Sunset Drive and continue 0.8 mile to the road's end at a turnaround with a horse hitching rail in Bob Straub State Park. The park prohibits camping.

The path starts by the restrooms and climbs across a grassy foredune to the wide beach. Head left for 2.3 miles to the end of the spit. Cars are allowed on this stretch of beach, so you'll see tire tracks and may find fishermen parked at the spit's tip. When you follow the beach left to the quiet bayshore side of the peninsula, however, you'll leave motors behind. The breath-holes of clams dot the soft white beaches of the still bay. On your left, grassy dunes gradually give way to a young forest of spruce, shore pine, and Scotch broom.

After you've trekked 1.6 miles from the spit's tip, the bayshore beach finally ends where the tide flats of a branching estuary inlet cut into the peninsula. Follow hoofprints inland to find a sandy trail through the woods. In 0.4 mile you'll reach a 5-way trail junction *(GPS location N45°10.75' W123°57.82')*. The network of sandy trails is unmarked and confusing, but if you turn right and keep right for 0.9 mile you'll follow a scenic ridge out along the bay. Then veer left and follow the largest trail at junctions for 0.5 mile to return to your car.

Oregon Coast Trail trekkers from Cape Lookout (Hike #26) should take the beach south 4 miles, ford the mouth of Sand Lake at low tide, continue 4 miles on the beach, and cross Cape Kiwanda.

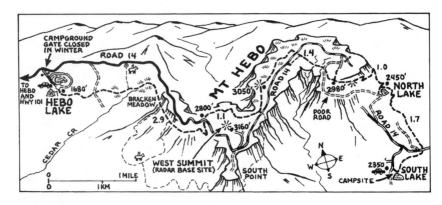

28   Mount Hebo

Difficult (to summit meadow)
8 miles round trip
1500 feet elevation gain

Difficult (shuttle to South Lake)
8.1 miles one way
1400 feet elevation gain

Views from the 3-mile-long, meadowed plateau atop Mt. Hebo stretch from Tillamook Bay to the white cones of the Cascade Range. This coastal peak is so high that snow often blocks access in January and February. By May the meadows are colored with wildflowers. Like Saddle Mountain to the north, this plateau is a remnant of a gigantic, 15-million-year-old basalt lava flow that spilled from Eastern Oregon to the sea.

Surprisingly, Indians crossing from the Willamette Valley to the coast found it easier to scale this mountain and cross its high meadows than to cut their way through the lowland rainforests. Pioneer Hiram Smith and a crew of Tillamook settlers improved the Indians' steep path in 1854. It remained the major horse route across the Coast Range until a lower elevation wagon road was built in 1882. The Forest Service rediscovered the historic path in 1975, upgraded it, and opened the 8-mile Pioneer-Indian Trail from Hebo Lake to South Lake in 1984.

Much of the route traverses a dense, 8000-acre Douglas fir forest planted in 1912 after a devastating fire. This was one of the Forest Service's first reforestation efforts, and unwisely relied on seed collected in the distant Rocky Mountains. Today the trees are not nearly so large as similar-aged, native Douglas fir stock better adapted to Oregon's coastal climate.

An Air Force radar station that was housed on the west summit of Mt. Hebo during the Cold War has been removed without a trace. During the Columbus Day storm of 1962 the station's wind gauge measured Oregon's mightiest gale

(170 miles per hour) before the gauge blew away.

To start the hike, drive Highway 101 south of Tillamook 19 miles (or north of Lincoln City 24 miles) to Hebo and turn east on Highway 22 for 0.2 mile. Just before the Hebo Ranger Station, turn left at a sign for Hebo Lake. Follow twisty, paved Road 14 uphill 4.7 miles, fork to the right at the Hebo Lake Campground entrance, and keep right for 0.2 mile to the trailhead parking area. Expect to pay a $5-per-car day use parking fee here. The rest of the year the campground is gated closed, adding 0.2 mile to the hike.

For a quick warm-up, you might want to stroll 0.5 mile on the wheelchair-accessible gravel path and boardwalk around Hebo Lake. The main Pioneer-Indian Trail starts at a signboard on the opposite side of the parking lot from the picnic shelter. This trail climbs for 2.9 miles, crossing a gravel road and a bracken-filled meadow, before reaching paved Road 14 at a saddle.

Cross Road 14 and continue on the trail another mile. This part of the Pioneer-Indian Trail contours around the mountain and follows posts across a broad plateau with meadows and viewpoints. Wild strawberries and Indian paintbrush grow here. It's also home to the threatened silverspot butterfly.

If you haven't arranged a shuttle car to the far end of the trail, choose a view-point as your turnaround point.

If you do have a shuttle car, or if you're game for a long hike, keep going on the Pioneer-Indian Trail. The path crosses Road 14 two more times and descends steeply to brush-rimmed North Lake. Keep left and continue 1.7 miles through the woods to trail's end at a campsite beside South Lake. If you intend to drive a shuttle car here, be warned that part of the road is rough. From Hebo Lake, continue 3.3 miles up Road 14 to a summit, fork right on a narrower continuation of Road 14 for 2 miles, turn right onto a rough dirt road past a "14" sign, and soon turn right again. After 1.6 bumpy miles join a good gravel road. Continue 0.4 mile and then turn right for a final 0.3 mile to the trailhead pullout on the left.

Other Options

Equestrians begin at a Road 14 trailhead 1.2 miles beyond the Hebo Lake turnoff. Two loop tours have been designed for horses here, the 3.2-mile New Loop and a 10.5-mile trip around South Point.

Niagara Falls (Hike #29).   *Opposite: Fishing on Hebo Lake.*

29   Niagara Falls

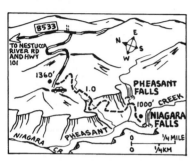

Easy
2 miles round trip
360 feet elevation gain

See photo on previous page.

Two 100-foot waterfalls spill into Pheasant Creek's secluded box canyon. An easy 1-mile path descends along a wooded creek to viewpoints at the falls' base.

Drive Highway 101 south of Tillamook 15 miles (or north of Lincoln City 28 miles) to the village of Beaver near milepost 80, and turn east on a paved road along the upper Nestucca River. After a 6.7-mile drive through pastoral dairy farmland, keep right at the settlement of Blaine. Now watch the odometer. In another 4.8 miles (between mileposts 11 and 12), turn right on an easy-to-miss paved road through a fenced field. This narrow road passes signs stating "8533" and "Niagara Falls Trail" and then turns to gravel. Go straight on the main road at all forks for 4.3 miles to another easy-to-miss junction at a pass. Turn right past a small "Trail" sign for 0.7 mile to a parking area on the left.

The trail sets off downhill through a forest of Douglas fir, salal underbrush, sword ferns, and the mossy arches of vine maple. Spring brings big 3-petaled trilliums, 5-petaled candyflower, and the delicately belled stalks of wild lily-of-the-valley. Look for yellow monkeyflower on creek banks.

The path crosses a splashing creek three times on footbridges, then traverses down a canyon slope to the base of Pheasant Falls' lacy 100-foot fan. Another 100 yards brings you to a picnic table at a viewpoint of Niagara Falls, a gauzy 130-foot ribbon launching off the lip of a vast amphitheater of sheer rock cliffs. The layers exposed here reveal that this rock was formed by a series of basalt lava flows.

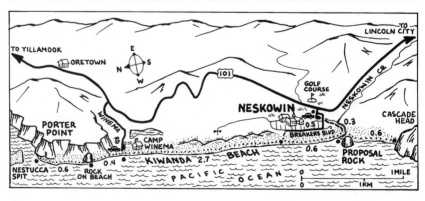

30   Neskowin

Easy (to Proposal Rock)
1.4-mile loop
No elevation gain

Easy (Camp Winema to Porter Pt)
2 miles round trip
No elevation gain

Right: Proposal Rock.

(Refer to map on previous page)

This beachfront village has been known as a romantic hideaway since the 1800s, when a sea captain is said to have rowed his lady love to Proposal Rock to pop the question. The forested little island is still a good place for an old-fashioned query. These days the rock is accessible on foot from Neskowin's beach at all but the highest tides, but beware of sneaker waves.

Drive Highway 101 south of Tillamook 33 miles (or north of Lincoln City 10 miles), turn west at a small "Neskowin" pointer, and go straight 100 yards to the Neskowin Wayside. From the far left end of the parking lot, walk across a street and follow a paved path straight along Neskowin Creek 0.3 mile to Proposal Rock.

Expect to wade to visit the rock, since it diverts Neskowin Creek. In fact, the sandy creek lapping the rock's base is a good place to let kids splash around a bit — warmer and safer than in the surf. The creek's name derives from the Salish word *Ne* ("place of") and *skowin*, reported to mean "plenty of fish."

If you want to climb Proposal Rock, a steep scramble trail at its right-hand edge leads up through spruce, alder, salal, and salmonberry to the top.

At low winter tides, the stumps of a sunken cedar forest emerge on the beach, evidence of massive earthquakes that drop Oregon's coastline ten feet every 300 to 600 years. The last one hit on January 26, 1700.

To tour Neskowin on a short loop, turn right along the beach for 0.6 mile. Head inland at a beach access just beyond a row of 11 identical condominiums. Turn right on paved Breakers Boulevard, pass 7 blocks of nice old cottages, and turn left on Salem Avenue to your car.

For a longer hike, you could simply walk north along the beach to its end at the Nestucca River. But that's a tiring trudge in loose sand. To skip to the highlight of that trek, drive 4 miles north of Neskowin on Highway 101, turn left on paved Winema Road for 0.6 mile, and park at a beach access.

From here it's a fun 1-mile stroll north to the driftwood jumbled at the river mouth beneath the cliffs of Porter Point. This is a quiet, wild spot, where you're almost certain to see harbor seals, cormorants, and loons.

The Oregon Coast Trail simply follows the beach here. To the north, long-distance hikers from Pacific City (Hike #27) have to plan a boat shuttle across Nestucca Bay or hike around the bay on roads. To the south, follow Highway 101 a mile to find the trail across Cascade Head (Hike #32).

31 Harts Cove

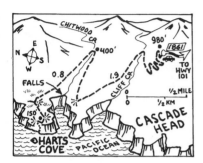

Easy (Cascade Head upper trail)
2 miles round trip
160 feet elevation **loss**
Open July 16 through Dec 31

Moderate (Harts Cove)
5.4 miles round trip
900 feet elevation **loss**

Cascade Head won its name when sailors spotted the waterfalls cascading from its oceanfront cliffs. The trail down to Harts Cove leads to a viewpoint of one of these dramatic falls. But the path also features an old-growth spruce forest, a flower-filled blufftop meadow, and a rocky shore where sea lions bellow. To protect endangered butterflies and wildflowers on the headland, the road to the trailhead is gated closed January 1 to July 15. The access road also passes the easy, upper trailhead to the more famous Nature Conservancy preserve on Cascade Head. Ambitious hikers can do both in a day.

From the junction with Highway 18 (just north of Lincoln City), drive north 4 miles on Highway 101. Just before a crest, turn left on gravel Cascade Head Road 1861, marked by yellow gate that's closed to vehicles January 1 to July 15. After 3.2 miles, a guardrail on the left marks the easy, upper trailhead to

Meadow at Harts Cove.

Chitwood Creek waterfall at Harts Cove.

the Nature Conservancy preserve on Cascade Head.

If you decide to take the Nature Conservancy path (see map on page 90), you'll amble through a forest of second-growth Douglas fir, spruce, and alder for a mile before emerging at the meadows. In summer expect white yarrow, plumes of goldenrod, tall pink foxglove, and Indian paintbrush. A hundred yards into the meadow the trail crests at the upper viewpoint. Most hikers will find it hard to turn back here. Remember, the farther you continue down the steep meadow trail, the farther you'll have to climb back up. A good compromise is an overlook halfway down, the only viewpoint of the rugged coves and islands to the north. Pets are banned on the Nature Conservancy trail.

If Harts Cove is your goal, drive an extra 0.9 mile on Road 1861 to a parking lot at road's end *(GPS location N45°03.90' W123°59.73')*. The well-graded trail switchbacks down through a hemlock forest 0.7 mile to a footbridge over pretty Cliff Creek. Next the path contours amid 6-foot-thick Sitka spruce and hemlock giants. Spring blooms here include big, 3-petaled trilliums, double fairy bells, and stalks of wild lily-of-the-valley. Fall brings orange chanterelle mushrooms.

A bench at the 1.4-mile mark offers a glimpse ahead to Harts Cove's headland. Don't take a brushy side path down to the left in the hopes of a better view; it doesn't have one. Instead continue on the main trail. In half a mile you'll cross Chitwood Creek, and in another 0.6 mile you'll enter the headland's fabulously scenic meadow, once part of the Taggard homestead.

Take the leftmost of several paths down the grassy bluff to find a cliff-edge viewpoint overlooking Harts Cove and Chitwood Creek's waterfall. The sea lions you hear so clearly are out of sight around a promontory.

To reach the shore (on a rugged path not suitable for children), climb back up from this viewpoint 50 yards to a junction and head seaward. A scramble trail descends to the lava rock edge of the headland, where deep water gently rises and falls, exposing a bathtub ring of barnacles, starfish, and sea palms.

32   Cascade Head   🚶 🐧 🌲

Moderate (from lower trailhead)
4.2 miles round trip
1200 feet elevation gain

Difficult (inland trail)
6 miles one way
1200 feet elevation gain

Cascade Head's panoramic, blufftop wildflower meadows were threatened by commercial development in the 1960s, but fans of the wild headland rallied to purchase the fragile area and donate it to the non-profit Nature Conservancy for preservation. Ironically, the impact of up to 10,000 nature-loving visitors a year now threatens the meadows' ecology.

Flower picking, hunting, camping, fires, bicycles, and dogs have been banned. The easy, upper trailhead to the headland meadows is closed six months of the year (see Hike #31) to protect threatened Oregon silverspot butterfly caterpillars. If you hike here from the lower trailhead (open all year), please *stay on the trail*. Even spreading out a picnic may inadvertently trample the meadow's rare checkermallows (5-petaled pink wildflowers) or the violets that serve as food for the rare caterpillars. You might also consider hiking the much quieter Cascade Head Inland Trail instead, a woodsy bypass route that lacks ocean views but avoids the fragile meadows.

If you're taking the Nature Conservancy Trail to the headland meadows from the lower, all-year trailhead, drive Highway 101 north 1 mile from the interchange where highways 101 and 18 join (just north of Lincoln City). Then turn left on Three Rocks Road for 2.3 miles and turn left on Savage Road 100 yards to the parking lot of the Knight Park boat ramp.

From Knight Park, the trail crosses Three Rocks Road and traverses the woods beside Savage Road. Stay on the trail because this section crosses private land.

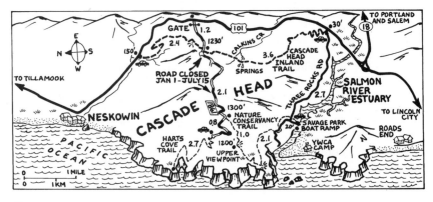

After 0.4 mile you'll end up along the road to the old trailhead, where parking is strictly prohibited. From this old trailhead, the path climbs into a forest of large, gnarled spruce for 1.1 mile to a meadow with a breathtaking view across the Salmon River estuary. In the distance are Cape Foulweather and Lincoln City's Devils Lake. Then the path steepens and climbs 0.6 mile to an upper viewpoint, the turnaround spot.

If you'd prefer a less crowded, more challenging hike at Cascade Head, instead try the Oregon Coast Trail through the inland rainforest. To find this path from the junction of highways 101 and 18 (just north of Lincoln City) drive 1 mile north on Highway 101, turn left at Three Rocks Road, and immediately park by a trail sign on the right. At times a little overgrown, the path switchbacks uphill through a second-growth spruce forest with pink salmonberry, red thimbleberry, and clusters of red elderberry in summer. In spring look for white trilliums, oxalis, and wild lily-of-the-valley. Much of the trail follows ancient roadbeds, regrown with alder. Expect a few muddy spots and some distant highway noise.

This portion of the Oregon Coast Trail is entirely within the Cascade Head Experimental Forest, where logging-oriented research has cut many of the area's old-growth trees. A stately grove of 6-foot-thick Sitka spruce remains in a hidden glen where springs feed the headwaters of Calkins Creek, 2.9 miles along the trail. A boardwalk crosses a skunk cabbage dale here.

After 3.6 miles, turn right on gravel Road 1861 for 100 yards. (It would be possible to leave a shuttle car at this trail crossing, marked by a roadside post 1.2 miles from Highway 101, but Road 1861 is closed to all traffic January 1 to July 15 each year.) The trail's final 2.4-mile section descends from Road 1861 through woods to a red barricade and brown hiker-symbol sign at a Highway 101 pullout 1 mile south of Neskowin.

Salmon River from headland.   Opposite: Sitka spruce rainforest at Cascade Head.

33   Baskett Slough Refuge

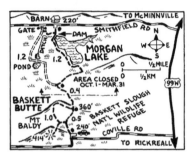

Easy (to Baskett Butte)
1.5-mile loop
200 feet elevation gain
Open all year, sunrise to sunset

Moderate (to Morgan Lake)
4.9-mile loop
260 feet elevation gain
Open April 1 to September 30

Above: Morgan Lake.

Each fall 22,000 dusky Canada geese fly from Alaska's Copper River delta to winter in the Willamette Valley. This refuge west of Salem welcomes them with diked ponds and unharvested fields of corn, rye grass, and wheat. Not surprisingly, the area has become a hit with other bird species, too. A short loop hike here visits a viewpoint and an oak forest. A longer loop to Morgan Lake is open April through September. Pets and flower picking are banned.

From Salem, take Highway 22 west to Rickreall, turn north on Highway 99W for 1.9 miles, and turn left on gravel Coville Road 1.5 miles to the trailhead parking lot on the right. If you're coming from Portland or Corvallis, look for the Coville Road turnoff on Highway 99W between mileposts 56 and 57.

Walk up the wide, mowed trail 200 yards and fork left. Old apple trees, wild rose bushes, and pale blue flax flowers line the path. Expect the chirp of crickets, the hollow coo of mourning doves, and the squawk of ring-neck pheasants.

After another 200 yards you'll reach a fork at a pass. To the left is the summit of Mt. Baldy, with a view across the Willamette Valley's patchwork of farms to the rumpled green Coast Range. Take the right-hand fork to find the mowed loop trail around Baskett Butte and into an oak forest. Beware of the abundant, triple-leaved poison oak plants masquerading as tree seedlings here.

At the 1-mile mark reach a T-shaped junction. To the right is the quick route back to your car. Turn left for the longer loop, open from May through September. This path descends to a junction at the site of an old barn. Follow trail signs to the right, along Morgan Lake, and back along a service road to end the loop at the old barn junction. Along the way look for redwing blackbirds perched on cattails, polliwogs in the ditches, and beaver-like nutria in the ponds.

34   Valley of the Giants

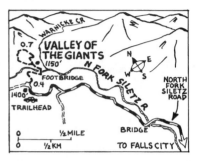

Easy
1.5-mile loop
400 feet elevation gain
Open except during fire season
    in late summer

This ancient grove, towering above the rushing headwaters of the Siletz River, is home to some of the largest trees in Oregon. While the hike here is not difficult, the drive is. Plan a full hour to negotiate the 28 miles of confusing, unmarked gravel logging roads between Falls City and the trailhead. The route includes two gates that are locked at 5pm, so don't head back too late.

Start by driving to Rickreall, where Highway 22 from Salem crosses Highway 99W between Corvallis and McMinnville. From this intersection, follow signs 4 miles to Dallas, and then follow signs to Falls City another 9 miles. At the far end of this town, curve left across a bridge onto Bridge Street. In 0.7 mile the street turns to gravel, and in another mile it becomes a one-lane timber company road, where log trucks rumble on weekdays.

A total of 14.9 miles from Falls City, the road turns sharply left to avoid a locked gate with a "Keep Out" sign. This is the site of Valsetz, a logging company town built as the terminus of the Valley & Siletz Railroad. In the 1980s the company that owned the town removed the buildings, drained the neighboring millpond lake, and gated the road to keep out nostalgic former residents.

Just 200 yards after turning left at the gate, turn right at a T-shaped junction. (Remember this turn; it's easy to miss on your return drive.) Keep right around the old Valsetz lakebed, now full of snags, foxglove, and alder.

A total of 8.2 miles from the gate you'll reach the South Fork Siletz River. If the wooden bridge here hasn't been replaced, this may be where you have to park. Beyond the bridge 0.2 mile take an uphill fork to the right. In another 0.3 mile, keep left at a fork. Now keep left at all junctions for 4.9 rough, pot-holed miles to a bridge over the North Fork Siletz River. Continue on the gravel road another 1.1 mile to a fork, and finally turn right for 0.5 mile to a sign for the Valley of the Giants Trail.

The trail itself descends among 450-year-old, 10-foot-thick Douglas firs, some rising 150 feet to their first branch. In June marbeled murrelets roost on the thickest of the high branches here. These small black-and-white birds spend the rest of their lives at sea. They only fly inland to lay their eggs, without benefit of a nest, on mossy, flat-topped branches 150 feet up in giant trees. A shortage of suitable old-growth trees has left the birds in trouble.

The path descends to the North Fork Siletz River, crosses on a steel footbridge, heads left past a picnic table, and then forks for a final, 0.7-mile loop through the area's grandest stand of big trees. White woodland flowers beneath the giants include star-flowered solomonseal, queens cup, trillium, and oxalis.

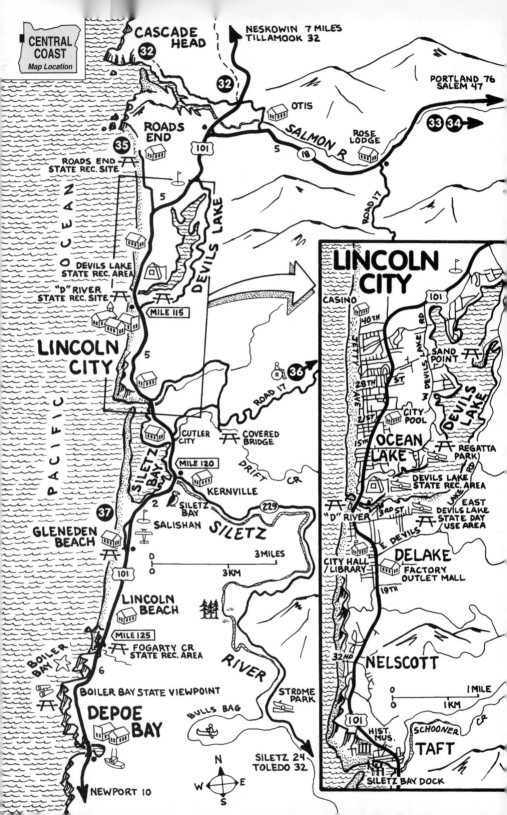

Siletz Bay and the Taft district of Lincoln City.

LINCOLN CITY

The longest town on the Oregon Coast, Lincoln City formed when five coastal communities voted to consolidate in 1964. Local entrepreneurs began billing their heavily-developed coastline as the "20 Miracle Miles." Then-governor Mark Hatfield dubbed the zone the "20 Miserable Miles," and in the resulting uproar many of the most garish motel signs and billboards were removed.

The area's natural scenery does border on the miraculous. Behind the beach, Devils Lake and Siletz Bay retain much of their pastoral setting. To the south, the seashore crinkles into a series of scenic coves at Fogarty Creek and Boiler Bay. Just beyond lies Depoe Bay, a village with the world's smallest harbor.

Oceanlake District

Shops line Highway 101 In the northernmost of Lincoln City's five boroughs. Best bets include the Siletz tribe's Chinook Winds casino on 40th, the maple bars at the 101 Inspirations Bakery on 17th, and the indoor public swimming pool off 22nd.

Devils Lake

Indian legends of a hungry lake monster gave this freshwater lake its name. Despite the monster threat, waterskiing and swimming are popular in the relatively warm lake.

Just north of the D River bridge is the Devils Lake Recreation Area with 87 campsites and 10 yurts (summer reservations accepted); paddleboat and sailboard rentals are nearby. On the opposite shore is the East Devils Lake Day Use Area, with picnic tables and a boat ramp used by waterskiers. To explore the quieter north end of the lake by canoe or sailboard, launch at Sand Point Park's beach (off East Devils Lake Road) or at one of the city parks along West Devils Lake Road.

D River State Recreation Site
Shortest river in the world, the D River flows a mere 200 yards from Devils Lake to the sea. The state park at the Highway 101 river bridge provides access to a busy — and reliably windy — beach. One of the world's largest kite festivals is held here each year on a weekend in late June and early fall, bolstering Lincoln City's claim to be "Kite Capital of the World."

Delake district
Once a city in its own right, Delake now is home to Lincoln City's library and city hall at South 9th and a large mall of factory outlet stores at 14th.

Nelscott district
This beach community is named for Nelson and Scott, the developers who founded it in 1926. The district's old-fashioned, literate ambience inspired local mystery author M. K. Wren to set several of her popular murder stories in a cat-dominated used bookstore. Bookish haunts and antique shops still abound.

Taft District
The area's best seal watching and family beach fun is at the Siletz Bay dock in Lincoln City's Taft district. To find it, turn west 2 blocks at the South 51st Street traffic light near milepost 118. Taft's old city hall on Highway 101 now houses the North Lincoln County Historical Museum, open Wed-Sun noon-5 from ay 15 to Oct 15, and Wed-Sat noon-5 in winter (but closed Dec 15-Jan 31). Admission is often free, but donations are requested.

Siletz Bay
Sawmills once poisoned this estuary, but time and care have brought about a remarkable recovery, with great blue herons and snowy egrets stalking among the driftwood on the bay's mudflats. A wildlife refuge encompasses the grassy tidal plain southeast of Highway 101's Siletz River bridge. The hottest birdwatching, however, is from Cutler City's bayfront park (turn west off Highway 101 near the antique mall at the south end of Lincoln City).

Siletz River
Tidewater backs 18 miles up the forested canyon of this untamed river. For a scenic 62-mile loop drive, take paved Highway 229 upriver to the village of Siletz (headquarters of the Siletz Indian Reservation and the Siletz Brewing Company), continue to Toledo, turn right to Newport, and return along Highway 101.

For an easy 8-mile canoe exploration of a wild, roadless riverbend known colorfully as the Bulls Bag, leave a shuttle car at Strome Park, a picnic area with a concrete boat launch 14 miles up Highway 229 from Highway 101. Then drive another 4 miles upstream and launch at Morgan County Park's ramp.

Fogarty Creek State Recreation Area
Picture-perfect and protected from the wind, this free park 6 miles south of Lincoln City features a cliff-rimmed beach where a lazy creek meanders past a

climbable sea stack. A trail under a Highway 101 bridge leads to picnic tables and a parking area in a spruce forest.

Boiler Bay State Scenic Viewpoint

The explosion of a gas torch set fire to the *J. Marhoffer* as she sailed past this rugged, lava-rimmed bay in 1910. The captain steered the flaming ship to the rocks, where, inspired by the courage of the captain's wife, all hands escaped to shore. All that remains of the ship is a barnacled boiler and driveshaft, accessible on the bay's rocky reef at low tide.

Low tide also exposes some of Oregon's richest tidepool life here. A short, rough trail down to the reef starts at an unmarked pullout. The official Boiler Bay State Scenic Viewpoint parking area is half a mile farther south on Highway 101. This area has lawns, picnic tables, and blufftop viewpoints. Bring binoculars to watch for whales. Several spouters have taken up year-round residence nearby.

Depoe Bay

In picturesque Depoe Bay, whale watching boats thread their way from the world's smallest natural harbor through a rock channel to the sea. At high tide a **spouting horn** in a smaller chasm nearby sprays saltwater across Highway 101; don't park where the road is wet. A **Whale Watching Center** on the seawall offers free whale movies and exhibits 10am-5pm daily in summer (otherwise 10am-4pm Wednesday-Sunday).

Among the arcade-like row of gift shops lining the highway you'll find saltwater taffy, carmelcorn, and **Gracie's Sea Hag Restaurant & Lounge**. The only Oregon destination listed in CalTech's student travel guide, the Sea Hag features seafood but stands out because barmaids bang booze bottles as rhythm accompaniment to hit tunes on request.

The town's name honors a Rogue River Indian who was forcibly moved to the Siletz Reservation and then lived near here. He spent so much time hanging around the Army depot in Toledo that soldiers dubbed him Depot Charley. A later attempt at decorum upgraded the moniker to Charles DePoe.

Homes on Salishan Spit (Hike #37).

35   Roads End

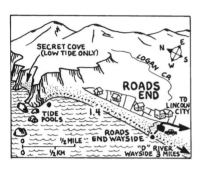

Easy
2.8 miles round trip
No elevation gain

Even when Lincoln City's beaches are crowded or windy, this sheltered strand just north of town is surprisingly quiet. With tidepools, islands, and a headland with a hidden cove, it's a fine place for a romantic stroll.

Take Highway 101 to the Lighthouse Square shopping center at the north end of Lincoln City and turn onto Logan Road. (If you're coming from Portland or Salem, drive 2.7 miles south from the intersection of Highways 101 and 18.) Follow Logan Road a mile to Roads End State Recreation Site, a parking lot on the left.

A short path descends to the beach at the pebbly mouth of a lazy little creek. Hike to the right. For the first mile, the beachfront bank is topped by a jumble of quaint old cottages. Then the beach narrows to its end at a massive headland.

The tough black basalt lava of the promontory's tip has protected a long, striped orange cliff of softer sedimentary rock that curves back along the beach. Other fragments of lava form ragged islands, where comic, long-necked cormorants dry their black wings atop guano-stained roosts. At low tide, look in pools here for starfish, mussels, and anemones—but don't disturb these animals.

Also at low tide, it's possible to clamber around the headland's tip to a secret cove's beach. Tarry here and you'll be trapped until the next low tide.

Roads End.

Drift Creek Falls before the rockslide that shortened the falls.

36   Drift Creek Falls

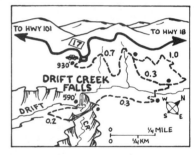

Easy
3 miles round trip
340 feet elevation gain

A dramatic, 240-foot suspension footbridge and a waterfall are your rewards for hiking this well-graded, packed gravel path through the woods.

If you're coming from Portland or Salem, take Highway 18 toward the Coast. After passing Rose Lodge and milepost 5 (short of Highway 101 by 5 miles), turn left onto paved Bear Creek Road for 9 miles. This road, often narrow and occasionally gravel, becomes Road 17 by the time you reach the trailhead. If you don't have the required $5-per-car parking permit, you can buy one here.

If you're coming from Lincoln City, take Highway 101 to milepost 119 at the south edge of town, turn east onto Drift Creek Road for 1.5 miles, turn right at a T-shaped junction, and 0.3 mile later, fork uphill to the left onto one-lane Drift Creek Camp Road (alias Road 17) for 10.2 twisty, paved miles to the large trailhead parking area on the right.

The trail descends through a second-growth Douglas fir forest with sword ferns, red huckleberries, vine maple, and salal bushes. In early spring, big white trilliums and tiny white oxalis bloom here. Keep right at all junctions for a mile to a 20-foot-wide creek on a bridge amid alders. The path next enters an old-growth grove of big hemlock, red cedar, and fir. At the 1.3-mile mark the trail spans Drift Creek's canyon on a dizzying suspension footbridge. Continue 0.2 mile down to trail's end at the base of a waterfall that spills into a misty pool beside the bridge.

For a return loop that adds 0.7 mile, much of it through an old-growth forest, recross both bridges and turn right on the North Loop.

37   Salishan Spit   🦉

Difficult
8.1 miles round trip
No elevation gain

Sandy peninsulas—known as spits—separate each of Oregon's coastal river bays from the sea. But only here, beside Siletz Bay, has the unstable dunescape been developed into a posh, private resort. Winter storms in 1972 and 1973 cut into the spit, destroying one partially built house and threatening others before bulldozers and truckloads of boulders stemmed the erosion. In the event of a major tsunami, of course, the spit would be swept clean.

In the meantime the spit's pleasant beach is open to the public, and is almost always empty—except for shorebirds and the nearly 200 harbor seals that lounge at the peninsula's tip. Perhaps the most fun part of the hike, though, is ogling the elaborate homes built by the well-to-do on a foundation of shifting sand.

If you are staying at the Salishan Spa & Golf Resort, or if you are a guest of a Salishan homeowner, you can start your hike at the Shops at Salishan, a cluster of upscale shops 3 miles south of Lincoln City on Highway 101 (between mileposts 121 and 122). Park near the spa and follow a nature trail along the dike separating the golf course from Siletz Bay. In half a mile the path crosses Salishan Drive to the beach.

If you don't have connections at Salishan you'll have to start a bit farther away, at the public beach access in Gleneden Beach. To find it, drive 0.8 mile south of Salishan, turn west onto Wessler Street at a sign for Gleneden Beach State Park, and drive 0.2 mile to a huge parking lot and small picnic area.

A short paved trail descends through a wind-dwarfed spruce forest to a soft sand beach flanked by crumbling orange sandstone bluffs. Wet-suited surfers

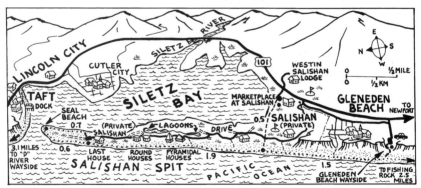

Harbor seals at the tip of Salishan Spit.   Opposite: Surfer at Gleneden Beach.

often catch waves here in the mornings. Seal heads peer from the surf.

As you hike to the right along the beach, the horizon ahead is dominated by the dark green cape of Cascade Head (Hike #32), and the Inn at Spanish Head, a 10-story concrete-and-glass bookshelf leaning against the cliffs of Lincoln City.

After a mile, the bluff ends and Salishan begins. The daring, angled rooflines of the gray houses here seem clipped from 1960s *Sunset* articles. Pass a pair of pyramidal palaces, then a duo of round domiciles, and, at the 3.4-mile mark, the last house. Another 0.6 mile brings you to the end of the spit, opposite the Taft dock. Disturbing the seals here is illegal, so don't venture too near.

Continue around the bayshore half a mile until the beach turns to mud. Then turn right across driftwood to the end of paved Salishan Drive. If you're a guest at the resort, you can return on a loop along this private road, rather than merely on the public beach. If you take the road, you'll pass lagoons and picturesquely placed houses for 1.9 miles. When you reach the golf course, turn left on the nature trail beside the golf course to the Shops at Salishan.

If you're hiking the Oregon Coast Trail south from Cascade Head (Hike #32), walk along Highway 101 for 5 miles to the Chinook Winds Casino, take the beach south through Lincoln City to Siletz Bay, skirt the bay on Highway 101 to Gleneden Beach, walk two miles on the sand to Lincoln Beach, and return to the highway shoulder for 9 miles to the Devils Punchbowl (Hike #38).

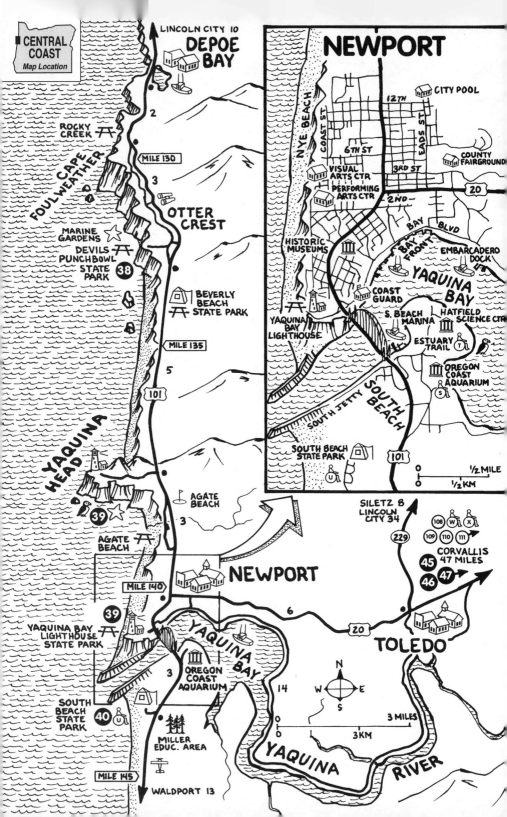

The Sylvia Beach Hotel in Newport's Nye Beach district (page 105).

NEWPORT

This romantic port is one of the oldest resort towns on the Coast. Top attractions include a world-class aquarium, two historic lighthouses, and a bustling bayfront. There's plenty of room for guests; Newport has more oceanview hotel rooms than any other city between San Francisco and Seattle.

Bay Front

In the quaint old streets along Yaquina Bay, whale watching tour offices, fish canneries, and clam chowder restaurants rub shoulders with commercial tourist attractions such as the Wax Works and Ripley's Believe It Or Not. Next to the Undersea Gardens, don't miss the **free public dock where sea lions bask**. At the west end of the Bay Front, near Newport's bridge, is an active **Coast Guard station.** At the east end are the Embarcadero docks, where you can charter a boat or rent crab pots.

Oregon Coast Aquarium

This modern aquarium features large outdoor exhibits of playful sea otters, curious seals, and chattering sea birds. Indoors are hands-on exhibits, a video theater, a gift shop, a cafeteria, and a huge Plexiglass tank of pulsing jellyfish. Best of all, a transparent underwater tunnel offers close-up views of sharks and deep-sea fish. Follow signs from the south end of Newport's bridge. Open daily 9-6 from Memorial Day through Labor Day; otherwise 10-5. Admission is $18.95 for adults, $16.95 for kids 13-17, $11.95 for kids 3-12, and $16.95 for seniors.

OSU Hatfield Marine Science Center

A block beyond the Oregon Coast Aquarium, this scientific research center's free displays explain tsunamis, weather forecasting, and salmon recovery plans. You'll also find carefully labeled exhibits of Oregon marine species, including an octopus lurking in a tank by the door. Hours are 10-5 daily (10-4 Thur-Mon in winter).

Yaquina Head

Inside Oregon's tallest lighthouse, built in 1873, narrow spiral stairs lead visitors up to a dizzying view. The lighthouse's scenic cape, Yaquina Head, was preserved in 1980 when Congress bought the headland from a gravel company that had planned to quarry it to sea level. Today the grounds are open 8am-5pm daily, with an interpretive center (open 10-4:30), stairs to a cobble beach, and a tidepool loop trail through a portion of the old quarry. Lighthouse tours are available noon-3pm Thursday-Tuesday. A viewpoint beside the lighthouse overlooks islands teeming with cormorants, murres, tufted puffins, and seals. Whale watching is excellent here too. Drive 3 miles north of Newport on Highway 101 and turn left. Expect a $7-per-car day use fee. See Hike #39.

Cape Foulweather

Highway 101 climbs to a viewpoint atop this headland, named by explorer Captain Cook on a stormy day in 1778. Bicyclists can ride around the cape's cliffy face on a twisty, lower portion of old Highway 101, crossing an artistic 1930s bridge. Just south of the cape, bike or drive to visit Devils Punchbowl State Natural Area—a panoramic picnic area on a cave-riddled sea bluff (see Hike #38).

Beverly Beach State Park

A short trail from this popular park leads under a Highway 101 bridge to long, often windy Beverly Beach. The campground with 256 sites and 21 yurts is open all year, with reservations accepted in summer. The park includes a picnic area and 0.9-mile loop trail along Spencer Creek. See Hike #38.

Historic Museums

One block east of Highway 101, an 1895 Victorian mansion and a log cabin in Newport's Historic District house the Lincoln County Historical Society's exhibits of pioneer artifacts. The museum is open Tue-Sun 10-5 from June to August and Thur-Sun 11-4 the rest of the year. Adults are $5 and kids age 3-12 are $3.

Toledo

Toledo lost its county courthouse to rival Newport in the mid 1900s. Today this well-preserved, off-the-beaten-track milltown features antique shops.

Sea otter at the Oregon Coast Aquarium.

Newport's Yaquina Bay Bridge.

South Beach

The **Oregon Coast Aquarium** anchors this Newport suburb south of the Yaquina Bay bridge. Take a tour of the popular **Rogue Ale microbrewery** beside the South Beach Marina. At the marina itself you can spend a romantic night on the **Newport Belle**, a 3-story riverboat moored permanently at Dock H, with 5 staterooms that run $150-165 and include a buffet breakfast. Reservations are at 541-867-6290 or *www.newportbelle.com*. Plenty of South Beach shops offer seafood and pirate-themed gifts. A mile down the road, amid the beachfront's grassy dunes, **South Beach State Park** has 285 campsites, 27 yurts (at $40), and a network of trails (see Hike #40).

Nye Beach

Art galleries, bed & breakfast inns, and romantic beachfront hotels cluster near 3rd and Coast streets in Newport's historic Nye Beach district. Ask to see the Dr. Seuss or Ken Kesey rooms of the **Sylvia Beach Hotel** (267 NW Cliff), a 1910 classic renovated with a literary theme. Rooms run $85-220 and can be reserved at 888-795-8422 or *www.sylviabeachhotel.com*. The **Newport Visual Arts Center** at 777 West Olive Street hosts juried art exhibits; it's free, and open 11am-5pm Tuesday through Sunday. The **Newport Performing Arts Center** (also at 777 West Olive) stages concerts, plays, and festivals. For a bed & breakfast inn nearby, try the **Grand Victorian** (105 NW Coast), a turreted, 3-story classic with rooms that run $100-180, including breakfast. Reservations are at 800-784-9936 or *www.grandvictorianor.com*.

Yaquina Bay

Flamboyant entrepreneur Colonel T. Egenton Hogg whirled into Newport in the 1870s promoting a transcontinental railroad that he claimed would turn the town into a new San Francisco. When canny locals responded by demanding high prices for his railroad right-of-way, Hogg angrily built his terminal 4 miles short of the city and instead ferried rail tourists the final miles across Yaquina Bay to the beach. Today a scenic, 14-mile bayside road between Newport and Toledo passes the abandoned railbed's trestle pilings. Oyster farms dot the route. For the bay's best birdwatching, however, park at the far left corner of the Hatfield Marine Science Center and stroll the short Estuary Trail to viewpoints.

The Devils Punchbowl. Below: Cape Foulweather from the punchbowl's cave.

38   Devils Punchbowl

Easy (to the Devils Punchbowl)
1.1 miles round trip
100 feet elevation gain

Moderate (to Beverly Beach)
4.3 miles round trip
150 feet elevation gain

When wave-carved caves met underneath the yellow sandstone bluffs of Otter Rock, their roofs collapsed, leaving a gigantic "punchbowl" at the tip of the panoramic headland. For an easy walk that's fun even with kids, explore the punchbowl from above and below, passing tidepools along the way. For a longer hike, walk the beach south to a woodsy loop beside the campground at Beverly Beach.

To start, drive 8 miles north of Newport (or 15 miles south of Lincoln City) on Highway 101 to the Devils Punchbowl State Scenic Area turnoff between mileposts 132 and 133. Then follow signs 0.7 mile to the park's day-use parking area.

Park the car and walk up the road a block—past a chowder restaurant and some shops—to a fenced overlook. What looks like orange paint on the punchbowl's sides is natural lichen. The bowl's soft sandstone would erode much quicker, but it's stacked atop an ancient lava flow of tough black basalt. The same lava flow left the many flat islands and reefs visible from here. Walk left around the picnic area to pick up more views on the way back to your car.

To visit the inside of the punchbowl and the Marine Gardens tidepools, walk 2 blocks along C Street (the other street by the parking lot). Just past the street's

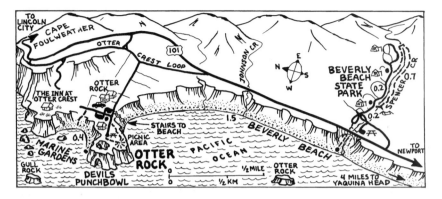

"Dead End" sign, take the trail to the left down through spruce woods to a hidden, quarter-mile-long beach. Low tide here exposes vast rock shelves where starfish and anemones crowd the cracks. Don't touch these animals, and don't walk on the mussels. Also beware of the extremely slippery green seaweed.

At the left end of the beach you can sneak into the Devils Punchbowl through either of two caves, though one is blocked at high tide.

For the longer hike along Beverly Beach, return to your car and cross the road to a 97-step staircase descending the other side of Otter Rock's headland. The beach here is a hot spot for surfers, and nicely sheltered from the north winds that bedevil many a summer beach picnic. This is also the route of the Oregon Coast Trail, which finally leaves the highway shoulder it follows for 10 miles from Gleneden Beach (Hike #37).

Walk south along Beverly Beach 1.5 miles to pebbly Spencer Creek and turn inland on a trail underneath the Highway 101 bridge. Don't cross the creek to the picnic area unless you've left a shuttle car there. Instead go straight to a campground fee booth (where you can pick up a nature trail brochure) and continue straight on a campground loop road to site C5T. Here a wide nature trail crosses Spencer Creek on a footbridge. The heavily used path loops 0.7 mile through second-growth alder and spruce along the creek's bank before ending at campsite E9T. Turn left and walk back to the beach along the campground road.

Gull Rock from the beach at Marine Gardens.

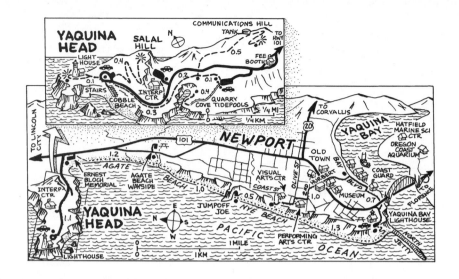

39 Newport Lighthouses

Easy (Yaquina Head exploration)
2.4 miles round trip
300 feet elevation gain

Easy (Old Town tour)
3-mile loop
250 feet elevation gain

Newport's two historic lighthouses are both popular tourist destinations, but they also serve as starting points for easy hiking explorations of Newport's scenic coast. Begin at the Yaquina Head lighthouse, on a dramatic cape with a modern interpretive center. Then drive into town to visit the older Yaquina Bay lighthouse, where a 3-mile loop takes you through Old Town to the bayfront.

To find Yaquina Head, drive 3 miles north of Newport on Highway 101 and turn left. Stop at the headland's entrance booth to pay the $7-per-car fee, and then continue half a mile to the large Interpretive Center parking lot on the right. After touring the displays here (open daily 9-5 in summer, 10-5 in fall, and Wednesday-Sunday 10-4:30 in winter), walk or drive another 0.3 mile to a turnaround at road's end, near the headland's tip.

From there a short, paved path leads to the 1873 Yaquina Head lighthouse, Oregon's tallest. The door is open 10-4 daily in summer, 11-4 in fall, and noon-4 Wednesday-Sunday in winter. Climb the 93-foot tower's spiral stair to the lantern room, with its two-ton lens of curved glass prisms. A deck at the tower's base overlooks islands where cormorants, murres, and seagulls nest. Watch for whale spouts.

Next return to the parking turnaround and take a staircase down to an unusual beach of black basalt cobbles, where you'll find tidepools at low tide. Harbor seals lounge on nearby islands. Then return to the parking turnaround. Near the restrooms you'll find a trail that switchbacks 0.4 mile up through wildflowers to Salal Hill and a bird's-eye viewpoint of the entire cape.

Before leaving Yaquina Head, drive down to the Quarry Cove trailhead to explore sandy paths through a former gravel quarry that is returning to nature. At high tide, seals lounge on rocks near the paved trail.

To visit Newport's older Yaquina Bay lighthouse, drive back to Highway 101 and turn south through town. Immediately before the Yaquina Bay Bridge, veer right at a state park sign to a picnic area below the turreted 1871 lighthouse. Newport's oldest building, it's open for free tours daily 11-4 (Wednesday-Sunday noon-4 in winter).

Locals claim the Yaquina Bay lighthouse is haunted, in part because the building was abandoned after only three years. Planners had intended for a supporting lighthouse to be placed 10 miles north at Cape Foulweather, but a local Army colonel ordered it built nearer instead, on the more accessible Yaquina Head. The mixup left the older Yaquina Bay lighthouse superfluous.

For the hike, go down stone steps from the lighthouse and cross the street to find stairs down to the beach. Then head north along the sand 1.3 miles until you reach the historic Nye Beach district, heralded by Nye Creek, a concrete street turnaround, and a quaintly-painted historic hotel. Walk up to a plaza, climb stairs to the right past the Newport Visual Arts Center gallery (open daily in the early afternoon), and go straight on Cliff Street to the Newport Performing Arts Center. Here jog left a block on Olive, turn right on Coast Street a block, go left on Second Street for 3 blocks, and then angle to the right on Hurbert Street to Highway 101 in Newport's Historic District. Continue on Hurbert Street, which turns into Canyon Way and passes the Canyon Way Bookstore, a labyrinthine literary wonderland.

At the end of Canyon Way, turn right along the bayfront past fish canneries and docks where sea lions lounge. Skirt the grounds of a historic Coast Guard station and duck under the Yaquina Bay Bridge to return to your car.

If you're trekking the Oregon Coast Trail, leave the south end of Beverly Beach (Hike #38) near the Moolack Shores Motel, follow Highway 101 south 2 miles to Agate Beach Park, follow the beach south to the Yaquina Bay lighthouse, and take Highway 101 south across the Yaquina Bay Bridge.

Inside the Yaquina Head lighthouse.   Opposite: The Yaquina Bay lighthouse.

40 South Beach

Easy (Estuary Trail)
0.7 mile one way
No elevation gain

Easy (Mike Miller Trail)
1-mile loop
100 feet elevation gain

Easy (to South Jetty)
2-mile loop
No elevation gain

These three short trails just south of Newport visit an estuary, an old-growth forest, and a jetty. The paths are easy enough that you can hike all of them in an afternoon. But pick just one if you're hiking with kids or if you're planning to round out the day with a visit to one of the aquariums here. Bicycles are limited to roads and paved paths in South Beach State Park.

The easiest of the three hikes traces the edge of Yaquina Bay's estuary. Drive to the south end of Newport's Yaquina Bay Bridge and follow signs to the Hatfield Marine Science Center, a research center with lots of public exhibits and well-labeled tanks of Oregon marine species. Park by the "Nature Trail" sign at the far left end of the parking lot. Before you start the hike, pick up a trail brochure for a $1 deposit in the science center's excellent bookstore.

The paved Estuary Trail is accessible even to strollers and wheelchairs. You're sure to spot great blue herons and shorebirds. At low tide, clam diggers often work the mud flats ringing the bay here.

The path curves through head-high yellow lupine and Scotch broom for 0.4 mile to a long boardwalk across an arm of the estuary. The odd tuberous plant

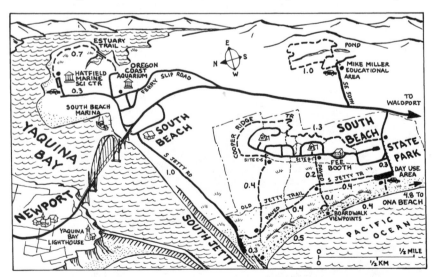

Estuary Trail boardwalk at Yaquina Bay.   Opposite: Pilings at Newport's South Jetty.

greening the mud flats here is pickleweed, a globally rare, edible species that thrives on saltwater and is sometimes collected as a salty salad green. Just beyond the boardwalk, the path ends at a road. Either follow the road 2 blocks to the Oregon Coast Aquarium or simply return as you came.

To try a 1-mile loop through an old-growth coastal forest, drive 1.2 miles south of the Yaquina Bay Bridge on Highway 101 to SE 50th Street. Near milepost 143, turn left at a sign for the Mike Miller Park Educational Area, follow a paved road 0.2 mile, and park on the shoulder by a map board on the left, just before a gate. This trail loops through a stand of 6-foot-thick hemlock and spruce. Twice the path crosses a long, marshy pond on scenic footbridges. Look here for osprey nests made of sticks on the tops of tall snags.

If you'd rather hike on the beach, drive Highway 101 south of the Yaquina Bay Bridge 1.4 miles, turn right at a sign for South Beach State Park, and drive straight 0.5 mile to the day-use parking area. Park by the restrooms and cross the grassy foredune to a broad, white-sand beach. Hike to the right 0.9 mile to the Yaquina River's South Jetty.

If you're camping at South Beach, start this hike instead at campsite B-1. Then take a paved quarter-mile trail to a boardwalk with viewing platforms, and walk right along the beach 0.5 mile to the jetty.

At the jetty, kite boarders and surfers ply the waves. Huge brown pelicans cruise past, at times plummeting into the water to scoop up fish. Climb the jetty for a view across the busy ship channel to the Yaquina Bay lighthouse. A row of pilings upriver marks the route of a railroad that brought jetty rock here.

To return on a loop, follow the jetty-top road inland 0.1 mile. Between two long gravel parking areas on the right, take a 10-foot-wide paved trail into the grassy dunes. Follow this path 0.2 mile until it is crossed by a smaller paved trail.

Here you have a choice. The shortest route back to your car is to continue straight on the big paved trail, perhaps with a detour to the boardwalk view-points. For a longer loop, turn left 0.4 mile, turn left on the Cooper Ridge Trail, and keep left at all junctions for 1.3 miles. This route follows a low wooded rise around the campground to the park entrance road, 0.3 mile from your car.

Long-distance Oregon Coast Trail trekkers arriving from the north across the Yaquina Bay Bridge (see Hike #39) should take South Jetty Road to the beach and follow the sand south 5.7 miles to Ona Beach Park (Hike #41).

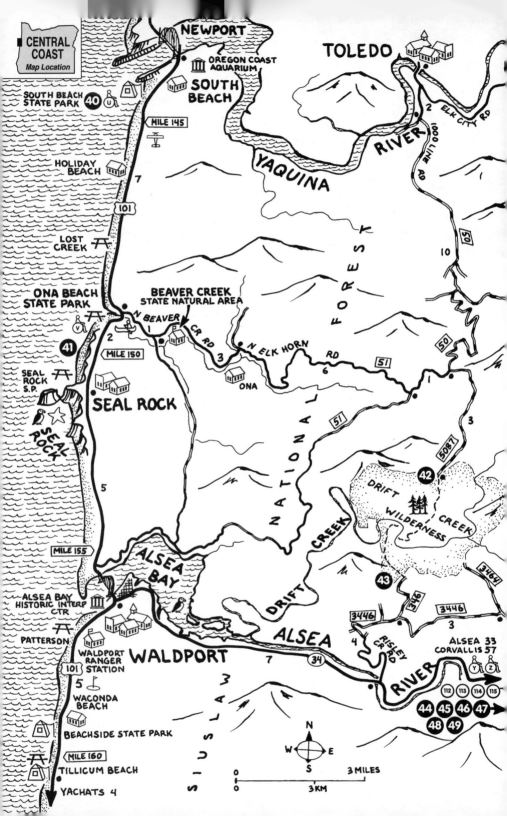

CENTRAL
COAST
Map Location

NEWPORT

TOLEDO

OREGON COAST
AQUARIUM

SOUTH
BEACH

SOUTH BEACH
STATE PARK **40** U

MILE 145

HOLIDAY
BEACH

ELK CITY RD

1000 LINE RD

YAQUINA

RIVER

2

50

101

7

10

LOST
CREEK

BEAVER CREEK
STATE NATURAL AREA

ONA BEACH
STATE PARK

N BEAVER

CR RD

N ELK HORN

RD

50

41

MILE 150

1

3

6

51

51

1

3

SEAL
ROCK S.P.

ONA

SEAL ROCK

50B7

5

42

DRIFT

CREEK

WILDERNESS

SEAL
ROCK

MILE 155

ALSEA
BAY

43

3467

316

ALSEA BAY
HISTORIC INTERP
CTR

3446

3446

3

PATTERSON

ALSEA

RIVER

4

RISLEY CR RD

ALSEA 33
CORVALLIS 57

WALDPORT
RANGER
STATION

WALDPORT

7

34

Y Z

101

5

112 113 114 115

WACONDA
BEACH

44 **45** **46** **47**

48 **49**

BEACHSIDE STATE PARK

SIUSLAW

N

MILE 160

TILLICUM BEACH

W   E

S

0   3 MILES

YACHATS 4

0   3 KM

Waldport's Alsea Bay Bridge.

WALDPORT

Waldport's name derives from the German word *Wald* ("forest"). Appropriately, the forest begins just behind the area's long, quiet beaches and extends inland to the old-growth groves of Drift Creek Wilderness and Marys Peak.

Alsea Bay Historic Interpretive Center

Waldport's original Alsea Bay Bridge, built in 1936 by luminary state engineer Conde McCullough, won a place on the National Historic Register in 1981 for its graceful arches. But the bridge was replaced ten years later when engineers found that salt air had weakened its concrete. At the south end of the new span's single, nostalgic arch is a surprisingly interesting free interpretive center with photographs and models telling the story of Waldport and its bridges. The free museum is open daily 9am-5pm (9am-4pm Tuesday through Saturday in winter). Bridge tours leave at 2pm daily in summer.

Seal Rock State Recreation Site

From the small picnic area in this blufftop park, a short paved trail descends to a sandy cove sheltered by rocky islands. Low tide exposes vast rock flats with tidepools. Bring binoculars to spot seals lounging on offshore reefs.

Ona Beach State Park

One of the most pleasant picnic areas on the coast, this park has lawns and a looping river that's perfect for canoes. A short paved trail crosses a dramatic footbridge to an ocean beach at the river's mouth. See Hike #41.

Alsea Bay

No jetties tame the mouth of the Alsea, so the river can still be capricious. A 1983 storm swept nearly a thousand feet off the end of the Alsea spit, undermining oceanfront homes. Today it's fun to watch seals basking on the mudflat islands that emerge from the estuary at low tide. Birdwatching is best at high tide, when rising water scoots shorebirds to the bank, where they're easier to spot. Crabbing is also popular. Rent crab pots and boats at The Dock of the Bay, on the waterfront in Waldport's Old Town.

Seal Rock.

Beaver Creek State Natural Area

Kayakers and hikers can now explore this new state park, still under development since its opening in 2010. If you're paddling, it's easiest to start at the ramp beside Highway 101 in Ona Beach State Park (see Hike #41). Head upstream 1.6 miles on broad, lazy Beaver Creek to a footbridge in the new park, where you can get out and stretch your legs on trails.

Hikers usually start at the Visitor Center, 1.2 miles inland from Ona Beach on North Beaver Creek Road. Dogs must be on leash. A barrier-free 0.2-mile loop from the visitor center passes a viewpoint. Then hike a boardwalk across the adjacent marsh 0.4 mile to the Beaver Creek footbridge. On the far shore, a 2.1-mile loop circles Snaggy Point, a hill with alder, spruce, and hemlock woods. In winter, access the trail system from a gated service road a mile south on South Beaver Creek Road.

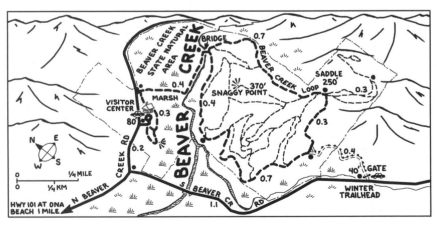

41 Ona Beach and Seal Rock

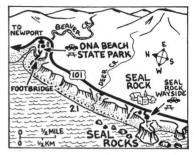

Moderate
4.2 miles round trip
100 feet elevation gain

Below: Footbridge at Ona Beach.

The Ona Beach picnic area and the island-ringed headland at Seal Rock rank among the most scenic spots on the central Oregon Coast. Although you could visit them by car, why not hike from one to the other along a quiet beach?

Start at Ona Beach State Park, near milepost 149 on Highway 101, south of Newport 7 miles. From the parking area, take the large paved trail straight ahead, past picnic lawns and restrooms. Cross a footbridge over lazy, looping, 100-foot-wide Beaver Creek. Then turn left along the bluff-edged beach toward Seal Rock. The beach narrows at high tide, so watch for waves.

Strangely, the lava forming Seal Rock matches flows found near Idaho in Hells Canyon. Seventeen million years ago, when the North American continent buckled as it rammed westward over the Pacific Ocean floor, immense flows of Columbia River basalt welled up through cracks near Hells Canyon. The lava surged down the ancestral Columbia River, which then entered the ocean here.

When you reach Seal Rock, do not try to climb directly up the headland's slippery face. Instead, at a small creek just before the third-to-last blufftop house (0.3 mile short of the cape) take an unmarked path up a brushy draw to a highway guardrail near Grebe Street, 300 yards from the entrance to Seal Rock State Park's picnic area. Short, paved trails from the picnic area lead to a viewpoint on the headland's neck and down to a beach and tidepools on the south side.

Long-distance trekkers on the Oregon Coast Trail from Newport (see Hike #40) will have to follow Highway 101 briefly at Seal Rock, return to the beach at Quail Street, follow the sand south 4 miles to the Bayshore Beach Club, and return to Highway 101 through Waldport to another beach access at Patterson Park (Hike #50).

42   Drift Creek North   🏕🌲🛶🐎

Difficult
7.6 miles round trip
1520 feet elevation **loss**

Right: Tree at the wilderness boundary.

So few ancient forests have survived in the Coast Range that Drift Creek's wilderness canyon really stands out. Two maintained trails descend through the old growth to this wild coastal stream, overhung with mossy maples. The northern Horse Creek Trail described here (compare Hike #43) passes the biggest trees. Both paths head downhill, so save some energy for the climb back to your car.

To start, drive 7 miles north of Waldport on Highway 101 to Ona Beach State Park, turn right on North Beaver Creek Road for 1 mile to a fork. Veer left for 2.9 miles to a T-shaped junction, and turn right onto one-lane, paved North Elk Horn Road 51. At another T-junction in 6.0 miles, turn left onto Road 5000 for 1.4 miles. Then fork right onto gravel Road 5087 for 2.8 miles to road's end.

The hike begins by following an old roadbed that was carefully converted to trail in 2008. After 0.6 mile you'll reach an old trailhead and climb on a narrower path into a rare, almost pure stand of old-growth western hemlock trees up to 5 feet in diameter. Later you'll pass 7-foot-thick Douglas fir and Sitka spruce. In spring look for white wildflowers: 6-petaled queens cup, shamrock-leaved oxalis, and wild lily-of-the-valley. In fall, orange chanterelle mushrooms dot the path's edge.

At the 2.6-mile mark you'll descend to a fork in the trail. Don't take the right-hand path, an abandoned section of trail that peters out at a landslide. Instead fork left, switchbacking down a forested ridge 1.2 miles to the trail's end at a campsite on a densely wooded bench above Drift Creek.

This is the turnaround point for most hikers. If you're feeling adventurous,

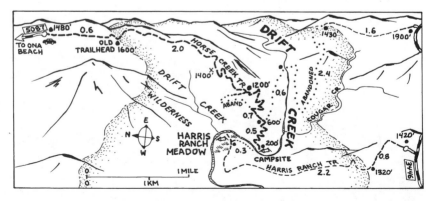

Drift Creek.   Below: Chanterelle mushrooms.

you can scramble down the steep, slippery bank 40 feet to the creek's shore. If you're really adventurous, you can wade the creek (usually knee deep), scramble up the far bank, and bushwhack downstream (to the right) 0.3 mile to Harris Ranch Meadow, where you'll find campsites, easy creek access, and the Harris Ranch Trail (Hike #43).

43   Drift Creek South

Difficult
6 miles round trip
1300 feet elevation **loss**

Overhung with mossy bigleaf maples, Drift Creek meanders through the densely forested canyons of the Coast Range's largest wilderness area. For the least difficult route to the creek, hike the Harris Ranch Trail down to an ancient homestead meadow in a creek bend. The hike back to your car is all uphill, so save some energy for the home stretch.

To start, drive Highway 34 east of Waldport 6.8 miles (or west of Corvallis

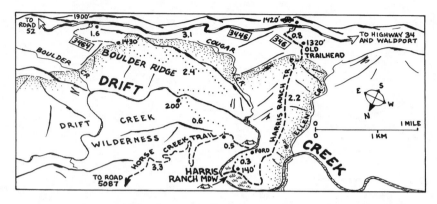

57 miles) to a bridge over the Alsea River. Turn north on narrow Risley Creek Road (alias Road 3446). If you see incorrect "Private Property No Drift Cr" messages spray-painted on the pavement, ignore them. After 2.5 miles of pavement and an additional 1.7 miles of gravel, fork left on Road 346 for 0.3 mile to the trailhead parking lot.

The hike begins along an old roadbed that has been converted to trail. When you reach the old trailhead after 0.8 mile the path descends through an old-growth rainforest of alder, 5-foot-thick Douglas firs, and droopy-limbed red cedars. Underbrush here includes salmonberry, vine maple, and lady fern. After 2.2 miles downhill, the trail enters a field of bracken and blackberries, a pre-World War II homestead pasture gone wild.

Go straight at an unmarked junction at the start of the meadow to find a large campsite beneath big streamside cedars. The bare bedrock banks of Drift Creek are great for picnicking or sunbathing. Red crawdads crawl through the shallows. After exploring the creekbank and the meadow, return as you came.

Other Options

Adventurers can connect this hike with the other maintained trail in the Drift Creek Wilderness (Hike #42), but it's not easy. From the meadow, bushwhack upstream 0.3 mile, ford the knee-deep creek, scramble up the 40-foot bank on the far shore, and look for the campsite where the Horse Creek Trail begins.

Old-growth trees at Drift Creek.

44 Chip Ross Park & Dimple Hill 🚲🐎

Easy (to Ross Park viewpoint)
1.5-mile loop
270 feet elevation gain

Difficult (to Dimple Hill)
7.6 miles round trip
1650 feet elevation gain

Right: Marys Peak from Dimple Hill.

Practically inside Corvallis, Chip Ross Park has become a favorite spot to jog, walk the dog, or stroll across a meadowed knoll for a view of the Willamette Valley. But a less known, quieter trail extends beyond the park, climbing 3 miles through the McDonald Forest to a viewpoint atop Dimple Hill.

Start by driving north of downtown Corvallis on 10th Street, which becomes Highland Drive. After 3 miles, at a pointer for Chip Ross Park, turn left on NW Lester Avenue for 0.9 mile to a gravel parking area and a few picnic tables at road's end.

Walk past a yellow gate and veer uphill to the left into a white oak forest with occasional small Douglas firs. Stay on the path to avoid the poison oak in the woods on either hand. After 0.5 mile you'll reach a large trail junction and face a decision. If you keep right you'll stay on the easy, broad trail that loops through Ross Park back to the parking area, along the way climbing through grassy meadows with benches overlooking the Corvallis area.

If you'd prefer the longer hike to Dimple Hill, however, turn left at the large trail junction and follow "Dan's Trail" signs into the McDonald Forest, Oregon State University's 11-square-mile research forest. The lower part of this path is closed to mountain bikes and horses from November 1 to April 14, when the tread can be muddy in spots. Near the start of this trail you'll have to veer right at a couple of poorly marked forks. Next the path switchbacks down half a mile, joins a spur trail from Jackson Creek Road, and heads west through the woods toward Dimple Hill. After switchbacking up to this peak's small summit meadow, you'll gain a view of Marys Peak (Hike #45) and the patchwork of farmlands surrounding Corvallis.

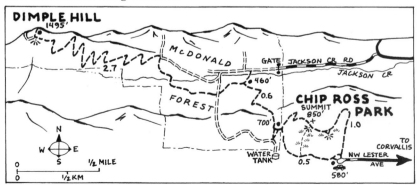

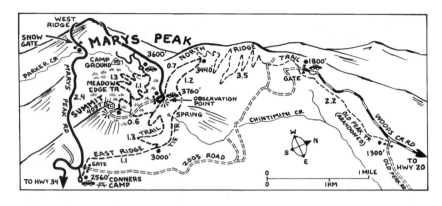

45   Marys Peak

Easy (road to summit)
1.2 miles round trip
340 feet elevation gain
Open April through November

Easy (Meadow Edge Trail)
2.4-mile loop
500 feet elevation gain

Moderate (East Ridge Trail)
5.4-mile loop
1250 feet elevation gain

Highest spot in the Coast Range, Marys Peak's wildflower-dotted summit meadows command views from the ocean to the Cascades. Four different trails ascend this mountain, ranging from easy paths to long, hard climbs. A National Forest parking pass is required, but is available at the trailhead.

Kalapuya Indians sent young men to the summit in quest of guiding spirit visions. The mountain's Indian name, Chateemanwi ("place where spirits dwell"), survives in the name for nearby Chintimini Creek. Numerous Marys have been credited for the peak's mysterious English name.

Indian legend offers an explanation for the summit's unusual alpine wild-flowers and noble fir forest—rare in the Coast Range. Apparently the trick-ster god Coyote stole Panther's wife, and Panther retaliated by kidnapping Coyote's son. In his anger, Coyote dammed the Willamette and flooded all but this peak's summit, which he spared as a refuge for plants and animals. Botanists see a thread of truth in the tale. Oregon's climate has warmed over the past 6000 years, forcing once-common Ice Age species to retreat to this mountaintop "island."

The easiest and only crowded hike at Marys Peak is the 0.6-mile stroll up a gated gravel service road from the observation point parking lot to the summit, beside two radio relay buildings. On a clear day, views extend from the ocean to Mt. Rainier and Mt. Thielsen. July colors the summit meadows with red paintbrush, purple penstemon, white yarrow, and blue butterflies.

To find the observation point trailhead, take Highway 20 west of Corvallis through Philomath, fork left onto Highway 34 for 8.8 miles and turn right on paved Marys Peak Road 9.5 miles to its end. (From Highway 101 at Waldport, take Highway 34 inland 48 miles and turn left.)

But why jostle with crowds? The Meadow Edge Trail is only a mile longer and offers a far quieter, more interesting loop to the summit. To start, drive Marys Peak Road only 8.8 miles up from Highway 34, turn right at the Marys Peak campground entrance, and 100 yards later fork left to a picnic area and trailhead. Keep left when the path splits after 150 yards. The trail climbs along the margin between a rare grove of huge, old-growth noble fir and a meadow. After 0.7 mile turn left at a junction, and 80 yards later turn right, to climb to the summit viewpoint. To finish the loop, head back down and keep left at all junctions.

For a shorter drive (but a longer hike), take the East Ridge Trail across a slope of dense, old-growth Douglas fir to the peak's high meadow views. Start by driving the Marys Peak Road only 5.5 miles up from Highway 34. At an "East Ridge Conner's Camp" pointer, turn right to a trailhead parking lot. The well-graded path soon enters a stand of 5-foot-thick Douglas fir. June wildflowers include 3-leaved vanilla leaf, white starflower, and yellow Oregon grape. After 1.1 mile, fork left and climb 1.3 miles to the observation point parking lot. (A detour here will take you up the gravel road to the actual summit.) To return on a loop, walk to the far end of the parking lot past a picnic table and take the North Ridge Trail down a forested crest 0.7 mile. At an unmarked junction, turn sharply right onto the Tie Trail, which passes a small spring and traverses back to the East Ridge Trail.

Other Options

The most challenging route up Marys Peak, the North Ridge Trail, switchbacks up through dense forest to the observation point parking lot, gaining 2000 feet in 4.2 miles. To find the trailhead, drive west from Corvallis through Philomath, fork right on Highway 20 for 1.8 miles (to milepost 48), and turn left on Woods Creek Road 7.6 miles to a locked gate.

Marys Peak.   Opposite: Ancient Douglas firs along the East Ridge Trail.

Easy (2 short loop hikes)
2.4 miles round trip
440 feet elevation gain

Moderate (2 longer loops)
4.8 miles round trip
1100 feet elevation gain

Two Benton County parks northwest of Corvallis showcase the history of Kings Valley. Inspect the site of a Civil War-era Army fort, visit two pioneer homestead farmhouses, or stroll alongside a splashing mountain creek. Dogs must be on leash.

The Kalapuya tribe in Kings Valley traditionally used fire to manage the land, burning off grass and fir seedlings. The resulting oak savanna provided food — edible camas flower bulbs, acorns, tarweed seeds, and easily huntable deer.

Beginning in the 1770s, however, smallpox and other "white man's" diseases killed up to 95 percent of the natives. Still, the Army rounded up Indians from all of western Oregon onto a reservation that encompassed the northern Coast Range.

Fort Hoskins opened in 1856, guarding the reservation at the intersection of two major Indian trails. The fort closed 9 years later and the site was sold to a family that lived and farmed there until 1992.

Meanwhile, another pioneer family settled 3 miles away on the other side of the Luckiamute River. Ashnah Plunkett, the first white child born in Kings Valley, had met her husband at a local dance. He was a California soldier serving as a drummer at Fort Hoskins. Together they built a white clapboard farmhouse along Plunkett Creek in 1875. Ashnah lived there until her death in 1933.

The Plunkett farm was bought in 1966 by Fred Beazell, an employee at a high-tech company in California's Silicon Valley. Fred married his long-time sweetheart Dolores in 1968 and convinced her to move to Oregon in 1991.

But Dolores Beazell died just two years later. Grieving, and without children, Fred decided to leave the 586-acre property as a memorial to his beloved wife.

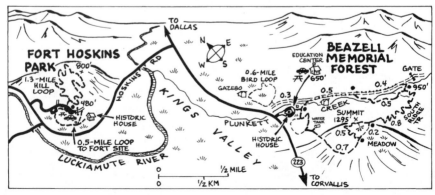

The Plunkett Barn at Beazell Forest.   Opposite: The Frantz-Dunn House at Fort Hoskins.

Today Benton County manages the Beazell Memorial Forest for recreation and forest ecology. Logging is permitted only to pay certain park expenses.

To drive here from Corvallis, head west on Highway 20 toward the Coast 10 miles (or drive east of Newport 45.5 miles). Turn north at a big sign for Kings Valley between mileposts 45 and 46. Follow Highway 223 for 4.8 miles to a sign for the Beazell Memorial Forest and turn right to a gravel parking turnaround.

Cross a picnic lawn to the Plunketts' 1930s barn, now modernized as an education center. Continue straight past the barn, veer left across a footbridge, and turn right on an old roadbed. This wide trail follows Plunkett Creek up a canyon shaded by mossy bigleaf maples, Douglas firs, and alders.

At the half-mile mark, fork to the right on the Plunkett Creek Loop, a smaller graveled path closer to the creek. After another half mile — and just 100 feet beyond a high, 60-foot railed footbridge — watch closely for a junction with the South Ridge Trail on the right. (If you cross a second high footbridge, you've gone too far.)

At this junction you face a decision. For a short hike, continue straight on the Plunkett Creek Loop and turn left on an old roadbed back down to your car. For a more vigorous hike, turn right on the South Ridge Trail. This longer route climbs in 20 switchbacks to a big junction with a mapboard. If you turn right here and keep right at junctions you'll climb 0.2 mile to a forested hilltop, zigzag down 0.3 mile beside a meadow, and follow an old roadbed 0.7 mile back to your car.

Next stop is Fort Hoskins Historic Park. Drive a few hundred yards back to Highway 223, turn right (north) for 1.7 miles to milepost 25, turn left on Hoskins Road for 1.8 miles, and turn right on the park's steep entrance road for 0.4 mile to a paved parking area where the road is gated closed. A picnic shelter in an old apple orchard here looks out across the fort site to the distant Luckiamute River and a few scattered farmhouses — all that remains of the town of Hoskins.

For a half-mile tour of the fort site, walk on down the gated road 200 yards and turn right on a wide gravel path. Just beyond the fort's parade grounds, detour briefly left down a road to the 1869 Frantz-Dunn House, built by the family that bought the fort. Then continue on the gravel loop trail back up to the picnic area.

For a longer hike, look for a small trail sign opposite the restrooms at the start of the paved parking area. Take this path up through Douglas fir woods 200 yards and fork to the right. The 1.3-mile loop that begins here switchbacks up a hill through an oak savanna, restored in the style of the old Kalapuyan tribe.

47   Peavy Arboretum 🌲🏠

Moderate
3.9-mile loop
900 feet elevation gain

Left: The Forestry Club Cabin.

Half a dozen self-guiding nature trails from Peavy Arboretum explore this corner of Oregon State University's 11-square-mile McDonald Forest. Because the short loops often overlap, it's tempting to combine them. The tour described here visits many of the area's highlights—a grove of ancient trees, a lake, and a viewpoint of Marys Peak. Running and jogging are not allowed.

Drive Highway 99W north of Corvallis 5 miles (or south of Monmouth 16 miles), turn west onto Arboretum Road for 0.8 mile, turn right at a Peavy Arboretum entrance sign, and then keep left at all forks for 0.3 mile to a parking area before a locked orange gate.

Pick up a map at a brochure box here. Then walk past the gate and follow the closed gravel road 0.3 mile up through a second-growth forest of Douglas fir, bigleaf maple, and sword fern. Just before the Forestry Club cabin, turn left beside a lawn 100 feet. Then turn left again across a footbridge on the Section 36 Loop.

This path climbs gradually through experimental ponderosa pine and Douglas fir plantations. Stick to the Section 36 trail at junctions, forking right after 0.1 mile and then keeping straight. After 1.4 miles you'll reach a T-shaped junction with the Powder House Trail. Turn left on this path, which crosses three gravel roads and climbs through a clearcut with sweeping views. Near the viewpoint you'll see the foundations of a dynamite storage building.

Then the Powder House Trail crosses another road beside a 1937 dynamite cap storage shed, and descends through a lovely, mossy grove of 6-foot-thick

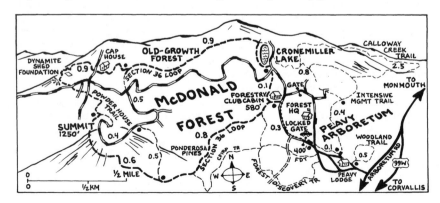

Douglas fir giants. Here you'll rejoin the Section 36 Loop. After keeping down-hill at junctions for a mile, turn right along the shore of Cronemiller Lake, a tree-rimmed reservoir where foresters hold annual log-rolling competitions. At the lake's far end, turn briefly right on a gravel road to find a sign for the trail to the Forestry Club Cabin. From there, walk back down the gravel road 0.3 mile to your car.

Other Options

If you're still going strong when you reach Cronemiller Lake, you can extend the loop by walking around the lake to the Calloway Creek Trail. Take this path and keep left at junctions for 2.9 miles. When you reach a parking area near Peavy Lodge, look for a 0.1-mile connector trail to the right that takes you back to your car.

48 Finley Wildlife Refuge

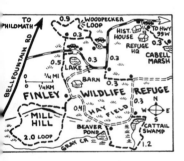

Easy (boardwalk to Cabell Marsh)
0.6 mile round trip
No elevation gain

Easy (Woodpecker Loop)
1.2-mile loop
100 feet elevation gain

Easy (Mill Hill Loop)
3-mile loop
100 feet elevation gain

Easy (Beaver Pond Loop)
3-mile loop
No elevation gain
Open April 1 to October 30

When the draining of Willamette Valley wetlands led to a decline of dusky Canada goose populations in the 1960s, the U. S. Fish and Wildlife Service used money from the sale of duck hunter stamps to convert this 8-square-mile farm into a bird-friendly patchwork of ponds, woodlands, and farmfields.

Several easy loop trails allow hikers to enjoy this rural birdland. Here too is the 1855 farmhouse of John Fiechter, a German whose success in the California gold rush financed a Greek Revival clapboard classic. Opposite the refuge headquarters, the restored home is open periodically for special events.

Drive Highway 99W south of Corvallis 10 miles (or north of Monroe 8 miles) to a Finley Refuge sign at milepost 93. Turn west on gravel Finley Road for 1.4 miles, turn left on Finley Refuge Road for 1.5 zigzagging miles, and park at the refuge headquarters on the left. A nature store in the headquarters is open Friday through Sunday from 10am to 4pm.

For the easiest of the four recommended walks, start at a kiosk outside the headquarters and take the 0.3-mile Homer Campbell Boardwalk to an observation blind overlooking Cabell Marsh, a diked wetland.

Then return to your car, drive another 0.8 mile west on Finley Refuge Road, and turn right at a sign for the Woodpecker Loop. Named for the five wood-pecker species that might be seen in this varied habitat, the broad gravel path begins in a grassy field with blackberries and wild roses, forks left through oak woodlands, climbs amid second-growth Douglas firs, and spans a boggy swale on a boardwalk. Near loop's end is an observation deck built around a huge oak. Views extend across the Willamette Valley to the Halsey mill, the Coburg Hills, and the snowy tips of Mt. Jefferson and the Three Sisters.

For the other two loop trails, drive 0.5 mile farther along Finley Refuge Road (keeping right at a fork) and park on the left in a gravel lot overlooking a fenced, bird-filled lake. Follow Mill Hill Loop signs to the right. In 0.3 mile, turn right along a gravel road for 300 yards to a junction at a curve. If Mill Hill's your goal, turn right at a "Trail" pointer, follow a mowed path straight to Gray Creek, and keep right around the low, wooded hill to complete the loop.

If you'd prefer the longer Beaver Pond loop (closed October 1 to March 31 to protect geese), stick to the gravel road at the Mill Hill turnoff. Follow the road 0.4 mile across a farmfield, and turn right at another "Trail" sign. This path passes a diked pond with ducks and nutria (alas, no beaver), makes several left turns, passes a diked cattail pond, and returns to the road. Turn right on the road 0.3 mile to a curve, turn left along a hedgerow another 0.3 mile, and turn right across a field to find the road back to your car.

Historic barn at Finley Wildlife Refuge.

49   Alsea Falls   🚶 🚴 🌲

Easy (to campground bridge)
1.2-mile loop
30 feet elevation gain

Moderate (to Green Peak Falls)
2.8 miles round trip
400 feet elevation gain

Right: Picnic table at McBee Park made from a single 75-foot plank.

Half the fun of visiting this Coast Range waterfall is discovering the scenic road that leads here between the rustic, time-forgotten hamlets of Alsea and Alpine. At the falls themselves you'll find a small campground, a pleasant picnic area, and a network of riverside trails extending to less-visited Green Peak Falls.

If you're coming from the Willamette Valley, drive Highway 99W just north of Monroe (or 16 miles south of Corvallis), turn west at a sign for Alpine, follow Alsea Falls signs 13.2 paved miles, turn right into the picnic area entrance, and park at the far end of the loop. If you're coming from Highway 101 at Waldport, head inland toward Corvallis on Highway 34 for 39 miles to the town of Alsea, turn right at a sign for the Alsea-Deadwood Highway for 0.9 mile, turn left on paved South Fork Road for 8 miles, and turn left into the Alsea Falls picnic area.

Start with a look at 20-foot Alsea Falls. Take a broad gravel trail from the far end of the picnic area parking lot and keep left for 100 feet to the top of the falls. A spur switchbacks down to the falls' base, a favorite spot for wading on hot days.

After admiring the falls, head back toward the parking lot but keep left 100 feet to a footbridge across the South Fork Alsea River. At a junction on the far shore, you'll face a decision.

For the easiest loop, hike upstream to the right for half a mile, recross the river on a bridge near the campground, and keep right to return to your car on another riverbank trail. This path ambles among second-growth hemlock and Douglas fir. Below the trees are giant old stumps, sword fern, moss-draped vine maple, shamrock-like oxalis, and salal bushes. Watch out for pointy-leaved stinging

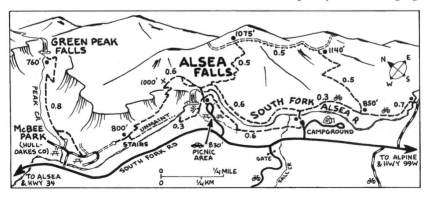

127

Alsea Falls.

nettles beside the trail.

If you'd rather see another waterfall, instead turn left after crossing the footbridge near your car. This path heads downstream for 0.6 mile. When the path joins a gravel road, continue straight for 100 yards. Then look for a hiker-symbol sign marking the trail's continuation uphill to the right. This path joins a trail from McBee Park (a picnic area owned by a timber company), follows Peak Creek up into an old-growth grove, and ends at a pool below Green Peak Falls' 60-foot waterslide.

If you're still going strong, there is a third loop option that adds another 2.4 miles. Return to the footbridge near your car, but instead of crossing the bridge continue straight 50 yards on the riverside trail upstream. Then turn left on the Side Winder Trail for 0.4 mile uphill, turn right along an old gravel road half a mile, turn right again on the steepish Buckhorn Trail for half a mile, and then turn right along the river to complete the loop.

Other Options

The only riverside trail open to mountain bikes is the 1-mile section upstream from the campground bridge, but after riding this you can continue on a challenging 8-mile loop on the other side of South Fork Road. Mapboards and signs show the route on paved roads, gravel roads, and rough single-track.

Cape Perpetua from Yachats.

YACHATS

When Indians from five far-flung tribes were corralled onto this rocky shore below Cape Perpetua in 1856, they named the spot Yachats (pronounced YAH-hots), meaning "at the foot of the mountain." The reservation was disbanded in 1875, and the remaining Indians were sent north to Siletz. Today an upscale, quiet little resort town clings to the dramatically rugged coastline here.

Yachats

Hollywood has filmed Yachats' wave-pounded coast often enough that even big-name stars have discovered this little town's funky shops, romantic bed & breakfast inns, and surprisingly suave restaurants. A restored 1930 church and museum in a cute log cabin is open daily (except Thursday) noon-3 on Third Street, a block west of Highway 101. At the north edge of town, Smelt Sands State Recreation Site overlooks a rocky shore with spouting horns, smelt fishermen, and an 0.7-mile wheelchair-accessible trail (Hike #50). At the south edge of town, the scenic, 1-mile Yachats Ocean Drive loops from Highway 101, passing a glorious picnic area and beach access at the mouth of the Yachats River.

Cape Perpetua

Cape Perpetua confronts the sea with a 700-foot cliff. Highway 101 clings to a ledge with viewpoints of the rugged lava shore between Yachats and the Heceta Head lighthouse. The black rock here erupted as part of a broad, undersea shield volcano over 40 million years ago. The rise of the Coast Range has lifted much of the 2000-foot submarine mountain above the waves.

Just south of the cape, stop at the Siuslaw National Forest's Cape Perpetua Visitor Center for excellent interpretive displays and advice from helpful staff (open daily 10-5:30 in summer, Friday-Tuesday 10-4 in winter). Expect a $5 parking fee. First-rate hiking trails start here (hikes #51 and 52). If you only have time for a very short walk, drive Highway 101 north 0.3 mile to a parking area for the

Devils Churn, a lava chasm that funnels waves to photogenic crashes. On the opposite side of the highway, a paved road leads to a small campground. Keep left on this road's various forks to drive to the top of Cape Perpetua, where a short stroll leads to a 1930s stone shelter with an unmatched view.

Neptune State Scenic Viewpoint
South of Cape Perpetua 2 miles, this picnic area amid windswept spruce accesses a small but beautiful beach at the mouth of Cummins Creek. Head south along the shore 0.4 mile, scrambling over lava outcrops to discover spouting horns and hidden beach coves. Or drive Highway 101 a mile south to the park's far end, and park at the Strawberry Hill turnout for the area's best tidepooling, views of seals on nearby rocks, and access to another beach.

Carl G. Washburne State Park
This overlooked, 65-site campground (with 2 yurts) is open all year, and often has room when bigger state campgrounds are full. Trails lead to a quiet beach and a creekside meadow popular with elk (Hike #53).

Heceta Head Lighthouse
In the Devils Elbow, a picturesque cove below the Heceta Head lighthouse, you'll find a lovely picnic area with a small beach, rocks at low tide, and islands crowded with sea birds. Expect a $5 parking fee. Trails lead up to the lighthouse and under Cape Creek Bridge's 220-foot arch (Hike #53). Volunteers give free tours of the lighthouse daily 11-5 from March to October, and Friday-Monday 11-2 in winter. The 1890s Heceta Light Station bed & breakfast has six rooms for $133-315, with reservations at 866-547-3696 or *www.hecetalighthouse.com.* The inn opens for free tours from noon to 5 Thursday-Monday in summer.

Sea Lion Caves
One of the few really worthwhile commercial attractions on the coast, this 100-foot-tall, sea-washed grotto still has dozens of wild, resident sea lions, despite the 200,000 tourists who ride an elevator down to see them each year. Adults are $14, seniors $13, and kids 5-12 are $8. Open daily 9-5 (9-4 in winter).

The Heceta Head Lighthouse (Hike #53).

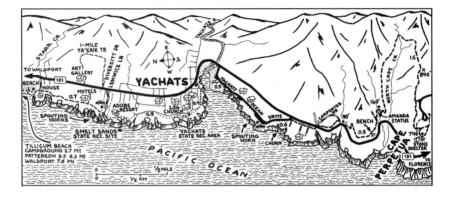

50 Yachats & Amanda Trail 🏃🌟

Easy (Smelt Sands to beach)
1.4 miles round trip
50 feet elevation gain

Easy (to Amanda statue)
2.1 miles round trip
200 feet elevation gain

Left: Cove near Smelt Sands.

  Two easy walks along the Oregon Coast Trail begin in the cute coastal town of Yachats. One hike leads north past spouting horns and crumbling bluffs to a long, broad beach. The other heads south of Yachats to a statue in the forest at Cape Perpetua honoring a blind Indian captive named Amanda.

For the first hike, drive Highway 101 to the north end of Yachats and turn west at a State Park sign onto Lemwick Lane. The gravel lane leads to the turnaround at Smelt Sands State Recreation Site. Walk to the right on a broad, graveled path. After 100 yards, watch for two spouting horns on the left. These geyser-like sprays shoot from cracks in the lava that have been widened by waves. The trail passes in front of a motel and ambles through fields of wind-mown salal, yarrow, and matted spruce trees.

After 0.7 mile the path crosses a house's gravel driveway and descends steps to a broad beach. If you're not ready to turn back, you can continue on hard-packed sand 6.3 miles to the Governor Patterson picnic area at the edge of Waldport. More realistic beachwalking goals are the grassy dunes beside Vingie Creek in 0.8 mile or the concrete stairs up a low orange bluff to the Tillicum Beach picnic area in 2.7 miles.

To try a new inland loop trail opened in 2013, walk back almost to the Smelt Sands trailhead, but turn inland on a path beside the Fireside Motel to Highway 101. Carefully cross the highway, walk a bit to the left to some art galleries, and

The Amanda Trail connects Yachats with Cape Perpetua.

head east through the private Gerdemann Botanic Preserve (no dogs allowed) on a public path 0.2 mile. Then turn right on the Ya'Xaik Trail for 0.6 mile through hillside woods back to Highway 101 at Diversity Drive, opposite the Smelt Sands entrance. Ya'Xaik (pronounced *YA-hike*) is the Alsea tribal name for Yachats.

For a different short walk along the Oregon Coast Trail, start on the south side of Yachats instead. From downtown, walk or drive south across the Yachats River Bridge and turn right on Yachats Ocean Drive for 0.6 mile to a parking pullout on the right. At middling high tides there's a little spouting horn at the north end of this parking pullout. Waves bang into a cliff and squirt up comically through a four-inch hole in the ground.

From the parking pullout walk south along Yachats Ocean Drive. Just before reaching Highway 101, follow "Oregon Coast Trail" markers to the right. For the next 0.2 mile the path parallels the highway, but is separated by a ditch. At Carpenter Drive, cross the highway carefully and turn right on a trail that climbs through the woods above the highway.

At the 0.6-mile mark you'll descend a wooden staircase to the highway shoulder beside a large sign, "Yachats: Gem of the Oregon Coast." Walk 100 feet along the shoulder and cross a few driveways to find the continuation of the trail.

Next the path switchbacks up into deeper spruce woods, with views to Cape Perpetua and the Cleft of the Rock Lighthouse, the only privately owned lighthouse in Oregon.

After the path crosses another small road, the route descends through a private tree plantation to a 50-foot footbridge over a pebbly creek. Here you'll find a small plaza and a four-foot concrete statue of Amanda. After the Rogue River Indian War in 1856, the Army forcibly removed the native people of Southern Oregon to a new reservation on the Central Oregon Coast. A patrol looking for stragglers in 1864 discovered Amanda, an elderly blind Indian woman, at a farm owned by a white settler on the Coos River. The soldiers marched Amanda to the reservation, along rocky headlands so rough that her bare feet left bloody tracks.

Amanda's memorial makes a good turnaround point. The trail ahead is increasingly rough for the next 1.5 miles to Cape Perpetua, where a stone shelter overlooks a panorama that extends, on clear days, 150 miles south to Cape Blanco.

51   Cape Perpetua

Easy (to tidepools and Devils Churn)
1.8-mile loop
100 feet elevation gain

Easy (to Giant Spruce)
2 miles round trip
100 feet elevation gain

Moderate (to viewpoint at shelter)
3 miles round trip
700 feet elevation gain

Most tourists at Cape Perpetua merely pause at the parking pullouts and drive on. They're missing a lot. Trails fan out from the visitor center toward old-growth forests, tidepools, and viewpoints you'll never see from a car window. The three easy hikes described here are short enough that a sturdy hiker can cover them all in an afternoon. If you don't already have a parking pass, expect a $5-per-car fee.

English explorer Captain Cook named the cape in 1778 while sailing into the teeth of a storm. Irritably, he noted in his journal that the same cape had loomed before him for five days straight. It was March 11, the holy day of St. Perpetua, and the faith-tested martyr's name apparently struck a chord.

Start by driving Highway 101 south of Yachats 3 miles (or north of Florence 23 miles) to the Cape Perpetua Visitor Center turnoff between mileposts 168 and 169. All three of the hikes begin at the visitor center's front door. For the shortest walk, follow the "Tidepools" pointer on a big map board to the left.

This completely paved trail descends to a tunnel under Highway 101 and then forks. To the left is a 0.4-mile loop that visits lava tidepools, a spouting horn that sprays at high tide from a undersea cave in Cooks Chasm, and a white shell mound (or "midden") left by a village of mussel-gathering natives as long ago as 6000 years. Collecting marine animals is banned here now.

If you take the other trail fork after the tunnel, you'll cross a footbridge and then walk along the highway shoulder 250 yards to a "Cape Cove Trail" sign

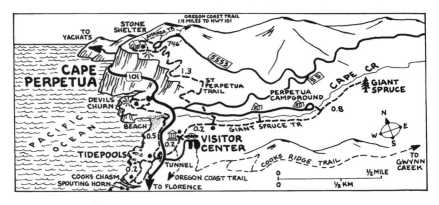

View from Cape Perpetua's stone shelter.   Opposite: Spouting horn at Cooks Chasm.

on the left. An unpaved spur of this path descends to a small, hidden beach. Keep straight another 0.2 mile to reach staircases down to tidepools and the Devils Churn. This seething, 50-foot slot began as a crack in the lava, but millennia of wave erosion expanded it to a long cave and then collapsed the roof.

For the next easiest hike from the visitor center, follow a "Giant Spruce" pointer on a path to the right and keep right at all junctions for a mile. You'll follow a broad gravel trail along alder-lined Cape Creek, opposite a campground. The 15-foot-thick Sitka spruce at trail's end sprouted some 400 years ago atop a rotting log, and as a result its arching roots now frame a tunnel.

For the most difficult and most rewarding of the three short hikes described here, follow the "Viewpoint" pointer 0.2 mile from the visitor center, turn left across Cape Creek, cross two paved roads, and switchback 11 times up a ridge to viewpoints in Cape Perpetua's wildflower meadows. Blue camas, red Indian paintbrush, and a few lupine bloom here in May and June. Keep left at the top to find the stone shelter built in 1933 by the Civilian Conservation Corps. Views extend 37 miles to sea, north to Cape Foulweather, and south 104 miles to Cape Blanco. The summit loop continues through spruce woods carpeted with wild lily-of-the-valley to a parking area. Walk right 100 feet to find the return trail.

If you're trekking the Oregon Coast Trail from Yachats (Hike #50), follow Amanda's Trail to Cape Perpetua's stone shelter, and descend to the visitor center.

52   Gwynn Creek   

Difficult (from visitor center)
5.8-mile loop
1100 feet elevation gain

Difficult (from Cummins Creek)
7.4-mile loop
1500 feet elevation gain

Some of the most spectacular old-growth Sitka spruce forests on the Coast drape the wild canyons south of Cape Perpetua. A 5.8-mile loop from the visitor center follows the crest of Cooks Ridge and traverses back through Gwynn Creek's secluded valley. The Forest Service charges $5 to park at the visitor center, but parking is free at the Cummins Creek Trailhead, where a longer loop around the beautiful Gwynn Creek valley begins.

For the short loop, drive Highway 101 south of Yachats 3 miles (or north of Florence 23 miles) to the Cape Perpetua Visitor Center turnoff between mileposts 168 and 169. Park and walk up to the RV/bus parking lot. The Cooks Ridge Trail begins by a map signboard in this upper parking area.

The path climbs along an ancient logging road 0.4 mile and then forks. Either fork is fine, because they rejoin in 0.3 mile at the top of the ridge. From here the trail follows the relatively level crest amid magnificent 6-foot-thick spruce and sword ferns for 1.6 miles to a junction in a saddle. Turn right on the Gwynn Creek Trail, which traverses gradually down a canyon slope.

Under the big trees on this route you'll find lots of orange-brown mushrooms from August to November: delectably edible chanterelles (with orange ribs underneath their caps) and deadly poisonous panther amanitas (with papery white gills underneath).

After 2.5 miles, the Gwynn Creek Trail descends to the creek and a T-shaped trail junction. Turn right to return to the visitor center. This 1-mile section of the Oregon Coast Trail follows the abandoned bed of a 1913 Florence-Yachats

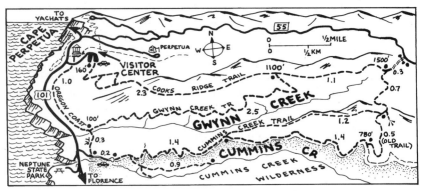

wagon road. Though the route is not far above Highway 101, the ocean views are great and the pounding surf drowns out traffic noise.

For the longer loop to Gwynn Creek, drive Highway 101 a mile south of the visitor center. Near Neptune State Scenic Viewpoint, turn inland at a sign for Cummins Creek Trailhead, and drive 0.3 gravel mile to a turnaround at road's end. The Cummins Creek Trail that begins here follows an ancient roadbed up the canyon without approaching the creek.

After walking up this wide trail 1.4 miles, veer uphill to the left on a well-marked footpath. This portion of the Cummins Ridge Trail follows a ridgecrest up through old-growth Douglas fir and spruce. After 1.9 miles you'll reach a T-shaped junction with the Cooks Ridge Trail. Turn left here for 1.1 mile, then turn left down the Gwynn Creek Trail 2.5 miles, and turn left again on the Oregon Coast Trail for 0.3 mile to its end at the road, 0.2 mile from your car.

Other Options

Although the official Cummins Creek Trail doesn't go to Cummins Creek, an unofficial path does. From the parking area, walk up the Cummins Creek Trail 300 yards and fork to the right on a smaller path. After 250 yards this trail hops a small creek and then forks. To the right, a short path deadends at Cummins Creek's bank in alder woods. The left fork continues 0.6 mile up the canyon bottom, scrambling over roots and logs, to its end at a small gravelly beach beside Cummins Creek.

Sitka spruce trees along Oregon Coast Trail.   Opposite: Cummins Creek.

Heceta Head

Easy (from viewpoint parking lot)
1 mile round trip
200 feet elevation gain

Moderate (from Highway 101)
2.6 miles round trip
600 feet elevation gain

Difficult (from Washburne Park)
5.9-mile loop
800 feet elevation gain

Oregon's most photographed lighthouse is open for tours — but only if you're willing to hike. Fortunately, the trails here are easy and spectacular.

Heceta Head (say *huh-SEE-tuh*) honors Bruno de Heceta, the Portuguese captain of a Spanish ship, who first sighted the cape in 1775. The lighthouse here was the last of Oregon's dozen coastal lighthouses to be built. Bricks for the tower were shipped from San Francisco to Florence and hauled over the hills on wagons. The 2-ton Fresnel lens, with 640 delicate, hand-ground prisms, was off-loaded onto the cape by surf boat.

For the shortest trail to the lighthouse, take Highway 101 north of Florence 12 miles or south of Yachats 15 miles. Just north of a tunnel, turn downhill into the Heceta Head Lighthouse State Scenic Viewpoint (formerly known as Devils Elbow State Park). Expect a $5 parking fee at this picturesque picnic area, beside a beach framed by the graceful 220-foot arch of a 1933 highway bridge. Low tide exposes a beach route to rocky islands, but access is banned to protect sea birds.

The lighthouse trail starts at the far end of the parking lot and climbs 0.3 mile through salal meadows and spruce groves to an old road. To the right is Heceta House, a white clapboard, 1893 Queen-Anne-style duplex that once housed the two assistant light keepers and their families. Still allegedly haunted by a young woman named Rue, Heceta House is now a pricey, elegant bed and breakfast. For reservations call 866-547-3696 or check *www.hecetalighthouse.com*.

From Heceta House, walk left along the old road 0.2 mile to reach the lighthouse. Volunteers offer free lighthouse tours 11am-5pm daily in summer and

Heceta Head.   Opposite: Heceta House.

Friday-Monday 11am-2pm in winter. The tour climbs 58 steps to a massive Fresnel lens rotating on a ball bearing track. Even if you can't climb the tower, bring binoculars to watch the antics of the 7000 long-necked, black Brandt's cormorants that roost April through August on the rocks below the railed yard. This headland has the species' largest mainland nesting colony. Tufted puffins, now rare here, were once so numerous that they gave Parrot Rock its name.

Two longer hiking routes to Heceta Head Lighthouse avoid the crowds and parking fee of the viewpoint parking area. For a moderate hike, drive 0.9 mile north on Highway 101 from the viewpoint parking area to a paved pullout on the right signed "No Overnight Parking." Walk 100 feet north and cross the highway to find a Beach Trail post. When the path forks after 50 feet, keep left. This trail climbs through an ancient, wind-swept Sitka spruce forest with salal, rhododendrons, and views up the coast as far as Cape Perpetua. After 1.3 miles the path switchbacks down to the lighthouse, the hike's turnaround destination.

For a longer loop hike that visits a beach and a beaver lake, drive 2 miles north on Highway 101 to milepost 176, turn west into the Washburne State Park day use area, and park at the far end of the picnic loop. Take the trail past the restrooms and follow the wide beach 1.2 miles to the left. At a brushy break in the bluffs, just 300 yards before Hobbit Beach ends, head inland on the Beach Trail. This path briefly tunnels up through the dense spruce forest as if burrowed by one of author J.R.R. Tolkien's fantasy creatures.

At a trail junction just before Highway 101, take the Oregon Coast Trail to the right 1.3 miles to the Heceta Head lighthouse and back. To complete the hike with a loop, cross Highway 101 and walk right 100 feet to find a small "Valley Trail" sign. Keep left on this path 1.7 miles to return to your car via an inland route that passes a beaver-dammed lake, China Creek, and the campground entrance.

Other Options

For a longer hike, detour 0.9 mile up a lovely loop along China Creek.

Long-range Oregon Coast Trail trekkers coming to Washburne Park from the north have to follow Highway 101 for 8 miles from the Cummins Creek trailhead (Hike #52). South of Heceta Head, the route follows the highway shoulder 3 miles to Baker Beach (Hike #54).

The Siuslaw River bridge from Old Town Florence.

FLORENCE

Dunes lie between the sea and this Siuslaw River port, where quaint shops pack the riverfront's Old Town. Shifting sand hills have backed up dozens of freshwater lakes in the forests nearby. Two of these sinuous lakes bracket popular Honeyman State Park. Farther inland, three trails through Coast Range rainforest canyons lead to surprisingly tall waterfalls.

Old Town

Founded in 1893, this delightful riverfront district between Highway 101 and the docks at the Port of Siuslaw is home to 36 boutiques and a dozen eateries. Parking can be tight on weekends. Start your exploration afoot at the gazebo and fishing dock in the cute pocket park at Laurel and Bay streets. Shops line the waterfront in both directions. First explore under the arched, 1936 Siuslaw River Bridge to the west. Then walk back to the wharf at Mo's chowder restaurant and continue along a boardwalk to the end of the marina.

Explore side streets to find the craft shops in the restored 1905 Florence Grade School at 278 Maple Street and the Fly Fishing Museum at 2nd and Nopal Streets.

Jessie M. Honeyman State Park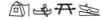

Kids slide down sand dunes straight into swimmable Cleawox Lake at this extremely popular park. Twenty-foot-tall pink rhododendrons bloom in April in the forest. This is Oregon's busiest state park campground with 355 campsites, and 10 yurts at $39-44. The campground's open year round, but you're unlikely to find a spot on summer afternoons without a reservation. The park's four day-use picnic areas include two free areas east of Highway 101 on forested Woahink Lake, where a boat ramp caters largely to waterskiers. A $5 day-use parking fee is charged at the two Cleawox Lake picnic areas west of Highway 101, but this is where you'll find the dunes. There's also a historic 1930s store by a swimming beach where paddleboats are rented in summer. For a map, see Hike #61.

Three Rivers Casino

The Coos, Lower Umpqua, and Siuslaw tribes operate a large, modern casino 3 miles east of Florence on Highway 126, with slot machines, gaming tables, a gift shop, restaurants, a hotel, and a display of Indian artifacts.

Harbor Vista County Park

The Siuslaw River's twin jetties jut across broad beaches to the sea. For the best view, visit this often overlooked park, where you'll also find a picnic area and a 38-site year-round campground with showers. Drive Highway 101 to the north end of Florence, turn west on 35th Street a mile, turn right on Rhododendron Drive a mile, and turn left on North Jetty Road. Expect a $3 parking fee.

North Jetty

After soaking up the view at Harbor Vista, continue a mile to a parking lot at North Jetty Road's end, a good place to let kids play on the beach or clamber on the jetty's boulders.

Weekends from mid-March through October, Seahorse Stagecoach offers hour-long beach rides from here north to Heceta Beach's Driftwood Shores resort. Before Highway 101 was completed in 1936, stages regularly plied the hard, wet sand of low tide. This updated coach has fat rubber tires, a bright red roof, big windows, and a wood stove. Departures still depend on low tides.

South Jetty

South Jetty Road, a mile south of Florence, divides the dunes into two worlds. North of the road, the river-edged Siuslaw Spit is reserved for hikers and wildlife—notably the thousands of tundra swans that winter in the dune-fringed marshes of the spit's interior. To the south, dune buggies roar through the sand hills from staging areas along the road. Expect a parking fee.

Sutton Creek Recreation Area

Quieter than Honeyman Park, this area 6 miles north of Florence also features lakes, dunes, and forest. A boat ramp along Highway 101 accesses large, forest-rimmed Sutton Lake (waterskiing permitted). Drive west 2 miles from Highway 101 at the recreation area sign to find Holman Vista, with an observation platform overlooking the dunes beside Sutton Creek. Open year-round, 80-site Sutton Campground straddles the creek a mile upstream (see Hike #54). Nearby, the 39-site Alder Dune Campground and picnic area is also open year-round, with a lake where kids can slide down a dune into the water.

Darlingtonia State Natural Site

The insect-eating pitcher plant *Darlingtonia californica* usually grows in bogs in the Klamath Mountains, luring flies and bees into its baseball-bat-shaped green throat with a honey-like smell. A short boardwalk from a picnic area in this forested wayside leads across a bog to one of the strange insectivore's northernmost colonies. Drive 5 miles north of Florence on Highway 101.

Siuslaw Pioneer Museum

Indian and pioneer artifacts are displayed in this museum at the corner of Maple and Second Streets in downtown Florence. Hours are 10-4 daily from May 1 to September 30 (noon-4 Tuesday-Sunday in winter). Adult admission is $3.

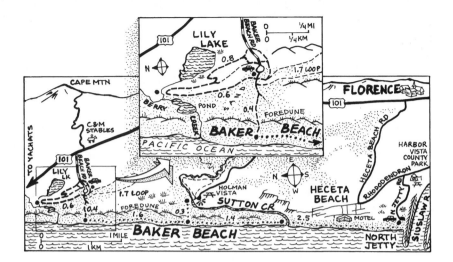

54 Baker Beach

Easy (to Baker Beach)
0.8 miles round trip
No elevation gain

Easy (to Lily Lake)
1.4-mile loop
30 feet elevation gain

Moderate (shuttle to North Jetty)
5.9 miles one way
No elevation gain

Right: Baker Beach dunes.

Though quite close to Florence, Baker Beach is a wild stretch of grassy dunes and bird-friendly estuary mostly known only to horseback riders. Hikers can explore the area on a network of short loop trails. If you can arrange a car shuttle, you can trek the length of Baker Beach, wade Sutton Creek, and continue south along Heceta Beach all the way to the Siuslaw River's North Jetty.

Drive Highway 101 north of Florence 7 miles. A bit beyond C & M Stables, turn west on gravel Baker Beach Road for 0.5 mile to its end at a large parking area with horse facilities. Bikes are banned and dogs are permitted on leash only.

Start out toward the roar of the ocean on a sandy old road that's gated closed to vehicles. The path heads across grass-covered sand hummocks with struggling, wind-matted trees. In early summer, blue lupine, wild strawberries, and prickly yellow gorse bloom here.

After just 50 yards you'll reach a signed trail crossing and face a decision. If you have children along who can't wait to get to the beach, you'd best keep going straight. The sandy path is a bit braided, but follow hoofprints and trail posts 0.4 mile to the beach. Note where the trail joins the beach, because the path can be hard to find on your way back.

If you have time to explore the dunescape first, however, turn right at the trail crossing to take the Lily Lake Loop. This path leads 0.6 mile to a pond in the dunes and then doubles back along the crest of a sand ridge that's overgrown with forest. At a fork at the 1.1-mile mark, turn left to switchback down to the reedy shore of Lily Lake. Keep right at the next trail junction to complete a 1.4-mile loop to your car.

For a longer trip, take the sandy path 0.4 mile to the beach and turn left along the hard-packed wet sand zone. There are enough sand dollar fragments here that, with patience, you'll find a whole one. The dry sand of the beach's driftwood zone is closed from mid-March to mid-September because the snowy plover, an endangered sandpiper-like bird, nests there then.

After 3 miles you'll reach Sutton Creek, ankle deep where it fans out across the beach. If you've arranged a shuttle to the North Jetty parking lot (see map), wade the creek and continue 2.5 miles. This final stretch traverses Heceta Beach, a busier shore lined with cottages and motels.

55   Sutton Creek

Easy (to Bolduc's Meadow)
1.3-mile loop
30 feet elevation gain

Moderate (to Sutton Campground)
4.3-mile loop
100 feet elevation gain

Sand dunes and rhododendron-filled forests line the banks of this meandering creek between Sutton Lake and the ocean. It's a haven for birds and beavers, and a network of loop trails makes it a good place for hikers, too.

Drive Highway 101 north of Florence 5 miles. Between mileposts 185 and 186 turn west at a Sutton Creek Recreation Area sign, and go straight on the paved road 2.2 miles to its end at the Holman Vista turnaround. Expect a $5 parking fee.

From the little picnic area here a paved, 100-yard trail beside the restrooms leads to a decked observation platform overlooking the creek — where you're likely to see great blue herons. On the horizon, above the grassy dunes of Baker Beach, notice the Sea Lion Caves' entrance building atop a rugged headland. If you don't mind getting your feet wet, it's fun to wade the knee-deep, relatively warm creek and explore across the dunes to the ocean.

For the loop hikes along the creek, however, take a trail cut through the salal bushes at the end of the picnic area's little lawn, marked by a post with a blue stripe. Left-hand forks of this path deadend at creek fords. On a hot day, it's tempting to wade the creek and slide down the dunes on the far shore straight into the water. To hike onward, however, keep straight for 0.8 mile to a bench with a view upstream to a footbridge. For the short loop, turn right at the bench on a half-mile trail that returns through the woods to your car.

For the longer loop, continue into Bolduc's Meadow, the site of a vacation resort from the 1930s to the 1970s. Don't cross the footbridge here. Instead continue straight, following a hiker symbol. After another 1.3 miles along the creek, you'll reach the campground's Loop A. Turn left 300 feet along the road to site A11, cut left to the B loop, walk left along this road 200 feet to site B16, turn left to cross the creek on a footbridge, and then turn left on a creekside path. In 0.2 mile you'll reach the soft sand of the dunes at a T-shaped junction. Turn left, skirt a sandy open area, and keep straight for nearly a mile before reentering the woods and switchbacking down to the footbridge at Bolduc's Meadow. Turn right to return to your car.

Baker Beach.   Opposite: Holman Vista.

56   Cape Mountain

Easy (to summit)
1.9-mile loop
500 feet elevation gain

Difficult (to Berry Creek)
8-mile loop
1100 feet elevation gain

Left: Nelson Ridge meadow on Cape Mountain.

The trail network on Cape Mountain was designed to be shared by horses and hikers, but you're unlikely to meet either horses or hikers. It's odd, really, because the trails loop through nice old-growth forests and meadows with ocean views.

This coastal mountain was called *Tsahawtita* ("grassy ridge") by local Indians because they burned off the forest here to simplify deer hunting. After the Forest Service built a fire lookout on the summit in 1932, the forest grew up and blocked most views. Today the only trailside structure is a *hitsi,* an Indian hunting shelter, reconstructed from a description by an early homesteader.

Drive Highway 101 north of Florence 7 miles. Just beyond C & M Stables (between mileposts 182 and 183), turn inland on Herman Cape Road for 1.1 paved mile and an additional 1.7 mile of one-lane gravel to the Dry Lake Trailhead on the left *(GPS location N44° 05.78' W124° 04.25').* Walk up to a campsite on the right and head toward the horse corrals to find the Princess Tasha Trail, which climbs through a mossy coastal forest of 5-foot-thick Sitka spruce and Douglas firs for 0.4 mile to a 4-way trail junction at a pass.

Here you could turn left and keep left at all junctions for 0.5 mile to Cape Mountain's summit. But the summit meadow is a bit disappointing, and most of the loop options back from the summit involve old roads (see map).

For a longer loop with better views, turn right at the 4-way junction to stay on the Princess Tasha Trail, which becomes the Scurvy Ridge Trail (after Olson Viewpoint's bench) and eventually passes the Indian shelter. Follow "Horse Water" pointers at the 2-mile mark, keeping left at trail junctions near the Horse

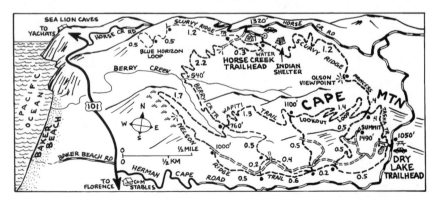

Berry Creek at Cape Mountain.

Creek Trailhead until you hit the Berry Creek Trail. This path briefly follows an ancient road to another viewpoint bench, but then the trail switchbacks down 1.8 miles to Berry Creek (almost always crossable with a good jump) and climbs 0.4 mile to a four-way junction.

The shortest route back to your car from this trail crossing is to go straight, but it's gentler and more interesting to turn right. This route crosses another fork of Berry Creek in an old-growth cedar forest, traverses a long forested slope, and then switches back atop a surprising ridgetop meadow that resembles a golf fairway. The Forest Service has logged and mowed half a mile of Nelson Ridge in an attempt to simulate the elk-friendly meadows that Indians created by setting fires. A bench here offers seacoast views that stretch to the distant Siuslaw River jetty.

To complete the loop, keep right at junctions to continue along the Nelson Ridge Trail back through woods to your car at the Dry Lake Trailhead.

57 Pawn and Pioneer Trails

Easy (Pawn Old Growth Trail)
0.8-mile loop
50 feet elevation gain

Easy (Mapleton Hill Pioneer Trail)
0.6-mile loop
200 feet elevation gain

Left: Pawn Old Growth Trail.

Just a few miles' drive apart, these two very short nature trails visit an old-growth forest and a pioneer wagon road. The drive here is half the fun, looping through forgotten homestead valleys of the Coast Range. Take Highway 126 east of Florence 1 mile, turn left onto North Fork Road for 11 miles to a junction, continue straight on Upper North Fork Road for 5.4 miles, and turn right across a bridge onto Elk Tie Road for 100 yards to the Pawn Old Growth Trailhead.

Along the 0.8-mile loop look for a 250-foot-tall Douglas fir and a cave-like red cedar trunk hollowed by fire. After the Coast Indian Reservation was opened to homesteaders in 1875, four families started the town of Pawn near here, named for the first letters of their names: Poole, Akerley, Worthington, and Noland.

For the next hike, drive back 5.4 miles and turn left across a bridge onto the North Fork Siuslaw Road for 2.4 miles. Park at a "Pioneer Trail" sign on the left, 400 yards after the road turns to gravel. This trail follows what once was the main route linking the Southern Willamette Valley and the Coast. In 1908, homesteaders upgraded the horse trail to a wagon road with 13 switchbacks and a covered bridge across McLeod Creek. The bridge collapsed in a 1929 snow storm, taking a 1926 Chevy with it. The roadbed, now nicely overgrown with mossy alders, bigleaf maples, and cedars, forms a portion of the 0.6-mile loop.

To drive back a different way, continue east on gravel North Fork Siuslaw Road. This is a replacement route built in 1927. When you reach the pass after 1.7 miles, keep left at a junction for another 2.1 miles. Then turn right on Highway 36 for 3.2 miles to Mapleton and the highway back to Florence.

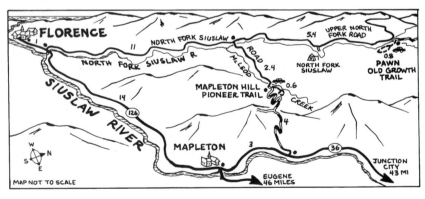

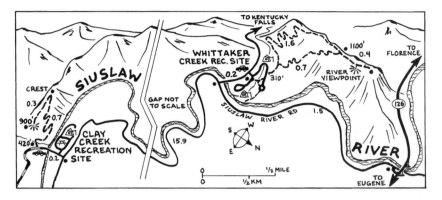

58   Siuslaw Ridge Trails   🚲 🏕

Moderate (from Whittaker Creek)
3.1-mile loop
800 feet elevation gain

Moderate (from Clay Creek)
2 miles round trip
600 feet elevation gain

Right: Footbridge at Whittaker Creek.

These two Coast Range trails climb through patches of old-growth forest to ridgetop viewpoints. Though the paths are 16 miles apart, they both start at little-known campgrounds on the same paved backroad.

Drive Highway 126 west of Eugene 33 miles (or east of Florence 26 miles) to a junction between mileposts 26 and 27. Following "Whittaker Cr. Rec. Area" signs, turn south along the Siuslaw River 1.6 miles, turn right for 0.2 mile, and turn right into the park entrance. Veer right 100 yards to park by a footbridge over Whittaker Creek. When the campground is closed in winter, park by the gate.

Cross the footbridge, turn left, and walk 100 yards on a campground road to an "Old Growth Ridge Trail" sign on the right between campsites 23 and 24. This trail climbs — steeply at times — through a Douglas fir forest with white spring wildflowers: fairy bells, trilliums, and shamrock-leaved oxalis. Yellow wildflowers here are wood violets and Oregon grape. Keep to the right at junctions to climb 0.7 mile to a ridgecrest. The return loop is to the left, but first turn right amid giant old-growth trees for 0.4 mile to a bench with a Siuslaw River view.

For the next hike, drive back to the Siuslaw River Road, turn right for 15.9 miles, and turn right again at a "Clay Creek Trail" sign. Drive straight past the campground entrance and park on the left just beyond a Siuslaw River bridge. The rough, narrow trail starts on the opposite side of the road, crosses Clay Creek on a footbridge, and climbs gradually through old-growth Douglas fir 0.7 mile to a saddle. Here the trail turns left along the ridgecrest amid red-barked madrone trees 0.3 mile to its end at a viewpoint with a glimpse of the Siuslaw River.

59 Sweet Creek Falls

Easy (to Sweet Creek Falls)
2.2 miles round trip
350 feet elevation gain

Moderate (all trails)
5.2 miles round trip
650 feet elevation gain

This sleepy Coast Range valley, with its beautiful cascading creek, was settled in 1879 by the Zarah T. Sweets, a family of Oregon Trail pioneers. Portions of an early wagon road have been incorporated in a dramatic trail past a dozen falls. Four trailheads along the route make it easy to hike the path in segments.

Start by driving Highway 126 to the Siuslaw River Bridge in Mapleton (15 miles east of Florence or 46 miles west of Eugene). Cross the bridge from town and immediately turn west on Sweet Creek Road for 10.2 paved miles. Then take a paved turnoff to the right to the Homestead Trailhead turnaround.

From here a graveled path heads upstream past a split, 10-foot waterfall. Later, the trail hugs a cliff through a canyon full of punchbowl-shaped falls. Four-foot-thick Douglas fir trees tower above the creekside alder and bigleaf maple. Black, robin-sized water ouzels fly just above the creek's surface before plopping underwater to prowl the creek bottom for insect larvae.

After 0.7 mile a path from a second trailhead joins on the left. Continue upstream 0.4 mile to a cliff-edged plunge pool at the base of 20-foot Sweet Creek Falls. A spur trail switchbacks up 150 yards to a viewpoint of an upper falls in a thundering slot. From the lower viewpoint, it's possible to cross the bridgeless creek on slippery boulders to reach the unmarked continuation of the trail, but the crossing's tricky in summer and all but impossible in winter, so most hikers will prefer to turn back.

To hike the valley's upper reaches, drive the paved road 1.3 miles beyond the

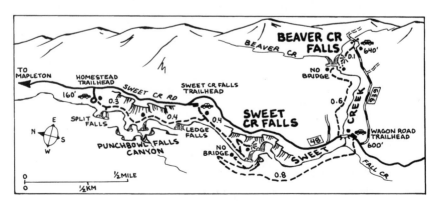

Falls on Sweet Creek.   Opposite: Catwalk in Sweet Creek's gorge.

Homestead Trailhead. Just after a bridge, park at the Wagon Road Trailhead on the left. Across the road, a path heads downstream 0.8 mile to a different viewpoint of Sweet Creek Falls. Just before trail's end, a spur switchbacks down to the bridgeless creek crossing mentioned above.

The 0.6-mile trail segment to Beaver Creek Falls is particularly nice. From the Wagon Road Trailhead, walk across the road's bridge to find a Sweet Creek Trail sign on the right. This portion of the path heads upstream to the base of a fan-shaped waterfall where Beaver Creek and Sweet Creek merge. Although the trail ends here without a bridge, it's not hard to hop the creek. On the far side, a 40-foot scramble up a slippery slope brings you to a railed viewpoint at the end of a very short trail from gravel Road 939. To drive here from the Wagon Road Trailhead, simply continue along the paved road 0.2 mile and take the first fork left for 0.5 mile to a parking area.

60   Kentucky Falls   

Moderate (to Kentucky Falls)
4.4 miles round trip
800 feet elevation **loss**

Moderate (Smith River to 3-mi bridge)
6 miles round trip
120 feet elevation gain

Difficult (entire trail, with shuttle)
8.7 miles one way
1400 feet elevation gain

Right: North Fork Falls.

Three of the Coast Range's most spectacular waterfalls tumble through the jungly rainforest of this remote Coast Range canyon. If you've hiked to these falls before, you might start at a lower trailhead and hike up the North Fork Smith River instead. Either way, set aside time for the drive here on twisty backroads.

Start by taking Highway 126 west of Eugene 33 miles — or east of Florence 26

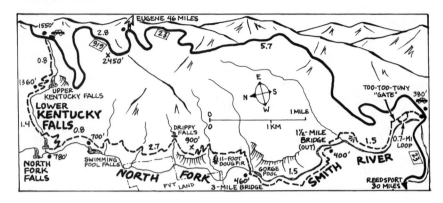

miles. Between mileposts 26 and 27, turn south at a "Whittaker Cr. Rec. Area" sign. In 1.6 miles turn right across a bridge at another Whittaker Creek sign. Follow this paved, one-lane road 1.5 miles and fork left onto Dunn Ridge Road for 7.0 twisty, uphill miles to a T-shaped junction at the end of pavement. Then turn left on Knowles Creek Road for 2.7 miles, turn right on gravel Road 23 for 1.6 miles, and finally turn right on paved Road 919 for 2.8 miles to the trailhead parking area on the right.

Walk up the road 50 yards from the parking area to find the trail on the left. Beneath the trail's old-growth Douglas firs, look for big white trilliums blooming in April and carpets of shamrock-leaved oxalis with little white blooms in May. Wet areas have spiny devils club, pink bleeding hearts, and salmonberries.

After half a mile the path switchbacks down to the base of tiered, 100-foot-tall Upper Kentucky Falls. In another 1.4 miles the trail ends at an observation deck in a misty grotto where curtains of water spill from the mossy cliffs on either hand. To the right is 100-foot Lower Kentucky Falls. A smaller trail scrambles down 100 yards from the deck to the North Fork Smith River and a better view of North Fork Falls' colossal 120-foot-tall fan.

If you're not yet ready to return to your car, hike 100 yards back from the Lower Kentucky Falls viewing platform and fork downhill to the right on the smaller North Fork Trail. This path extends 6.5 miles down the North Fork Smith River. From this end, the best goal is 0.8 mile away, a 6-foot waterfall that tumbles into a 140-foot-long pool. On hot days it's fun to swim in this oval pool or to sunbathe on the bedrock ledges surrounding it.

A better way to hike the North Fork Trail, however, is to start at the lower end. To find this trailhead from Eugene, follow the driving directions to Kentucky Falls (above), but when you return to pavement near the end of the drive, don't turn right on Road 919. Instead turn left onto Road 23 for 5.7 miles.

To find this trailhead from Reedsport, take Highway 101 north 0.8 mile and turn right on Smith River Road for 14.8 miles. Just before a bridge, turn left on North Fork Road 48A for 7.4 miles of narrow pavement and an additional 2.3 miles of gravel to a fork. Bear right, following a "Mapleton" pointer, for another 0.6 miles on gravel to a road triangle. Veer right onto paved one-lane Road 23 for 4 miles to a large sign for the North Fork Smith Trailhead on the left.

The volunteers who built the trail through this beautiful river canyon claimed that the forest here was enchanted by "Too-Too-Tunies," mischievous sprites that misplaced their tools and teased their dogs. Today the most mischievous creatures you're likely to find are the Douglas squirrels that flick their tails and race about tree trunks, scolding passersby.

From this lower trailhead the North Fork Trail sets out through an old-growth forest of Douglas fir and hemlock. Continue straight 0.3 mile until you reach the signed Too-Too-Tuny "gateway," a pair of giant firs that squeeze the trail ahead. If you're truly pressed for time you could turn left here on a wheelchair-accessible path that loops back to your car. Otherwise, sally onward.

After 1.5 miles you'll reach the site of a former bridge across the North Fork Smith River. This is another possible turnaround spot, but when the river is low in summer and fall you can cross and continue another 1.5 miles (on a brushier trail) to an intact footbridge across the river. Just before this 3-mile bridge the trail passes a rock-lined gorge where the river forms a 100-foot pool 5 feet deep—a nice swimming hole on a hot day.

Day hikers generally turn back at the 3-mile bridge, because the trail ahead climbs steeply away from the river. Still, there are attractions along the route ahead: a Douglas fir 11 feet in diameter, the dripny waterfall of a side creek, the river's best swimming hole, and Kentucky Falls itself. Of course the easiest way to see these sights is to do the entire trail one way, returning by shuttle car or bicycle on the paved road between trailheads.

Kentucky Falls.

Honeyman Park

Easy (dunes exploration)
1.7-mile loop
250 feet elevation gain

Easy (trail between lakes)
2.4 miles round trip
No elevation gain

Most visitors to this extremely popular park bask in the sand dunes, paddle in the lakes, or simply stay in the campground. But the best way to investigate Honeyman Park's scenery is to hike through the dunes or to take a trail between the two forest-rimmed lakes.

Drive Highway 101 south of Florence 3 miles (or north of Reedsport 18 miles), turn west into the park entrance, and follow "Sand Dunes Picnic Area" signs 0.3 mile to a parking lot where a $5 day-use fee is charged.

A sandy trail at the end of the lot promptly leads to the open dunes beside Cleawox Lake. In summer, kids slide down the sand straight into the swimmably warm water here. Hike through the soft sand to the far end of the lake. Ahead you'll see a "tree island," a forested hill bypassed by the advancing dunes. Because zooming, noisy dune buggies are allowed in the 1.5-mile-wide strip between that tree island and the ocean beach, hikers seldom venture there.

Tree island and dunes at Honeyman Park.   Above: Cleawox Lake.

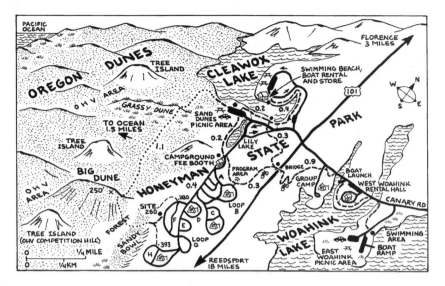

Instead turn left at the end of Lake Cleawox and climb to the crest of a grassy dune. From here you can see south to a second tree island. To its left is the tallest dune in the area, a bare, 250-foot-tall sand hill. Head cross-country half a mile to the wind-rippled summit of this monster dune, where views extend across the undulating sandscape to the sea. Then romp down the steep east face — directly away from the ocean — and duck through a strip of forest on one of several crude but heavily used sandy paths. In 100 yards you'll emerge in a large sandy bowl rimmed by forest. Cross this basin and climb to the campground trail, marked by a gap in the rim. The left fork of this sandy forest trail leads you to campsite 260 on Loop F. From there, turn left on the road and keep left for 0.4 mile to the campground entrance fee booth. Just beyond, a trail to the left skirts Lily Lake 0.2 mile back to your car.

If you'd rather hike between the park's lakes — or if you want to avoid paying a day-use parking fee — park at the free East Woahink Picnic Area. To find it, turn east from Highway 101 (away from the campground entrance) onto Canary Road. After 0.5 mile, turn right down the East Woahink entrance road to the large parking area. Walk part way back up the entrance road to find a trail on the left marked "Cleawox Lake Day Use Areas." If you follow these signs and keep left at all junctions for 0.5 mile you'll cross a road bridge, skirt the lakeshore around the West Woahink rental hall, cross another road bridge, and duck briefly through the woods to the group camp entrance on Canary Road.

Follow signs to the left to find a paved bike path that crosses Highway 101 on a pedestrian overpass. If you're biking, stick to this wide path and campground roads. If you're hiking, walk 100 feet beyond this bridge and veer right on a path that descends, crossing two roads to a paved trail along Cleawox Lake. To the right 0.4 mile the lakeshore trail ends at a swimming beach with summer paddleboat rentals and a historic 1930s stone bathhouse converted to a souvenir shop. To the left 0.2 mile is the Sand Dunes Picnic Area — where the dune loop exploration begins.

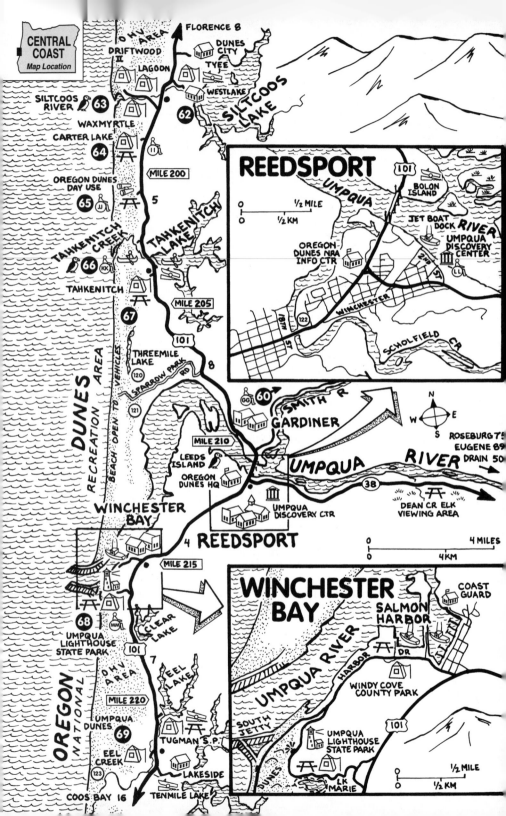

Reedsport's Umpqua Discovery Center.

REEDSPORT

The Umpqua River curves to the sea through the largest expanse of coastal dunes in North America. The slowly advancing dunes have backed up more than a dozen large, many-armed freshwater lakes into the forest. The area's largest harbor is near the ocean at Winchester Bay.

Oregon Dunes National Recreation Area

With 36 virtually unbroken miles of beach, this is the place to run barefoot along a dune's rippled crest or slide down a sand chute. Wild rhododendrons up to 20 feet tall fill the forests with pink blooms in April. Birds of 247 species find habitat in the dunes area, especially in the estuaries and the marshy "deflation plains" behind the beach's grassy foredune. While all of the National Recreation Area is open to hikers and horseback riders, few venture into the half where OHVs (off-highway vehicles) are allowed to zoom through the sand.

A good first stop is the Oregon Dunes Visitor Center (open 8am-4:30pm Monday-Saturday in summer, weekdays in winter) in Reedsport at the junction of Highways 101 and 38. Then pull into the Oregon Dunes Day Use Area north of Reedsport 10 miles on Highway 101, where volunteer hosts give tips on geology, ecology, and recreation from 10am-2pm daily in summer.

Umpqua Discovery Center

This modern interpretive center on Reedsport's old riverfront features the Umpqua River's ecology and history. Don't miss the walk-through exhibits that simulate the sights and sounds of life in an Indian village, in a logging camp, on a 19th-century waterfront dock, in a one-room schoolhouse, and in an old-time barbershop. Hours are 10am-5pm Monday-Saturday and noon-4pm Sunday from June 1 to September 30. In the off season it's open Monday-Saturday 10am-4pm and Sunday noon-4pm. Admission runs $8 for adults, $7 for seniors, $4 for kids 5-16, or $20 per family.

Siltcoos River

Only 3 miles long, this lazy river meanders through the sandy forest between huge Siltcoos Lake and the ocean. Along the way it passes near four popular Forest Service campgrounds. East of Highway 101, 15-site Tyee Campground has the river's only boat ramp. Canoe exploration upstream to Siltcoos Lake is easy, but paddling downstream to the sea requires portaging at a low concrete dam. There are three large campgrounds west of Highway 101, but Driftwood II is a staging area for noisy off-highway vehicles. See Hike #63.

Tahkenitch Lake

Tahkenitch is an Indian word for "many-armed," and indeed this 3-square-mile lake is so sinuous it has nearly 100 miles of shoreline. A boat ramp along Highway 101 is popular with fishermen and waterskiers. A dam blocks lake boaters from exploring Tahkenitch Creek, but if you carry a canoe or kayak 160 yards down the Tahkenitch Creek Trail (Hike #66), you can paddle the lazy creek 2 miles downstream alongside the dunes to the bird-rich estuary.

Dean Creek Elk Viewing Area

A herd of over 100 Roosevelt elk is almost always within sight of this viewing pullout in a pasture beside Highway 38, east of Reedsport 3 miles.

Winchester Bay

Just inside the Umpqua River jetties, Winchester Bay's Salmon Harbor has become Oregon's largest sport fishing marina. The town itself is a salty blend of fish markets, charter boat offices, and tackle shops. Windy Cove County Park, across the street from the marina, has picnic tables and a 97-site campground.

Umpqua Lighthouse State Park

A 2-ton, 800-prism Fresnel lens still rotates atop the 65-foot tower of this 1894 lighthouse, blinking its trademark sequence of two white flashes and one red. Tours of the tower cost about $5 (students $3). Tours are available 10-4 daily from May 1 to Sept 30 (Fri-Sun in spring/fall). Call 541-271-4631 to arrange off-season tours for groups of 6 to 10. A stone's throw down the road, the state park has picnic tables, swimming, and a 44-site campground beside little, forest-rimmed Lake Marie (Hike #68). The park rents 8 yurts ($56-80) and 2 log cabins ($39-40).

South Jetty

Two jetties angle together at the south edge of the Umpqua River mouth, enclosing a triangle of saltwater. An oyster and mussel company has set up business here, and it's a good spot for canoeing or birding too. To find it, take Harbor Drive west from Winchester Bay to the Ziolkouski parking area. Beyond this parking lot, Harbor Drive continues 2 miles along the very broad, very flat beach, passing two more parking areas. Vehicles aren't allowed on the beach, but the lots are staging areas for off-highway vehicle (OHV) exploration inland to the 400-foot-tall Umpqua Scenic Dunes. See Hike #69.

William M. Tugman State Park

Resident mallards and geese waddle through the picnic lawns of this state park beside Eel Lake, popular with fishermen and power boaters. The 94-site, forested campground is open year-round, has 16 yurts, and is seldom crowded. Drive 10 miles south of Reedsport on Highway 101 and turn inland.

62   Siltcoos Lake

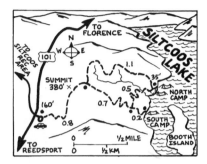

Moderate
4.3-mile loop
600 feet elevation gain

This loop through the woods leads to secluded campsites on the shore of vast Siltcoos Lake. The trailhead parking area is on the inland side of Highway 101, immediately opposite the Siltcoos Recreation Area turnoff 8 miles south of Florence (or 13 miles north of Reedsport) at milepost 198. A trailhead parking pass can be bought here for $5 if you don't have one already.

Take the trail up to the left amid Sitka spruce and Douglas fir. Large sword ferns, slender deer ferns, and orange salmonberries line the path. Many of the huge stumps in the forest still bear springboard notches where loggers stood to cut the trees in the 1930s. Orange chanterelle mushrooms thrive in the second-growth woods from August to November, but do not confuse them with the poisonous, white-gilled panther amanitas also common here.

After 0.8 mile the path heads downhill and forks. Keep right at all junctions for 0.9 mile to South Camp, a single lakeside tent site surrounded by alder and salmonberry brush. Distant sailboats tilt across the lake. Fishermen troll through the inlets. Across the lake is wooded Booth Island, with a cabin and dock.

Head back up the trail and keep right for 0.5 mile to find North Camp, a nicer collection of lakeshore campsites amid firs. The trails in this camp are a bit confusing. Keep right at every fork until you've visited all three campsites. Then turn around and keep right again to find the loop trail back to your car.

If you'd like to canoe to these campsites, drive 1.5 miles north on Highway 101 and turn east at a Siltcoos Lake sign for half a mile to a boat ramp. Paddle 1 mile south to the shore opposite the start of Booth Island.

Siltcoos Lake.

63   Siltcoos River

Easy
3.1-mile loop
50 feet elevation gain

Left: Snowy plover closure sign.

    The estuary where the Siltcoos River loops from the forest to a quiet beach is one of the richest birdwatching sites in Oregon. Even if you have never before seen a kingfisher, an osprey, or an egret, the chances are good you'll spot one here. Along the way, the river trail passes some of the most beautiful scenery in the Oregon Dunes. A special $5 parking fee is charged at the trailhead.

    Drive Highway 101 south of Florence 8 miles (or north of Reedsport 13 miles) to the Siltcoos Recreation Area turnoff at milepost 198, and take the paved road 0.9 mile to the Stagecoach Trailhead parking area on the left.

    Hike left on the Waxmyrtle Beach Trail between the Siltcoos River and the road 0.2 mile and turn right across a campground entrance bridge over the river. On the far side, turn right again on a riverside trail. Look here for kingfishers perched on branches above the water. These robin-sized birds with oversized heads and pointed bills suddenly dive into the water to spear fish.

    Ignoring left-hand spur trails from Waxmyrtle Campground, you'll climb along a bluff edge with a sweeping view across the estuary. If a black-and-white hawk-like bird cruises past, it's probably an osprey. The stork-like birds standing stilt-legged in the river shallows are snowy egrets (if white) or great blue herons (if gray).

    The trail leaves the shore pine woods, joins an abandoned sandy road, and follows it to the beach. Turn right 0.6 mile to the river mouth. The dry-sand-and-driftwood zone near the river is off limits from March 15 to September 15 because snowy plovers lay their eggs there then. These rare birds resemble

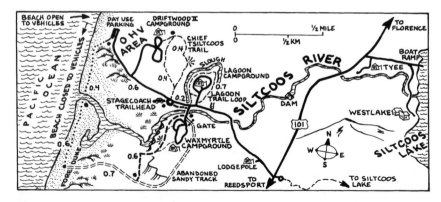

The Siltcoos River estuary from the Waxmyrtle Trail.

sandpipers but have a white shoulder yoke and search for food in dry sand rather than near the waves. A 1994 survey found only 60 snowy plovers on the Oregon Coast, but their numbers now seem to be increasing.

You can return as you came, of course, but to make a loop, take off your shoes and wade calf-deep across the river where it fans out across the beach. Then hike 0.4 mile north along the beach, head inland following footprints across the start of the grassy foredune, cross the day-use parking lot, and follow the paved road 0.6 mile to your car.

Other Options

The Lagoon Trail loops 0.7 mile around Lagoon Campground, tracing the bank of an oxbow slough that once was part of the Siltcoos River. The trail starts opposite the Waxmyrtle Campground entrance bridge. Yet another short loop, the 0.8-mile Chief Tsiltcoos Trail, begins opposite the Stagecoach Trailhead and explores an forested sand dune beside Driftwood II Campground's OHV area.

If you're trekking the Oregon Coast Trail from Florence, cross the Siuslaw River bridge, turn right on South Jetty Access Road, and follow the beach south 16 miles, fording Siltcoos and Tahkenitch Creeks (see Hikes #64-67). Then turn inland on Sparrow Park Road and Highway 101 for 8 miles to Reedsport.

64   Taylor Dunes

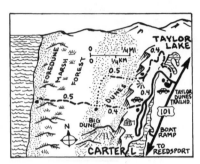

Moderate
2.7-mile loop
100 feet elevation gain

Here you can hike across the range of coastal dune ecosystems—forest, high dunes, foredune, and beach—in just a mile. If you're staying at the popular Carter Lake Campground you can start the hike on a shortcut trail there. Other hikers will need to park at the nearby Taylor Lake Trailhead. Parking passes are required, and can be bought on site.

Drive Highway 101 south of Florence 9 miles (or north of Reedsport 12 miles), turn west near milepost 199 at the Carter Lake Campground entrance road, and promptly turn left to the Taylor Dunes Trailhead.

The trail skirts little Taylor Lake and climbs 0.4 mile to a dunes viewing platform at the end of the graveled path. From here follow posts through the sand 0.5 mile to the Carter Dunes Trail. Turn right for the beach, following posts with blue-striped tops.

The route crosses areas of sand, shore pine forest, and Scotch broom. Just before the beach you'll cross a deflation plain that's marshy in winter, abuzz with mosquitoes in June, and abloom with big, blue king's gentians in August. Before exploring the beach, memorize where the unmarked trail crosses the foredune. The Siltcoos River is 1 mile to the right and Tahkenitch Creek is 4 miles left.

To make a loop on your way back from the ocean, go straight to the Carter Dunes Campground and walk left 0.4 mile along the road to your car.

Carter Lake Dunes.   *Opposite: Coast strawberry.*

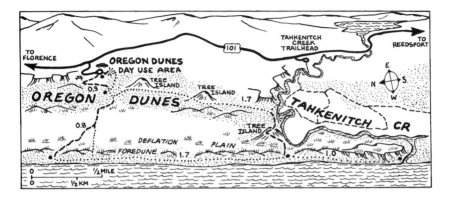

65   Oregon Dunes

Easy (to ocean)
2.2 miles round trip
150 feet elevation gain

Moderate (to Tahkenitch Creek)
4.8-mile loop
250 feet elevation gain

Visitors who simply photograph the view from the Oregon Dunes Day Use Area are missing the best scenery in this seafront Sahara. It's just over a mile from the overlook's picnic area to a remote, windswept beach. Even better is a 4.8-mile loop hike to beautiful Tahkenitch Creek, through dunes and tree islands.

Looking across the dunes, it's easy to wonder why this part of the coast has so much sand in the first place. Rivers are pulverizing rocks all the time, and grains of the toughest minerals — especially transparent quartz — are carried to sea as sand. Oregon's offshore sand beds are 70 to 180 feet thick. Storms and waves dredge some of this sand up to the beach each spring. Along most of the Coast, headlands and bluffs block the prevailing west winds from blowing the sand farther inland. But here, in the lowlands between Florence and Coos Bay, wave after wave of wind-driven dunes have marched ashore. Each onslaught buries forests before gradually petering out and sprouting forests of its own.

Man accidentally changed the dunes' traditional cycle by introducing European beachgrass in 1910. Originally intended to stabilize sand near jetties and railroads, the stubborn grass spread along the beach, creating a 30-foot-tall foredune. Because this grassy dike stops sand from blowing off the beach, the inland dunes have been cut off from their supply of sand. The last dunes still marching eastward are expected to disappear within a century. Already they have left behind a broad deflation plain, a marshy area stripped by winds to wet sand. As brush and trees take root on the plain, a young, half-mile-wide forest is growing up between the beach and the dunes.

To find the Oregon Dunes Day Use Area, drive Highway 101 south of Florence 10 miles (or 11 miles north of Reedsport) to a turnoff between mileposts 200 and 201. Expect a $5 parking fee. From the parking area's turnaround, take a paved path to the right. This trail switchbacks 0.3 mile down through the forest into the dunes themselves.

Once in the open sand, head toward the roar of the ocean, first following posts in the dunes and then a trail across the deflation plain. In early summer look at the edge of the young forest for the blooms of yellow Scotch broom, white coast strawberry, and blue seashore lupine.

Crest the foredune and head left along a remote, windswept stretch of beach. Seals peer from the waves. Pipers and gulls run ahead along the waves' edge. Shells of razor clams, scallops and sand dollars litter the beach.

After 1.7 miles, turn inland at a brown hiker-symbol sign atop the foredune. This path touches a bend of lazy Tahkenitch Creek, curves left across a willow marsh full of driftwood logs, and climbs around the shoulder of a tree island—a forested hill surrounded by dunes. After another stunning viewpoint of Tahkenitch Creek, this time where the dunes are shouldering the creek aside, the trail vanishes into the open sand. Head straight across the sand to find trail posts marking the route along the left side of two tree islands. After a mile of hiking in loose sand, climb back to the Oregon Dunes Day Use Area and your car.

Viewpoint deck at the Oregon Dunes Day Use Area.

66   Tahkenitch Creek

Easy (short loop)
1.6-mile loop
50 feet elevation gain

Moderate (to ocean)
2 miles round trip
80 feet elevation gain

Right: Sand dollar on the beach.

An easy trail network follows this lovely, meandering creek through the dunes. If you don't mind taking off your shoes for a short wade, you can cross the creek to a rarely visited ocean beach strewn with sand dollars. Start by driving Highway 101 south of Florence 12 miles — or north of Reedsport 9 miles — to the Tahkenitch Creek Trailhead near milepost 202. Parking passes are required, but can be bought here.

Park at the end of the turnaround and hike down through a coastal forest of Douglas fir, evergreen huckleberries, and rhododendrons. Cross an 80-foot bridge over the languid creek, ignore several right-hand spurs leading down to the creek, and cross a sandy opening to a junction marked by a post. Turn right into shore pine woods and keep right for 0.2 mile to the hike's best creek viewpoint — a sandy bend walled by 50-foot dunes. Look on the shore for yellow monkeyflowers in summer, and deer hoofprints year round.

Decide at this creekside stop if you're willing to take off your shoes. In summer the creek is shallow, sandy-bottomed, and warm, so it's tempting to wade, especially if you've brought kids. If you do cross the creek, climb up the steep dune on the far shore and keep left across the open sand to a trail that enters the forest of a "tree island," a wooded hill surrounded by dunes. This path traverses the tree island, crosses a deflation plain, and scales a grassy foredune to a wild and remote stretch of beach. Vehicles are never allowed here, and even hikers are rare. If you plan to explore along the beach, be sure to note where the trail

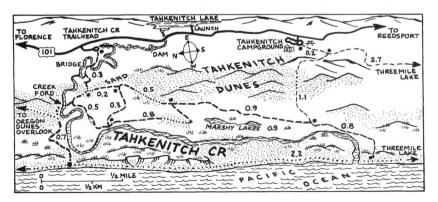

crossed the foredune so you can find your way back.

If you choose not to wade the creek, or if you want to return on a loop, start back from the creek and keep right. After 0.4 mile on this path through the woods you'll reach a post marking another junction.

For the shortest loop hike, turn left here. If you're still going strong, however, turn right. This right-hand path follows a long sandy opening with a few abandoned telephone poles — all that remains of the Coast Guard road built along the shore in World War II to spread the alarm in case of a Japanese invasion. Then keep left to return to your car.

Other Options

A 0.9-mile spur from the Tahkenitch Creek trail network connects to the loop described under Tahkenitch Dunes (Hike #67), which includes a longer beach access route.

Tahkenitch Creek at the ford. *Opposite: Sanderlings.*

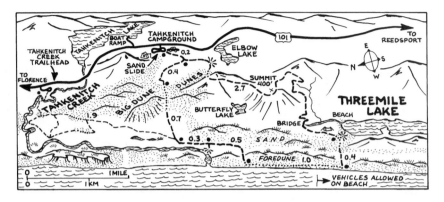

67 Tahkenitch Dunes

Moderate (to dunes and ocean)
4.2 miles round trip
400 feet elevation gain

Difficult (to Threemile Lake)
6.4-mile loop
650 feet elevation gain

In addition to huge sand dunes and a secluded ocean beach, this hike offers an optional return route through the forest, passing a remote, 3-mile-long lake. Dogs must be on leash on the beach and kite-flying is banned to protect nesting birds.

Drive Highway 101 south of Florence 13 miles or north of Reedsport 8 miles. Between mileposts 203 and 204, turn west into Tahkenitch Campground, and then go straight into a trailhead parking loop. Parking passes are required, but can be bought here.

The path that starts here climbs 0.2 mile amidst 20-foot-tall rhododendrons that bloom in April and May. At a junction, turn right for another 0.4 mile to the open dunes. If you're hiking with kids, it might be best to make these dunes your destination, rather than vowing to reach the ocean. Exploring the sand hills here is like playing in a giant sandbox.

For a more substantial hike, however, follow posts across the open dunes toward the ocean. This route leads to a trail through a shore pine forest. Keep left at a junction with the Tahkenitch Creek trail, skirt the creek's estuary for 0.6 mile until the main trail veers right through grassy dunes to the beach *(GPS location N43° 47.33' W124° 10.36')*.

For the loop, head left on the broad beach a mile. After 0.7 mile you'll pass a large steel I-beam planted in the sand with a sign announcing the start of an area where vehicles are permitted. Expect tire tracks on the sand for the next 0.3 mile. Then look for a trail sign atop the foredune *(GPS location N43° 46.57' W124° 10.57')* and

Threemile Lake.

take a path inland 0.4 mile to a signpost in the open dunes. The loop trail turns left here, but first continue straight 200 yards to a viewpoint on a sandy bluff above Threemile Lake. The lake is in fact 3 miles long, but it's wedged between such steep slopes that the best access to the lakeshore's beach is a 200-foot sand slide straight down from this viewpoint. Scientists have unearthed saltwater mussel shells from prehistoric campsites along the lake, a find suggesting that this was once a salty estuary connected to the sea.

To continue the loop, climb left 200 yards to a campsite in the woods overlooking Threemile Lake. From here the easy-to-follow 2.9-mile trail back to your car traverses densely forested ridges where chanterelle mushrooms sprout in fall.

68   Lake Marie

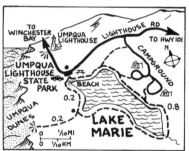

Easy
1.4-mile loop
50 feet elevation **loss**

The stroll around this lovely little lake in Umpqua Lighthouse State Park hardly takes an hour. But it's easy to fill out the day by exploring the Umpqua Dunes, swimming in the lake, camping, or examining the nearby lighthouse.

Start by driving Highway 101 to milepost 217 (south of Reedsport 5 miles or north of Coos Bay 22 miles). Follow signs for Umpqua Lighthouse State Park west a mile, bypass the campground entrance, and park at a lakeshore picnic area on the left. Walk down to the small swimming beach and turn right on a shoreline path cut through 8-foot walls of coastal shrubbery, including April-blooming rhododendrons and two kinds of bushes with tough-skinned, edible blue berries—salal, with 3-inch leaves, and tiny-leaved evergreen huckleberry.

Lake Marie.   Below: Umpqua Dunes.

After 0.2 mile the path forks. Take a detour on the right-hand spur. This fork soon emerges from the forest at the Umpqua Scenic Dunes, a 7-mile-long stretch of sand hills. Unfortunately, dune buggies are allowed to zoom through the areas near the park, so be on guard if you decide to trek half a mile west through the sand to reach the ocean beach at Harbor Drive's Ziolkouski parking area.

Back at Lake Marie, if you take the trail's other fork (and keep left and at all other junctions), you'll circle the lake back to your car in another 0.8 mile, passing an old-growth grove of 4-foot-thick Sitka spruce along the way.

There is no trail to the Umpqua River Lighthouse, but if you drive 0.2 mile up the road from the picnic area you can park at a viewpoint by the 65-foot tower—built in 1894 after a shaky start. When California Gold Rush miners trekking overland from Oregon discovered gold on the Klamath and Rogue rivers in 1850, a ship of entrepreneurs led by Heman Winchester sailed from San Francisco to find the mouths of those rich rivers. They wound up here, liked it, and stayed. Six years later, the Oregon Territory's first lighthouse was built on the sandy spit across the Umpqua River. After an 1861 storm toppled the tower into the river, the present lighthouse was built in a safer spot atop this bluff.

69   Umpqua Dunes

Easy (to start of dunes)
1-mile loop
50 feet elevation gain

Difficult (to ocean)
5.4 miles round trip
100 feet elevation gain

The biggest dunes in Oregon stretch west of Eel Creek Campground in a vast seafront Sahara. No off-road vehicles disturb the immense quiet here. Although the hike from Eel Creek to the beach begins and ends on marked paths, most of the route crosses a stark, trackless dunescape of wind-rippled sand.

Start by driving Highway 101 south of Reedsport 11 miles (or 16 miles north of

Coos Bay). South of Eel Creek Campground 0.3 mile, turn into the well-marked John Dellenback Trailhead, where you'll find picnic tables and restrooms beside a creek bend. Parking passes are required, but can be bought here.

The Dellenback Trail to the Umpqua Dunes starts at a signboard on the right, crosses Eel Creek on an 80-foot bridge, and launches into a Douglas fir forest with evergreen huckleberry bushes and 15-foot-tall rhododendrons. This is actually an ancient sand dune, overgrown with woods. Ignore a side trail to the left (the return of the easy loop). Then cross a paved campground road at the 0.3-mile mark and continue 0.2 mile up into the woods to the start of open dunes.

For the easy loop back to your car, keep left across the sand to find the return trail through the woods. If you're headed for the ocean beach, however, the only markers guiding the way are infrequent, blue-banded posts. Your best bet is to climb the long, tall, dune in front of you. This is an oblique dune, named because it forms at an oblique angle to both the summer's northwest winds and the winter's southwest storms. Constantly moving, oblique dunes can be hundreds of feet tall and over a mile long. The sandy troughs on either side of this one have beachgrass, dwarf blue lupine, and an occasional marshy pool.

Follow the long dune's crest nearly a mile toward a tree island—a forested hill bypassed by the shifting sand. Skirt the tree island's right-hand edge and continue straight half a mile to the line of trees marking the edge of the deflation plain. Winds off the ocean stripped this plain down to wet sand, allowing grass, shrubs, and trees to sprout. In summer, look for yellow monkeyflowers here.

Turn right on a trail along the grassy edge of the deflation plain. After 0.2 mile, a sign marks where the path turns sharply left, ducking through a shore pine forest. The trail crosses a marsh on a plank bridge. In winter, water can cover the trail here a foot deep. Then the path crests the grassy foredune to the broad, nearly empty beach.

If you still have lots of energy, you can head left along the beach 2.5 miles to the scenic, rarely visited mouth of Tenmile Creek. Otherwise return as you came, finding your way back across the open sand by heading first to the tree island's left edge and then toward two gray water tanks on a forested hill far inland.

Other Options

If you're trekking the Oregon Coast Trail south from Reedsport, walk Highway 101 south 4 miles to Winchester Bay, turn right a mile to the South Jetty, and take the beach south 20 miles alongside the Umpqua Dunes. At Horsfall Beach, turn inland at an OHV center and follow roads 4 miles to Coos Bay.

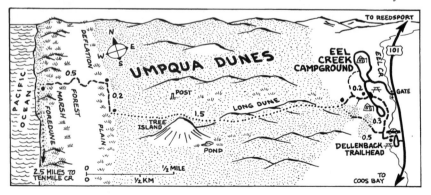

Coos Bay waterfront.

COOS BAY

Although Coos Bay and North Bend grew side by side in Oregon's "Bay Area," the coast's largest metropolitan center, the two timber towns refused to merge in a 1943 election, and have remained rivals ever since. Maps of walking tours through each town's historic district are available in their respective visitor centers along Highway 101. To the north of the Bay Area, sand dunes line the coast. To the south, waves crash against the rocky cliffs of Cape Arago. And inland are the forests that supply the logs stacked on the bay's docks.

Coos Bay Waterfront

Tugboats, yachts, and huge ocean-going freighters tie up at the deep-water port alongside downtown Coos Bay. Inspect the ships by strolling the boardwalk opposite the visitor center at Highway 101 and Commercial Avenue.

Coos Art Museum

A permanent print collection makes this the most highly regarded art museum on the Oregon Coast, 3 blocks from the waterfront in an Art Deco former post office at 235 Anderson Avenue. Open Tue-Fri 10-4 and Sat 1-4. Admission is $5 for adults, $2 for seniors and students.

Marshfield Sun Printing Museum

The city of Coos Bay spent its first 70 years known as Marshfield. From 1891 to 1944 the town's news appeared weekly in the 4-page *Marshfield Sun*. The newspaper's ancient printing press, typecases, and equipment remain in working order in this free museum, open Tue-Sat 1-4 in summer or by calling 541-266-0901, at Coos Bay's Fir Street and Highway 101, north of the visitor center 8 blocks.

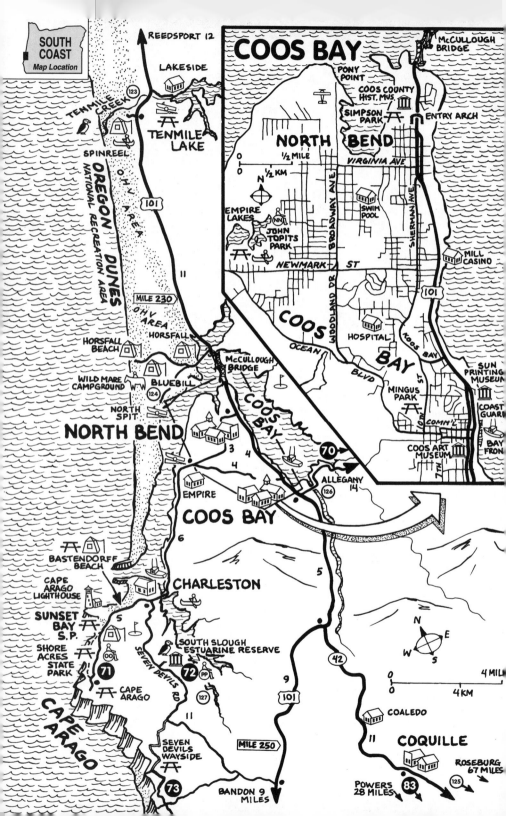

North Bend

This town was founded by the Simpsons—a dynasty of shipbuilders and timber barons whose posh seaside summer estate has been preserved as Shore Acres State Park. During the Depression, North Bend was reduced to paying its public employees with myrtlewood tokens. Prosperity began to return in 1936 with the construction of the graceful, mile-long **McCullough Bridge**, largest of the Oregon Coast spans designed by luminary Oregon highway engineer Conde B. McCullough. In the same year, North Bend built a steel **entry arch** across Highway 101 that remains a source of civic pride.

Beside North Bend's entry arch, the artifacts and displays in the **Coos Historical and Maritime Museum** are open 10-4 Tue-Sat for $4 (kids under 12 free). Behind the museum is Simpson Park, with a picnic area and playground.

At the south edge of North Bend's bayfront, the Coquille Indian tribe has converted an abandoned sawmill into the **Mill Casino,** a resort with slot machines, bingo, three 24-hour restaurants, and an upscale hotel.

Empire Lakes in Topits Park

The two lakes in this relatively undisturbed, 120-acre forest park off Newmark Avenue in Coos Bay are ideal for canoeing. Four miles of mostly paved paths explore the shores.

Tenmile Lake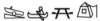

Largest of the sinuous lakes in the forest behind the Oregon Dunes, Tenmile Lake can be accessed near the town of Lakeside at a county park with a boat ramp, barrier-free fishing dock, and picnic area.

The best canoeing and birdwatching, however, are on Tenmile Creek, which meanders 5 miles from the lake to the sea. Put in at Spinreel Campground (an off-highway vehicle staging area). Because off-highway vehicles (OHVs) are banned from the estuary and the dunes to the north, this area is tops for trailless hiking too (see also Hike #69).

Horsfall campgrounds

Dune buggies rule the southern end of the Oregon Dunes National Recreation Area. All campgrounds here are staging areas for OHVs (off-highway vehicles)—except Wild Mare, a 12-site equestrian campground with corrals. Horsfall and Horsfall Beach campgrounds resemble parking lots, with sites marked off on the pavement. Forested Bluebill Campground abuts Bluebill Lake, a marshy springtime birdwatching site circled by a 1-mile hiking trail.

North Spit

Coos Bay's North Spit is a quiet retreat for beachcombing, fishing, huckleberry picking, and exploring grassy dunes. From 1999-2008 it was also home to the *New Carissa*, a 594-foot freighter that grounded here. From Highway 101 north of Coos Bay, turn west at a "Horsfall Dune and Beach" pointer, drive 4.4 miles to the BLM's **North Spit Boat Launch** parking area, and then hike a sandy track 2 miles west to the former shipwreck's beach.

Nearby, the **Wetlands Trail** loops 1.1 mile through dunes and woods, showcasing a Weyerhaeuser wetlands mitigation project. Expect to spot osprey. Park at the **North Spit Overlook**, 1 mile before the North Spit Boat Launch.

Charleston
Just inside Coos Bay's ocean jetties, this fishing village has a large marina, a boat ramp, whale watching tour boats, and a Coast Guard station.

Bastendorff Beach County Park
Next door to Sunset Bay, this mile-long beach extends to Coos Bay's south jetty, a good strolling goal for those who enjoy watching waves, ship traffic, birds, fishermen, and sunsets. The park's year-round, 99-site campground takes no reservations. A picnic area and playground are nearby.

Sunset Bay State Park
Perhaps the state's best ocean swimming beach is sheltered within Sunset Bay's scenic, cliff-rimmed cove beside this state park's large picnic area. Low tide exposes tidepools on sandstone reefs at the base of cliffs on either side of the cove (the north side is best), but take care when climbing the rocks, and do not touch or walk on tidepool animals. Across the road is a popular year-round campground with 130 sites and 8 yurts (summer reservations accepted). See Hike #71.

Shore Acres State Park
North Bend timber baron Louis Simpson bought this dramatic seaside estate as a 1906 Christmas surprise for his wife. Today Simpson's mansion is gone, but a state park preserves the formal English garden, Japanese garden, and rose garden. Rhododendrons and azaleas of 22 varieties bloom March through June. Nearby, a glass-walled observation building overlooks the shore's cliffs, where waves pound reefs of tilted sandstone strata. Visit in winter to watch the most impressive storm waves and see the gardens' 250,000-light holiday display (Thanksgiving to New Years Eve). Expect a $5 parking fee. See Hike #71.

Cape Arago State Park
Bring binoculars and a picnic basket to this rugged bluff at road's end west of Charleston. The binoculars will help you spot the seals and sea lions barking on the reefs of Shell Island. Take the picnic basket down the 0.3-mile North Cove Trail, which passes tables amid windswept trees on a panoramic ridge. The cove's tidepools and sandy beach are off-limits March 1 to June 30 to protect seal pups. A similar trail from the cape down to smaller, less visited, and perhaps more scenic South Cove is open year round. South Cove's tidepooling is among the best in Oregon. Confusingly, the Cape Arago Lighthouse is not on Cape Arago, but rather is 3 miles north on Point Gregory, and was returned to the Coos tribe, so it is not open to the public. View it from Bastendorff Beach or the trail at Sunset Bay. See Hike #71.

South Slough Estuarine Reserve
A first-rate interpretive center explains the importance of the tidal salt marshes that snake into the forested hills along this arm of Coos Bay. The center is open 10-4:30 daily, but closes on winter Sundays and Mondays. Drive Seven Devils Road south of Charleston—a scenic option to Highway 101 between Coos Bay and Bandon (see Hike #72).

Better yet, launch a canoe at Charleston, ride the incoming tide 4 miles up the slough and return on the ebb tide. Maps, tips, and tide tables are at the visitor center.

70 Golden and Silver Falls

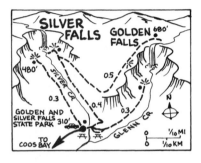

Easy (to top of Golden Falls)
1.8 miles round trip
370 feet elevation gain

Moderate (all trails)
3 miles round trip
570 feet elevation gain

Below: Silver Falls.

A pair of nearly 200-foot-tall waterfalls plummet into this remote Coast Range canyon amid huge myrtlewood trees and 6-foot-thick Douglas firs. Golden Falls was not named for its color, but rather for Dr. C. B. Golden, first Grand Chancellor of the Oregon Knights of Pythias.

At the south edge of Coos Bay, turn east off Highway 101, following "Allegany" signs for 13.5 miles through a number of intersections. From the store at Allegany, follow state park signs 9.4 miles to road's end at a small picnic area. The final 5 miles of this route are one-lane gravel unsuited for motorhomes.

From the parking area, a trail crosses Silver Creek on a footbridge and then forks. The right-hand fork leads through a grove of massive myrtlewood trees 0.3 mile to trail's end at a viewpoint of Golden Falls.

For better views, take the left-hand fork. This path climbs past old-growth Douglas fir with rhododendrons, ferns, and evergreen huckleberries. After 0.4 mile, a left-hand spur leads to the base of Silver Falls. The 160-foot fall spills from a bulbous cliff like long white hair, but thins in late summer to a ribbon.

The main trail continues uphill, following the narrow route of a precarious, long-abandoned road along sheer, unrailed cliffs to the top of 200-foot Golden Falls. Don't allow unattended children near this dizzying viewpoint. A brushy path upstream soon peters out. If you want to hike more, return to your car, cross the parking area, and take a 0.3-mile path up through the woods to a viewpoint with a different perspective of Silver Falls.

71   Shore Acres

Easy (to Simpson Cove)
0.6 miles round trip
80 feet elevation gain

Moderate (to Cape Arago)
4.4-mile loop
550 feet elevation gain

Breakers crash against the tilted sandstone cliffs of Cape Arago's rugged coast. Sea lions bark from offshore reefs. Wavelets lap the beaches of hidden coves. If this seems an unlikely backdrop for a formal English garden, welcome to the surprises of Shore Acres State Park. It's possible to drive to many of the attractions here, and tips for car travelers are detailed on page 174. But to explore this unusual coastline thoroughly, you'll need to hike at least a portion of the trail between Sunset Bay and Cape Arago.

To find Shore Acres from Highway 101 in Coos Bay, follow signs 9 miles to Charleston, and then continue straight 4 miles. A mile past Sunset Bay State Park, turn right into the Shore Acres entrance, pause at the entry booth to pay the $5 parking fee, and park by the oceanfront lawns at the far end of the parking area. Dogs are not allowed outside of cars in Shore Acres.

First walk to the observation building overlooking the sea cliffs. The waves below are slowly leveling the yellow sandstone's tilted strata, creating weirdly stepped reefs in the process. The plateau you're standing on was similarly leveled by waves thousands of years ago before the coastline here rose.

Turn left along the cliff edge a hundred yards and veer left to find the entrance to the fabulous formal gardens that remain from the 1906 estate of timber baron Louis Simpson. Explore the pathways here until you reach the Japanese garden at the far end. Then follow the sound of surf through a gate to the paved path along the oceanfront and turn left to descend to Simpson Cove. This hidden bay's

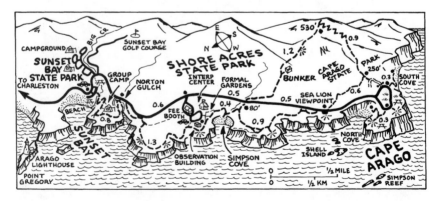

charming beach makes a good turnaround point for hikers with children.

For a more substantial hike, hop the cove's inlet creek, take an unpaved path up a forested gully and keep right at all junctions for 0.9 mile to the Simpson Reef Overlook, a highway pullout with a view of hundreds of seals and sea lions.

To return on a loop, cross the road from the overlook to a trail that traverses through a coastal rainforest of fir, spruce, waxmyrtle, and alder 0.6 mile to a T-shaped junction. Turn left, climbing steeply at times for 0.9 mile, and turn left on a downhill trail. After 0.6 mile look sharp for a path back to your left to find a roofless 4-room concrete bunker, a military observation post from World War II. Then continue 0.6 mile down to the paved road, jog left 50 feet on the road to a path on the other side, and keep right for 0.4 mile to return to your car.

Other Hiking Options

To see more, start at Sunset Bay instead. Drive 3 miles west of Charleston, pull into the Sunset Bay picnic area on the right, and park by the restrooms at the far end of the parking areas. Cross a footbridge to the right of the restrooms, follow the creek to the right 100 yards to the last picnic table and turn left on a trail up the forested hillside. Keep to the right at all junctions for the next 0.8 mile. When you reach the paved road, turn right along the shoulder 200 yards and climb a stile over a guardrail to the right. The path parallels the highway 300 more yards before angling into the woods on the long-abandoned entry road to the original Simpson mansion. Just 60 yards into the forest, however, turn right on an unmarked trail. This path passes a dozen cliff-edge viewpoints before leading to the Shore Acres observation building—the start of the hike described above.

Oregon Coast Trail trekkers from Coos Bay should follow roads 13 miles to Sunset Bay, hike the loop described here, return toward Coos Bay 3 miles, turn right on Seven Devils Road 6 miles, and turn right 3 miles to the beach at Seven Devils State Recreation Site (Hike #73).

Shore Acres State Park.   Opposite: The park's formal English garden.

72 South Slough Estuary

Moderate
3.4-mile loop
300 feet elevation loss

The city of Coos Bay was once called Marshfield, but the name no longer fits. Ninety percent of the bay's original marsh fields have been destroyed — diked, drained, or filled for development. Now wildlife biologists are understanding the importance of these lost tidal wetlands. When freshwater salmon smolts migrate to sea, for example, they need to linger in estuaries to gradually adjust to saltwater. Clams, herons, raccoons, and hundreds of other species rely on the rich life of the mudflats once derided as worthless sloughs.

The nation's first Estuarine Research Reserve was established here in 1974 on 7 square miles of abandoned farmland and cut-over forest bordering Coos Bay's South Slough. Displays in a modern interpretive center explain how breached dikes and regrowing forests are allowing wildlife to flourish, but a network of easy trails nearby allows you to investigate the reserve first hand.

From Highway 101 in Coos Bay, follow signs 9 miles west to Charleston. A few hundred yards beyond that harbor town, turn left on Seven Devils Road. After 4.3 miles, turn left onto the South Slough Estuarine Reserve entrance road for 0.2 mile and pull into the interpretive center's parking area on the left.

Take a look at the interpretive center's excellent displays, and then walk across the road to the Ten-Minute Trail. Follow this path downhill 200 yards, turn right on the Middle Creek Trail for half a mile, and cross a gravel road to the Hidden Creek Trail. This path switchbacks down through a young forest of alder, hemlock, and Port Orford cedar. Among the dense brush are three kinds of edible berries in late summer: tough-skinned blue salal, tiny red huckleberry,

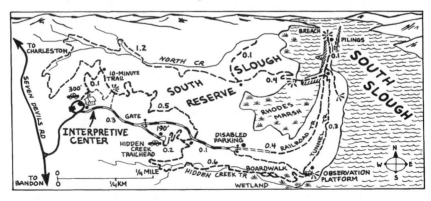

Boardwalk through skunk cabbage.   Opposite: Pilings along South Slough.

and pointy-leaved evergreen huckleberry. The path follows a small creek down to a boardwalk through an alder bog full of the huge, boat-shaped leaves of skunk cabbage. In spring, the gigantic yellow blooms of these plants intentionally give off a decaying stench to attract the flies required to pollinate them.

After 0.6 mile the Hidden Crek Trail reaches an observation platform amidst big Sitka spruce and rhododendrons, with a view across the estuary's salt marsh. Continue straight on the Tunnel Trail 0.4 mile to the "Sloughside Pilings," remnants of a railroad line used to dump logs into the slough for transport by raft to the sawmills at Coos Bay. The trail ends at the tip of a breached dike where tidewaters now flood through, converting pastureland back to marsh.

To make a loop you could turn around and simply go straight at all junctions for a mile, but it's far more interesting to loop back on the slightly longer North Creek Trail. For this loop, return 200 yards from the Soughside Pilings and turn right, crossing the inlet to Rhodes Marsh on a dike and a 70-foot bridge. Although dogs are allowed on leash on other trails in the reserve, pets are banned on this wildlife-sensitive path. Keep straight 1.6 miles and then turn right on the Ten-Minute Trail back to your car.

Coquille River lighthouse (Hike #74).

BANDON

Wildfires spreading through gorse — a thorny, yellow-flowered weed — burned nearly all of downtown Bandon in 1914 and 1936. Surprisingly, Bandon's rebuilt Old Town is one of the most charming on the coast. North of town is a sandy spit along the Coquille River with a lighthouse and a campground in Bullards Beach State Park. To the south, bird-covered islands and craggy sea stacks line the ocean beaches.

Old Town Bandon

Once local shipbuilders helped give this port the largest fleet between San Francisco and Astoria. Then two devastating fires broke Bandon's commercial power. But now recreation, arts, and retirees are fueling new growth. Archways beside Highway 101 span the entrances to Old Town, a 3-block collection of art galleries, boutiques, eateries, charter boat offices, and craft shops — all wedged beside a river marina with docks, piers, and a boat launch. See Hike #75.

You might start your visit at the **Face Rock Creamery,** on Highway 101 at the entrance to Old Town, where you can sample the squeaky curds of fresh gourmet cheese.

Bullards Beach State Park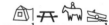

In a forest behind overgrown dunes, this park's year-round campground with 185 campsites and 13 yurts is sheltered from the beach's north winds (see Hike #74). Horse trails through the old dunes converge on an 8-site equestrian camp. Picnic lawns are a stone's throw from the Coquille River and a popular boat ramp.

Coquille River Lighthouse

At the far south end of Bullards Beach State Park, this picturesque lighthouse was built in 1896, rammed by a schooner in 1906, replaced by an automated beacon in 1939, and restored in 1978. Nostalgia buffs added a small solar-powered light in 1991. Volunteers lead tours up the tower stairs when the small museum and gift shop inside is open (10am-5pm daily from May through October). See Hike #74.

Bandon Dunes golf courses

Spreading across nearly two miles of oceanfront bluffs reminiscent of Scotland or Ireland, world-class 18-hole golf courses have replaced the gorse thickets 6 miles north of Bandon with dramatic fairways. Bandon Dunes, Pacific Dunes, and Bandon Trails are open to the public, but charge $100-295 per round.

Seven Devils State Recreation Site

The Seven Devils are a series of steep coastal ridges that bedeviled early road builders. One of the gorse-covered canyons between ridges holds this picnic area and lawn beside Merchants Beach (see Hike #73). Because vehicles are not allowed onto the sand here, it's quieter than Whisky Run Beach to the south.

Bandon Marsh Wildlife Refuge

Shorebirds, geese, ducks, and osprey visit this rich, hard-to-access 289-acre salt marsh. Observe the area with binoculars from Bullards Beach (Hike #74).

Cranberry bogs

Bandon's claim to be cranberry capital of the world is backed by 800 acres of cranberry bogs, the rectangular marshes visible along Highway 101. The nation's oldest cranberry festival is celebrated here on the second weekend of September. In fall the bogs are flooded so the bright red berries float for harvest. Most of the local crop is sold through the Ocean Spray Cooperative to color juice drinks.

Face Rock State Scenic Viewpoint

The best view of Bandon's craggy islands is at this blufftop picnic area on Bandon's Beach Loop Drive. Coquille tribal legends explain why the largest island resembles the uplifted face of a stony Indian princess, while a cluster of small pointy islands look like a cat and her kittens (see Hike #75).

Bandon Historical Society Museum

This museum's varied collections include Indian artifacts, photos of Bandon's devastating fires, and exhibits on logging, fishing, and cranberry farming. The museum is located on Highway 101 at 270 Fillmore, in a 1930s building that served as Bandon's city hall until 1970. Hours are 10am-4pm daily. Kids are free but adults can expect to pay a $3 admission.

New River

Created by an 1890 flood, this lazy river parallels the beach for 10 miles from Floras Lake to Twomile Creek, isolating the state's most secluded beach and a choice birdwatching site. The Bureau of Land Management (BLM) has developed a trail network (see Hike #76) to showcase the odd river and its overgrown dunes. Canoeists often face strong winds, and must portage 0.5 mile to the boat ramp when the access road is gated closed (Mar 15 to Sept 15). Pets must be leashed.

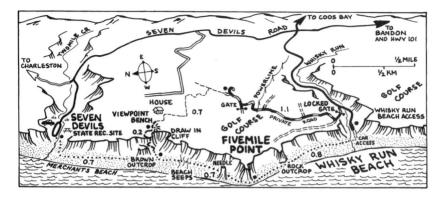

73   Fivemile Point

Moderate
3.2 miles round trip
200 feet elevation gain

Right: Fivemile Point.

A gold rush hit this secluded area in 1853 after prospectors found sparkling flakes in a layer of black beach sand. The wide-open boomtown of Randolph sprang up along Whisky Run's creek. Ships off-loaded cargo at neighboring Merchants Beach. But two years later the gold was gone. Wagoneers moved Randolph lock, stock, and barrel to the Coquille River, 4 miles away.

Vehicles are still allowed onto the sand at the Whisky Run beach access, so it's more fun for hikers to explore this area from the quieter Seven Devils picnic area, just to the north. From there an easy walk leads to the wave-swept islands and tidepools at Fivemile Point. These beaches are among the most reliably windy places in Oregon—an advantage for kite fliers who pilgrimage here, but a hazard for golfers at the posh Bandon Dunes course atop the bluffs.

Start by driving Highway 101 north of Bandon 5 miles (or south of Coos Bay 19 miles). Between mileposts 257 and 258 turn west on Seven Devils Road for 5 miles. Then turn left into the Seven Devils State Recreation Site entrance to a parking turnaround at a beachside picnic lawn. The canyon slopes are blanketed with gorse, a spiny shrub that blooms yellow from March to May. In its native Ireland, gorse forms hedges that corral livestock. Here it spreads with abandon and twice fueled fires that burned Bandon.

The hike starts out to the left along the beach from the Seven Devils picnic area, so you'll need to cross Twomile Creek. In summer you can hop over, but in winter you'll balance across on drift logs. Then stroll 0.7 mile toward

Fivemile Point. Just 200 yards beyond a brown rock outcrop that shoulders onto the beach, look closely for a post to the left. This marks a fun little detour — a path that tunnels up 0.2 mile through windswept Sitka spruce and salal to a bench at a blufftop viewpoint. Turn back here to avoid private property.

Then continue south along Merchants Beach another 0.7 mile to the tip of Fivemile Point. Low tide exposes rocks and ledges with tidepool animals here. Sea birds perch on scenic pinnacles in the surf. Sea lions squirm on reefs offshore. Except at the highest tides it's possible to make your way around Fivemile Point to Whisky Run Beach, so you can unpack a picnic on whichever side of the headland has less wind.

74   Bullards Beach

Easy (lighthouse exploration)
1.4 miles round trip
No elevation gain

Moderate (from beach parking)
5-mile loop
No elevation gain

Left: Coquille River lighthouse.

Just across the Coquille River from Bandon are a picturesque lighthouse, a hikable jetty, and an estuary beach great for birdwatching. To explore the area, drive Highway 101 north of Bandon 3 miles (or south of Coos Bay 21 miles), turn west at a Bullards Beach State Park sign and drive straight past the campground entrance and picnic areas for 1.3 miles to a T-shaped junction.

If you'd like to hike a 5-mile loop around the Bullards Beach peninsula, turn right to a beach parking area and walk left along the wide beach 1.7 miles to the lighthouse. To shorten the hike (a good idea if it's windy or if you've brought kids), simply turn left at the T-junction and drive to the lighthouse.

The youngest of the Oregon Coast's principal lights, this 47-foot tower was

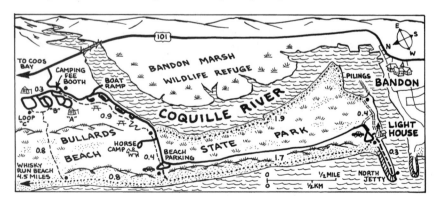

built on a Coquille River island in 1896. When ships continued to founder here (one nearly rammed the lighthouse in 1906), the Army built jetties by blasting apart Bandon's Tupper Rock, a site held sacred by the Coquille Indian tribe. Since then sand has collected behind the jetty, connecting the lighthouse's former island to Bullards Beach. In 1990 the site of Tupper Rock was returned to the Coquilles, who built a retirement home there.

When the lighthouse is open (2pm-5pm from Monday to Thursday and 11am-5pm from Friday to Sunday between May and mid-October), you can peruse the displays inside and ask volunteers to lead you up the tower's stairs. Then go back outside and walk 0.3 mile out to the North Jetty's tip, where waves crash against mussel-encrusted boulders. Watch here for sea birds — black cormorants, black-and-white murres, and enormous, diving brown pelicans.

Next return to the lighthouse and continue straight on a sandy car track atop the riverside jetty. Keep straight on this jeep road 0.4 mile to its end at a beach with a view across the river to Bandon's docks. This is a good turnaround point for hikers with kids. If you're doing the 5-mile loop, however, continue 1.9 miles along the river's soft beach to the end of sand at the park's entrance road. Then follow the road shoulder left 0.4 mile to the beach parking area.

If you're trekking the Oregon Coast Trail south along the beach from the Seven Devils State Recreation Site (Hike #73), cut inland through Bullards Beach State Park and walk Highway 101 south 3 miles to Bandon's Old Town.

75 Bandon Islands

Easy (to Coquille Point)
3.3-mile loop
100 feet elevation gain

Moderate (to Face Rock Wayside)
4.8-mile loop
100 feet elevation gain

Difficult (to Devils Kitchen)
8.6-mile loop
150 feet elevation gain

Right: Face Rock.

This hike begins in Bandon's Old Town, follows the beach past craggy islands in the surf, and then returns along city streets atop the seashore cliffs. To start, turn off Highway 101 through an archway proclaiming "Welcome to Old Town Bandon," drive a block to the riverfront, and turn left a block to a big parking area beside the boat basin.

First explore Old Town a bit by strolling around the three main blocks of gift shops, boutiques, and galleries. Then set off toward the ocean, following First Street along the riverfront. This street curves left at a white clapboard building built by the Coast Guard in 1939. Shortly afterward turn right on Jetty Road, a narrow street that once was the town's boardwalk to the beach. Because Jetty Road has no sidewalk, it can be more pleasant to climb over some boulders to the right (after the Lighthouse Bed & Breakfast) and follow the river beach most

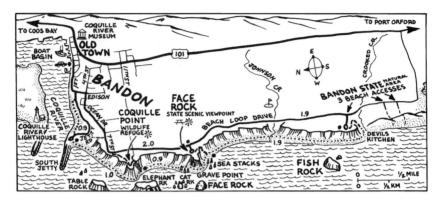

of the way to Jetty Road's end at the South Jetty.

The jetty was built in 1906 to stem a rash of shipwrecks on the Coquille River bar. When the *Oliver Olson* rammed the jetty so hard in 1953 that the ship couldn't be pulled free, the South Jetty was extended by building right over the ship's hull. Now sailors complain the uneven lengths of the river's two jetties make the bar more treacherous than ever.

 From the jetty, turn left along the ocean beach—here, the official route of the Oregon Coast Trail. To sea, Table Rock's flat top swarms with seagulls, cormorants, and murres. Bring binoculars to spot the red-beaked puffins that arrive in April. They nest in tunnels up to 30 feet long that they dig in the sides of the island's dirt top. To protect easily frightened seabirds, climbing and tidepooling are banned on all Bandon's islands and sea stacks—even those easily accessible at low tide.

After a mile on the beach you'll cross a sandy gap between Coquille Point and Elephant Rock, a huge island shaped like a big-eared elephant with sea caves for eyes. For the short loop, climb a staircase on the far side of Coquille Point to a paved path that follows the edge of the blufftop back toward town 0.3 mile. When this path ends, follow 7th Street a block and turn downhill to the left on a paved path to city streets at Jetty Road, which you can follow to return to your car.

For the longer loops, however, continue 0.9 mile along the beach to a collection of weird, pointy sea stacks at the tip of Grave Point. The cluster of small islands visible from here are Cat and Kittens Rocks. Face Rock is the large island resembling an uplifted face. According to a Coquille tribal legend, the face belongs to Ewauna, daughter of Chief Siskiyou, who had traveled here to a great potlatch feast in his honor. Ewauna had never seen the ocean before, so one night she sneaked to the beach for a moonlight swim. In the water she was grabbed by the evil ocean spirit Seatka. But she refused to look into his eyes, knowing that this was how he controlled his victims. Instead she fixed her stare on the North Star, and defiantly gazes there even today.

For the moderate loop hike, climb a staircase just beyond Grave Point to the picnic area at Face Rock State Scenic Viewpoint, and from there follow Beach Loop Road left to Old Town as described above. For the longest recommended loop hike, however, continue 1.9 miles farther along the beach to the Devils Kitchen, a sandy cove sheltered from the wind by a cliff. Walk inland to the back of the cove and go left up a trail into the trees to a picnic area. Then walk out to Beach Loop Drive and turn left along it 3.9 miles to Old Town.

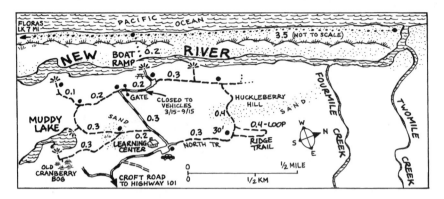

76   New River

Easy
2.3-mile loop
30 feet elevation gain

Right: New River

After an 1890 flood scrambled the drainage of this sandy coastal plain, a new river was left paralleling the beach for miles north of Floras Lake. This moat isolated the beach so well that smugglers ferried $17 million of marijuana bales ashore in 1977. Their forfeited ranch has since regrown gracefully into the landscape. The beach is still accessible only by boat, but trails explore the riverbank, forested dunes, and a lake. Pets must be on leash.

Start by driving 9 miles south of Bandon on Highway 101 (or 18 miles north of Port Orford). Near milepost 283, turn west on Croft Lake Road for 1.6 miles until it turns to gravel and forks. Veer right for 0.2 mile and then fork to the left through a gate (closed at night) for another 0.2 mile to a parking area.

Don't hike down the main road to the left. Instead veer right past a "Trail North" sign on an ancient ranch road amid windswept shore pine. After 0.3 mile, detour to the right on the Ridge Trail, an 0.4-mile path that loops out along an overgrown dune where 10-foot rhododendrons bloom in April and May. At the end of the Ridge Trail, turn right to continue on the main path. Then keep left at junctions for the next 0.7 mile to the boat ramp's small picnic area. From here the New River resembles a long lake, with the roar of unseen surf beyond the far shore's dunes.

Next walk up the gravel road 0.2 mile and go straight on the Muddy Lake Trail. If you keep left at junctions along this path you'll return to your car in 0.7 mile, but it's worth exploring three side trails along the way—to a New River viewpoint, to a birdwatching site at Muddy Lake, and to a former cranberry bog.

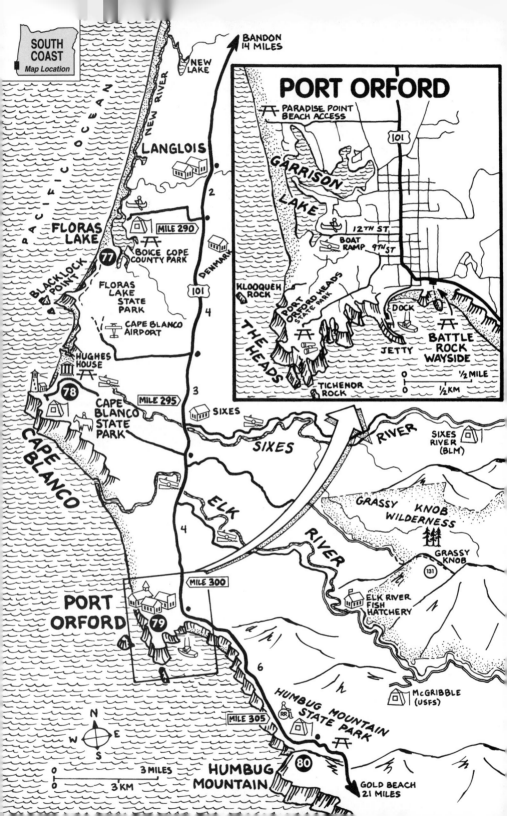

SOUTH COAST
Map Location

BANDON
14 MILES

NEW LAKE

NEW RIVER

PACIFIC OCEAN

LANGLOIS

2

MILE 290

FLORAS LAKE

77

BOICE COPE COUNTY PARK

DENMARK

101

4

FLORAS LAKE STATE PARK

CAPE BLANCO AIRPORT

BLACKLOCK POINT

HUGHES HOUSE

78

MILE 295

CAPE BLANCO STATE PARK

3

SIXES

CAPE BLANCO

SIXES

RIVER

SIXES RIVER (BLM)

ELK

4

GRASSY KNOB WILDERNESS

RIVER

GRASSY KNOB

131

MILE 300

ELK RIVER FISH HATCHERY

PORT ORFORD

79

6

McGRIBBLE (USFS)

HUMBUG MOUNTAIN STATE PARK

RR

MILE 305

N
W E
S

0   3 MILES
0   3 KM

HUMBUG MOUNTAIN

80

GOLD BEACH 21 MILES

PORT ORFORD

PARADISE POINT BEACH ACCESS

GARRISON LAKE

101

12TH ST

BOAT RAMP   9TH ST

KLOOQUEH ROCK

PORT ORFORD HEADS STATE PARK

THE HEADS

DOCK

JETTY

BATTLE ROCK WAYSIDE

TICHENOR ROCK

0   ½ MILE
0   ½ KM

Battle Rock on Port Orford's beach.

PORT ORFORD

Westernmost city in the lower 48 states, Port Orford overlooks a sheltered cove with a natural ocean harbor that has attracted settlers since 1851.

Cape Blanco State Park

Cape Blanco's plateau juts more than a mile to sea. A picturesque 1870 lighthouse at the cape's tip opens for tours ($5 per family, $2 for adults, free for kids under age 16) Wed-Mon 10am-3:30pm from April through October (see Hike #78). A nearby 50-site campground, open year round, has 4 cabins for $39-40. Also in the park are an 8-site horse campground and the Hughes House, a gorgeously restored 1898 home that's open from April through October, 10am-3:30pm Wed-Mon, for free.

Port Orford harbor

Each afternoon a harbor crane hoists the Port Orford fishing fleet, boat by boat, from the ocean for storage atop a dock for the night. Fishermen hawk their catch. Skin divers in wet suits often prowl the underwater reefs nearby.

Floras Lake

When developers in 1910 promised to make this lake a seaport by cutting a canal through the dunes to the ocean, the boomtown of Lakeport drew 400 eager settlers. The town vanished when surveys proved the lake is higher than the ocean, so that a canal would only drain it. Today, reliable winds make this sandy lake the Oregon Coast's most popular windsurfing and kiteboarding center for beginners. **Boice Cope County Park** offers a beach, boat launch, and 34 campsites. Tent sites are $16; day use is $2. The adjacent **Floras Lake House Bed & Breakfast** offers 4 rooms for $155-185 and can link you up with lessons (reservations: 541-348-2573 or *www.floraslake.com*). Turn west off Highway 101 onto Floras Lake Road 2 miles south of Langlois. See Hike #77.

Battle Rock

Pull into a parking lot beside Highway 101 at the south edge of downtown to visit this rock island on Port Orford's beach. In 1851, nine white settlers huddled here for 15 days, killing Indians with cannon fire before escaping by night.

Port Orford Heads State Park

From a museum in a historic 1934 Coast Guard barracks (open 10am-3:30pm Wednesday-Monday from April through October), easy trails lead to breathtaking clifftop viewpoints on Port Orford's headlands. See Hike #79.

Garrison Lake

Within Port Orford's city limits, this forest-rimmed, many-armed lake is stocked with trout. It's best explored by canoe from the boat ramp west of Highway 101 on 12th Street. Aquatic weeds hinder swimming or power boating.

Elk River

Drive 3 miles north of Port Orford and turn right on scenic Elk River Road 7.5 miles to visit a salmon hatchery. Experienced kayakers run the difficult whitewater chutes and emerald green pools of the 6 river miles above the hatchery.

Humbug Mountain State Park

A short path from this park's 95-site, year-round campground leads under a Highway 101 bridge to a pocket beach at the foot of Humbug Mountain's ocean cliffs. See Hike #80.

Humbug Mountain from Port Orford's harbor.   Opposite: Windsurfers at Floras Lake.

77 Floras Lake

Moderate (lake to orange bluffs)
3.5-mile loop
100 feet elevation gain

Difficult (lake to Blacklock Point)
8.3 miles round trip
250 feet elevation gain

Moderate (airport to Blacklock Point)
3.8 miles round trip
50 feet elevation gain

A hot spot for beginning windsurfers and kite boarders, this sandy lake in the coastal dunes has also become a secret mecca for hikers and backpackers exploring the wildest part of the state's coast. Quiet trails lead along forested bluffs and untrod beaches to Blacklock Point, a headland where time seems to have stopped centuries ago.

Drive Highway 101 south of Bandon 16 miles (or north of Port Orford 11 miles) to milepost 290, turn west on Floras Lake Loop, and follow signs for 2.8 zigzagging miles to Boice Cope Park. At road's end, just after the campground entrance, turn left into a lakeside parking lot. Expect a $2 day-use fee.

Cross a footbridge across Floras Lake's outlet (the New River) and keep left on a lakeshore trail. You'll pass a beach full of windsurfers and kite boarders preparing their gear for launch. After half a mile, when the trail peters out in the sand, head right 200 feet through a gap in the grassy foredune to the ocean beach.

Walk left a mile along the seashore toward Blacklock Point. After half a mile orange bluffs begin rising beside the beach. At the 0.8-mile mark, watch out for waves that smack all the way to the cliffs at high tide. Beyond this squeeze, the beach widens at a forested canyon where a creek sinks into the sand.

Turn inland here, keeping on the left-hand side of the creek, to find a path that climbs into the woods. After 200 yards the trail forks — and you'll face a decision.

If you're ready to head home, turn left and keep left for a short loop that returns to Floras Lake's shore. If you'd like to see Blacklock Point, however, turn right. This portion of the Oregon Coast Trail dips to a creek bridge and climbs

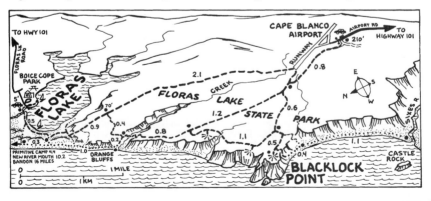

Hiking from Floras Lake to Blacklock Point.   Opposite: Cape Blanco's lighthouse.

to a forested plateau. After 0.8 mile, turn right on a path that skirts the bluff's edge. Two short side trails to the right detour to spectacular coastal viewpoints.

In 1.1 mile you'll reach a junction marked with an Oregon Coast Trail post. Turn right toward Blacklock Point. After half a mile the trail passes backpacking campsites under the headland's last trees. Campers need to bring water because there is no reliable source nearby. Keep left for 100 feet to a trail fork at the start of the headland meadow. If you go straight you'll explore the headland's tip on increasingly precarious paths. If you fork left you'll switchback down to a beach with sea stacks and giant jumbles of driftwood logs. Once you hit this beach it's hard not to stroll a mile south to the Sixes River, where a stream ripples calf-deep across the strand.

It's true that there is a shorter route to Blacklock Point. This shortcut is not as scenic but it is open to bicycles. Hikers will need to wear boots because the path always has mud puddles. To find this trailhead, drive Highway 101 north of Port Orford 7 miles (or south of the Floras Lake turnoff 4 miles). Between mileposts 293 and 294, turn west off Highway 101 at an "Airport" pointer and follow paved Airport Road for 2.9 miles to a parking area at the gated airport entrance. The trail begins to the left of the gate as a barricaded dirt road paralleling the runway through dense shore pine woods. After 0.8 mile keep left at an unmarked junction. Follow "Blacklock Point" arrows at junctions for the next for 1.1 miles, forking twice to the left and once to the right before emerging at the headland's tip.

 Oregon Coast Trail trekkers heading south from Bandon should follow the beach 5.8 miles, ford the New River's mouth (usually calf deep), and continue through protected snowy plover habitat 5.8 miles to a signed primitive backpacking campground on the left, in a meadow beside the New River. Then walk the beach another 4.7 miles to Floras Lake, take trails to Blacklock Point, follow the beach south, and ford the shallow Sixes River to Cape Blanco (Hike #78).

78

Cape Blanco

Easy (exploration near lighthouse)
1 mile round trip
100 feet elevation gain

Moderate (north beach tour)
4-mile loop
250 feet elevation gain

Oregon's westernmost point was named *Cabo Blanco* ("White Cape") on a disastrous 1602 Spanish sea exploration. Most of the crew died of scurvy, and no white men returned for 173 years. Park trails offer views of the picturesque headland and its windswept lighthouse, flashing a white beam to sea since 1870.

Drive 4 miles north of Port Orford on Highway 101 and turn west at a Cape Blanco State Park sign. If you've only time for a quick hike, drive straight for 5 miles to the parking area at the lighthouse gate. When the gate is open (10am to 3:30pm Wednesday through Monday from April through October), you can drive out to tour the lighthouse. Then come back and park here by the gate.

A post beyond the gate on the right marks the Oregon Coast Trail. This path descends through a meadow of wind-matted salal bushes and white yarrow for 0.3 mile to the cape's windy north beach. After exploring the driftwood (and the marine life exposed on rocks at low tide), return to your car, follow the road left 100 yards, and turn right at another Coast Trail post. Along this path 0.2 mile is a meadow viewpoint and picnic table overlooking the cape's other beach. Bring binoculars to scan the distant islands of Orford Reef, where whales often spout.

For longer hikes, it's best to start at the Sixes River boat ramp. To find it from

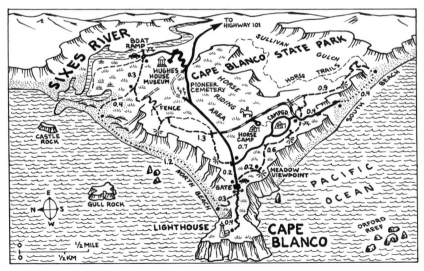

Highway 101, drive 4 miles on the park's entrance road and turn right at a sign for the Hughes House. Down this road 0.2 mile is a restored 1898 home (see page 189). Keep right on gravel another 0.2 mile to road's end at a boat ramp.

Beyond a gate, two mowed paths cross a pasture. Take the left-hand trail for 0.3 mile, and then fork to the right for 0.4 mile to the beach. Walk left along the beach 1.2 miles toward the lighthouse. A stone's throw before the beach runs out of sand, look for a trail up a meadowed slope to the left. Climb this path 0.3 mile to the lighthouse road parking lot described above.

To return on a loop, turn left along the road 0.2 mile. At a trail post opposite the campground entrance, take a mowed path left across a meadow. Then keep left at all junctions for the next 1.3 miles, passing cliff-edge viewpoints and brushy fields popular with deer before descending to the meadow by your car.

79   Port Orford Heads

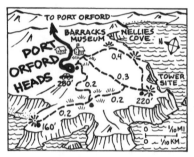

Easy
1.2-mile loop
200 feet elevation gain

Port Orford's rugged shore claimed so many lives in shipwrecks that the Coast Guard built a lifeboat station on a headland here in 1934. Whenever lookouts at the station's tower reported a ship in danger, guardsmen would tumble out of their barracks, race down a 504-step staircase to Nellies Cove, and launch a 36-foot self-righting lifeboat. The station closed in 1970, but the barracks now houses a museum and short trails tour the headland's meadows.

Drive Highway 101 to a state park sign at milepost 301 in Port Orford, turn west on 9th Street for 0.2 mile, and then curve left onto Arizona Street for 0.8 mile to a parking turnaround. Walk a gravel path 50 yards up to the free barracks museum, a quaint shingled building with historic photographs and Coast Guard memorabilia, open 10am-3:30pm Wednesday-Monday, April through October.

Behind the barracks, take a concrete path up across a picnic lawn a few feet and turn left onto a barkdust path marked "Cove Trail." This route has stunning views of the turbulent ocean cove where the station's boathouse once stood. After 0.4 mile you'll reach a railed site of the former lookout tower, with a view across Port Orford's bay to the dark hump of Humbug Mountain (Hike #80).

From the tower site, walk up a cement path 50 yards and fork left on a barkdust path that romps across a wind-mown salal meadow. Summer wildflowers here include yellow composites, purple heal-all, red paintbrush, blue lupine, white yarrow, and fuzzy cats ears. Keep left for 0.4 mile to a viewpoint above rocky islands where harbor seals lounge. Note Cape Blanco and Garrison Lake to the north. Then turn around and keep left for 0.4 mile to your car.

The 1932 Rogue River bridge at Gold Beach.

GOLD BEACH

Miners sluiced Gold Beach's sand in the 1850s for gold flakes washed from the Klamath Mountains by the Rogue River. Today the Rogue is prized for different treasures—whitewater, wilderness, and wildlife.

Rogue River

At times the irascible Rogue River is a string of sunny green pools, lazily drifting past salmon-fishing black bears and circling osprey. But the river can also be misty mayhem, boiling through Mule Creek Canyon's Coffeepot or raging over the giant pinball course of Blossom Bar Rapid's boulders. The best views are from trails (Hikes #85 and 87) or from boats (see below), but there's plenty of scenery along the 35-mile paved road from the Gold Beach bridge to the hamlet of Agness. Two campgrounds along the way (Lobster Creek and Quosatana) offer river beaches with nearby boat ramps.

Jet boat trips

In 1895, mail boats began braving the Rogue River's rapids to supply isolated settlers. This tradition has evolved into a fleet of 50-seat jet boats whisking tourists into the Rogue's wilderness. Loudspeakers announce herons, seals, and deer. Stops at rustic lodges allow passengers to buy lunch. The 64- to 104-mile tours cost about $50 to $95 and leave Gold Beach at about 8:30am and 2:30pm from May 15 to October 15. Jerry's Rogue Jets (800-451-3645, *www.roguejets.com*) dock downstream from the south end of the Gold Beach bridge, beside a free museum of Rogue River memorabilia.

Rafting the Rogue

Kayakers and rafters who tackle the wildest 40-mile stretch of the Rogue River usually launch at Grave Creek (15 miles west of Wolf Creek exit 76 on Interstate 5), float about 3 days, and take out at Foster Bar in Illahe. During the restricted season from May 15 to October 15, only 120 permits are issued for each day, chosen by lottery from ten times that many applications. Apply for the lottery between December 1 and January 31 at *www.blm.gov/or/resources/recreation/rogue/floatspace-lottery.php*. If you don't win a permit, you can plan a trip in the off-season's iffy weather or pay for a commercially guided trip (at least $500).

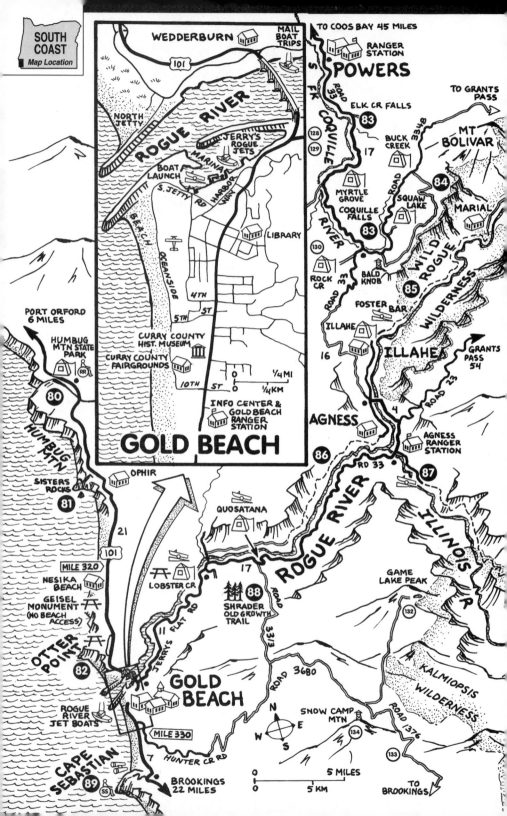

80   Humbug Mountain

Difficult
5.5-mile loop
1710 feet elevation gain

Right: Humbug Mountain.

When an army of settlers landed in Port Orford in 1851 to find a route inland to the new Rogue River gold mines, Captain William Tichenor assured them the task would be easy. They need only climb this imposing coastal peak to see the gold mine country on the far side, he claimed. A scouting party labored through ancient forests to the summit and named the mountain Tichenor's Humbug, because all they saw on the far side was more ocean. Today, of course, the ocean vistas and ancient forests are precisely why this loop hike is so attractive.

Drive Highway 101 south of Port Orford 6 miles (or north of Gold Beach 21 miles) and park at a Humbug Mountain Trailhead sign a quarter mile north of the state park's campground entrance. (If you're staying at the campground, take a footbridge across the creek and a tunnel under the highway to the trail.)

The trail starts in a glen of huge maple and myrtlewood trees, with sword ferns and black-stalked maidenhair ferns. The well-graded path soon climbs into an old-growth forest of Douglas firs, some 6 feet thick. After a mile the trail forks at the start of the loop. The shorter, slightly steeper West Trail to the right passes the hike's best viewpoint (looking north to Redfish Rocks, Port Orford, and Cape Blanco). Where the routes finally rejoin, take a short uphill spur to the small, steep summit meadow of grass and bracken fern, and the hike's only view south to the Gold Beach coast. Return via the trail's other fork.

 If you're trekking the Oregon Coast Trail from Cape Blanco (Hike #78), follow the beach south 5 miles, fording the tricky, chest-deep Elk River. Walk streets through Port Orford. Then take the beach south 2 miles and Highway 101 a mile to the 3.8-mile trail shown on the map below. Then take the highway south.

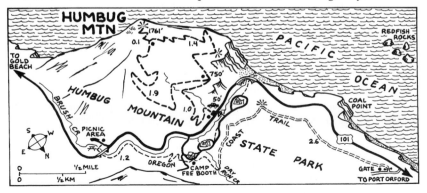

81   Sisters Rocks   🚶👨‍👧☆

Easy
1 mile round trip
230 feet elevation gain

Above: Frankport Beach from Sisters Rocks.

Surf rumbles through sea caves in these three monumental rocks, the largest of a cluster of islands between two scenic, rarely visited beaches. Rusting metal at Frankport Beach recalls a dock used from 1893 to 1905 to ship locally gathered tanoak bark to the S.H. Frank leather tannery in San Francisco. Sause Brothers Ocean Towing bought the old port in 1955 and quarried rock there until 1983. In the early 21st century, state lottery funds saved this land as an undeveloped park.

Start by driving Highway 101 south of Port Orford 13 miles or north of Gold Beach 14 miles. Between mileposts 314 and 315 (and 1.3 miles south of Prehistoric Gardens' roadside dinosaur statues), look for a nameless state park sign. Turn west beside a bluff on a very rough, rocky side road *(GPS location N42° 35.73' W124° 23.97')*. Park here and walk down the ancient road past a locked metal gate.

After 0.3 mile a left-hand fork of the road descends to Frankport Beach. The right-hand fork ends at a gravel plain between two of the monumental sisters. Scramble 100 feet up the largest of these semi-islands, straight ahead, to what looks like a crater but is actually the mouth of a giant sea cave. The other entrances to this cave are around the left-hand side of the rock. Explore the tide pool area here at your own risk because of slippery rocks and unexpected large waves.

82   Otter Point

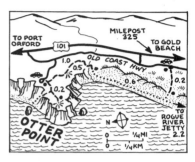

Easy
0.4 miles round trip
100 feet elevation gain

Below: View south from Otter Point.

No signs on Highway 101 alert travelers to this scenic, wave-pounded headland north of Gold Beach. As a result, few people have discovered the state park trails that descend to secluded beaches nestled against the little cape.

Drive Highway 101 north of Gold Beach 3 miles. Near milepost 325, at a sign marked "To Old Coast Road," drive west one block to a T-shaped junction, turn right for 0.6 mile, and turn left at a state park sign to a turnaround.

Follow the main trail out through the headland's meadow 0.2 mile to the tip of Otter Point. Summer wildflowers here include blue iris, red paintbrush, and white wild strawberries. What looks like heather is actually crowberry, with unpalatable black fruit. Notice that the cape's exposed rock strata are turned on edge like sliced bread. These layers began as mud deposited 150 million years ago on the seafloor 500 miles south of here. When faults slid the Pacific Ocean plate north, the compacted mudstone scraped off onto the continent and tilted sideways. On the horizon are other reminders of that colossal collision — Cape Sebastian to the south (Hike #89) and Humbug Mountain to the north (Hike #80).

To reach the beach, start walking back toward your car. A short scramble trail on the left drops precariously to a hidden beach on the north, while an official trail near the parking area descends to the right 0.5 mile to the broad south beach.

Oregon Coast Trail trekkers from Humbug Mountain follow Highway 101 south 9 miles to Euchre Creek at Ophir, take the beach 5 miles to Nesika Beach, cross the highway near the Geisel Monument, hike gravel Old Coast Highway 2 miles to Otter Point, and walk the sand 2.8 miles to the south jetty at Gold Beach.

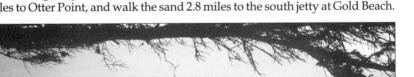

Coquille River Falls

Easy (Elk Creek Falls)
0.2 miles round trip
No elevation gain

Moderate (Big Tree)
2.4 miles round trip
800 feet elevation gain

Easy (Coquille River Falls)
1 mile round trip
400 feet elevation **loss**

Two waterfalls and the world's largest Port Orford cedar are the goals of these three trails in the mountains along the South Fork Coquille River. The paths are short enough that you can hike them all in an afternoon.

To drive to the first trail from the north, follow Highway 42 part of the way between Coos Bay and Roseburg. At a junction 3 miles east of Myrtle Point, turn south 17 miles to Powers and continue toward Agness 6.9 paved miles to the signed Elk Creek Falls pullout on the left. If you're coming here from the Highway 101 bridge at Gold Beach, take Jerrys Flat Road 32 miles to the Rogue River bridge near Agness and continue straight on Road 33 toward Powers for 25.6 miles (including 4 miles of gravel) to the Elk Creek Falls trailhead between mileposts 57 and 58.

At the trailhead, the path forks. First head left on a level trail that ends in 150 yards at a grotto beside Elk Creek Falls' 60-foot cascade. Then decide whether you want to climb 1.2 miles to see Big Tree. If so, return to the trailhead and take the other fork. Lined with delicate maidenhair fern, this path switchbacks up a steepish ridge where 15-foot rhododendrons bloom pink in June. After a mile, turn right on a grassy roadbed 100 yards. Then turn left on the trail's continuation. At a junction in a picnic area, turn left to Big Tree, a 239-foot-tall, 12-foot-thick Port Orford cedar.

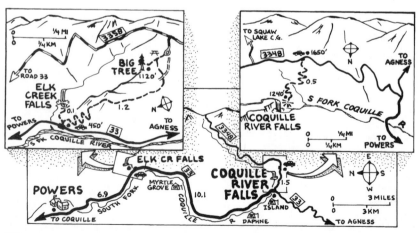

The next short hike leads to Coquille River Falls, where the South Fork Coquille River splits in two and thunders over a 100-foot cliff. To find the trailhead return to your car, drive south toward Agness 10.1 miles and fork left on paved, one-lane Road 3348 (toward Squaw Lake Campground) for 1.5 miles to the signed pullout on the left.

The Coquille River Falls trail switchbacks downhill for half a mile through an old-growth forest of Douglas fir and red cedar. The forest floor has sword ferns, shamrock-leaved oxalis, and Oregon grape. The path ends at a viewpoint of the big waterfall, but little Drowned Out Creek also splashes past the trail in a series of mossy 10-foot cascades. The exposed bedrock here is very slick, so use care if you insist on venturing onward 50 feet to a second viewpoint, or if you dare to scramble to the pools and chutes at the base of Coquille River Falls.

84   Hanging Rock

Moderate
4 miles round trip
1200 feet elevation gain
Open mid-April through November

Left: Hanging Rock.
Opposite: Coquille River Falls.

The view from this house-sized boulder is breathtaking even if you don't dare stand on the overhanging lip, a dizzying 3600 feet above the Rogue River. The hike here is nice in June, when acres of blooming rhododendrons along the Panther Ridge Trail are joined by yellow iris, white beargrass, and fawn lilies.

If you're driving from the north, take Highway 42 (between Coos Bay and Roseburg) to a junction 3 miles east of Myrtle Point. Turn south 17 miles to Powers, continue another 17 paved miles toward Agness, and fork left on paved, one-lane Road 3348 toward Glendale for 8.7 miles. Opposite the cute, free, 2-site Buck Creek Campground, turn right on gravel Road 5520 for 1.2

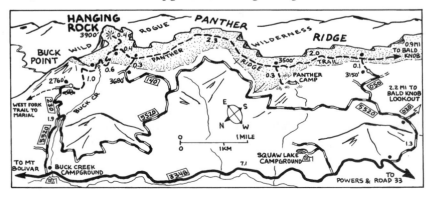

miles. Then turn left on steep Road 230 for 0.7 mile, keeping right at junctions, to the trailhead at road's end *(GPS location N42° 45.36' W123° 55.92')*.

If you're coming here from Gold Beach, take Jerrys Flat Road 32 miles up the Rogue River to the bridge near Agness, continue straight on Road 33 toward Powers 15.6 miles (including 4 miles of gravel), turn right on Road 3348 for 8.7 miles, turn right on gravel Road 5520 for 1.2 miles, and turn left on Road 230.

The Panther Ridge Trail climbs a slope where sparse old-growth Douglas firs leave light enough for rhododendron, salal, manzanita, and chinkapin to thrive. After a mile the trail rounds Buck Point's knoll and drops to a glen where huge cedar trees surround a spring at the head of Buck Creek (dry by July).

Next the path switchbacks up a dry ridge where orange tiger lilies bloom in July. Turn left at a T-shaped junction for 0.4 mile to reach Hanging Rock's stupendous cliffs *(GPS location N42° 44.44' W123° 55.79')*. Directly below, the tips of great fir trees bristle up from the Wild Rogue Wilderness. The Devils Backbone, a craggy ridge, seems to dive down through the forests toward a crash landing at Paradise Bar.

Other Options

The 7.1-mile Panther Ridge Trail continues west along the Rogue valley rim to Road 020 at Bald Knob. Whether or you hike or drive to Bald Knob, consider spending $35 to rent the lookout there, a 16-foot-square room on a short tower. With propane heat, fridge, lights, and stove, the cabin is open from Memorial Day weekend until closed by winter snow. Check *www.recreation.gov* for reservations.

85   Rogue River Trail

Difficult (to Flora Dell Falls)
8.6 miles round trip
600 feet elevation gain

Very Difficult (to Marial)
16 miles one way
· **950 feet** elevation gain

Very Difficult (to Grave Creek)
40 miles one way
2800 feet elevation gain

At Inspiration Point, the trail through the Rogue River's wilderness canyon has been blasted out of sheer basalt cliffs. More than 100 feet below, kayaks and rafts drift through green-pooled chasms toward the roar of Blossom Bar's whitewater. In other places the river trail ducks into forested side canyons with waterfalls. Sometimes the path emerges at grassy river bars with ancient ranch cabins and gnarled oaks. Hikers always share this wilderness gorge with the plentiful wildlife drawn by the river—kingfishers, black bears, deer, and eagles.

If backpacking the entire 40-mile path from Illahe to Grave Creek sounds daunting, consider an 8.6-mile day hike as far as Flora Dell Falls. If you don't mind shuttling a car on long, gravel roads you can hike one way on the 16-mile segment between Illahe and Marial. The most comfortable way to rough it, however, is to

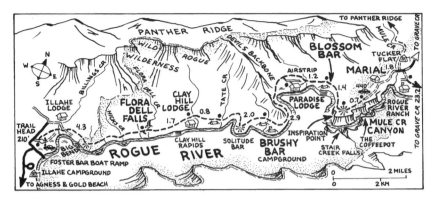

hike lodge-to-lodge, spending nights in rustic trailside inns.

Hikers may want to avoid mid-winter, when cold rains are the rule. It's also best to skip August, when the rocky, exposed slopes often shimmer with 100-degree heat. Poison oak is common, so learn to recognize its shiny triple leaflets. Bicycles and horses are not allowed. Backpackers should bring a lightweight stove, because campfires within 400 feet of the river are allowed only if they're packed up in firepans without a trace. Because black bears had become accustomed to raiding poorly cached food at night, campers at popular sites are required to store their food in the hoists and bear boxes provided. Elsewhere, campers must hang food bags at least 10 feet high and 5 feet from a tree trunk. A wilderness map and trail guide is available at the ranger station in Gold Beach.

The river's name comes from the Takelma and Tututni Indians, whom the early French trappers called *coquins* (rogues). When gold attracted white interlopers,

Mule Creek Canyon from Inspiration Point.   *Opposite: Kayakers below the trail.*

the tribes retaliated in 1855 by massacring settlers. The Army pursued the Indians to this remote canyon, where the soldiers were besieged by a superior force of well-armed warriors. The Army's trenches are still visible above the trail at Illahe's Big Bend Pasture. Relief troops from the east turned back when Indians rolled rocks on them from the steep slopes a quarter mile upstream of Solitude Bar. When soldiers from Gold Beach arrived, however, nearly 1200 Indians were taken captive and forcibly moved 150 miles north to the Siletz Reservation.

To find the trailhead, turn off Highway 101 at the south end of the Gold Beach bridge and follow Jerrys Flat Road (which becomes Road 33) up the Rogue River for 32 miles. Just after crossing a river bridge, fork to the right at a sign for Illahe and follow a one-lane, paved road 3.5 miles to the trailhead spur on the right.

From the trail register, the path skirts Big Bend Pasture for half a mile through the woods, crosses some fields and a dirt road, and then contours along a wooded slope above the river. In its first 4.3 miles, the path bridges five streams (Billings, Buster, Dans, Hicks, and Flea creeks) before reaching Flora Dell Creek. Here a 20-foot waterfall showers into a swimmable pool beside the trail. Fifty yards before the creek, a side trail descends to a bedrock bank of the deep, green river, a good place to eat lunch while watching drift boats and jet boats pass. Beware of lush poison oak along the side trail to the river.

For a day hike, turn back here. If you're planning an overnight trip, continue upriver. In 1.7 miles you'll pass Clay Hill Lodge. A night here runs $150 per person (kids $100), but includes meals. Book well in advance at *www.clayhilllodge. com*. For a backpacking campsite, either continue 0.8 mile to Camp Tacoma just before Tate Creek or hike an additional 2 miles through Solitude Bar's scenic gorge to Brushy Bar, a forested plain with a large campground and a guard station that's staffed May 15-Oct 15.

Beyond Brushy Bar 2.9 miles, take a side path to the right across a grassy airstrip to Paradise Lodge. Drop-in hikers are welcome at the bar and buffet restaurant

Flora Dell Falls.

CAPE FERRELO glows with lupine wildflowers along the
Oregon Coast Trail in Boardman State Park (Hike #91).

THE SILTCOOS RIVER (Hike #63) meets the sea in the Oregon Dunes near campgrounds and trails.

OLD TOWN FLORENCE (see p141) features shops and restaurants along the Siuslaw riverfront.

SOUTH SLOUGH ESTUARINE RESERVE (Hike #72) includes a visitor center and trails to the bay's tidal zone.

CAPE PERPETUA (Hike #51) is a scenic spot to visit a spouting horn, tide pool, giant spruce, or lookout shelter.

A MILE LONG, the graceful 1936 Conde McCullough bridge spans Coos Bay.

THE OREGON DUNES

ACTIVE DUNES move slowly inland, burying forests.

Along most of the Oregon Coast, bluffs block the prevailing west winds from blowing beach sand inland. But in the lowlands of the Oregon Dunes, wave after wave of wind-driven dunes have marched ashore. Each onslaught buries forests before gradually petering out and sprouting forests of its own.

Man accidentally changed the dunes' traditional cycle by introducing European beachgrass to stabilize sand near railroads in 1910. The stubborn grass spread along the beach, creating a 30-foot-tall foredune. Because this grassy dike stops sand from blowing off the beach, the inland dunes have been cut off from their supply of sand. The last dunes still marching eastward may disappear within a century.

Sand dollar.

BEACHGRASS has created a foredune, blocking sand.

BAKER BEACH (Hike #54) is the north end of the dunes.

DUNES shoulder aside Tahkenitch Creek (Hike #66).

REEDSPORT'S Umpqua Discovery Center (see p157) includes well-designed walk-through exhibits.

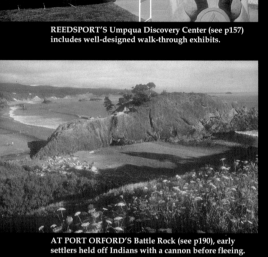

AT PORT ORFORD'S Battle Rock (see p190), early settlers held off Indians with a cannon before fleeing.

THE ROGUE RIVER (Hike #85) winds through a wilderness canyon accessed best by trail or float boat.

BIRDS OF THE COAST

Because birds must nest on land, thousands of sea birds flock to rocky islands and headlands each summer. Some of the best places to watch them are at Yaquina Head (Hike #39), Shore Acres (Hike #71), and Coquille Point (Hike #75).

BROWN PELICAN. With gigantic 7-foot wingspans, rows of pelicans cruise past jetties, flying low.

OYSTERCATCHER. This bird struts about tidepool rocks, prying open mussels with its long red bill.

TUFTED PUFFIN. This 15-inch sea bird lands on islands and tall sea cliffs to nest in dirt tunnels.

COMMON MURRE. Like skinny penguins, thousands of murres crowd sea rocks to guard their eggs.

CORMORANT. This long-necked bird dives deep for fish and then poses on rocks, drying its wings.

SEAL OR SEA LION?

Most likely that dog-like shape you've spotted in the surf is a **harbor seal**. About 5 feet long and weighing up to 300 pounds, they like to lounge on sand spits near river mouths.

Steller sea lions are ruddier and three times as large. Look for them at Newport's docks and on offshore rocks.

HARBOR SEALS rest on Salishan Spit (Hike #37).

SEA LIONS swim at the Oregon Coast Aquarium (see p105).

Elephant seals are ten times larger, but breed only near Cape Arago (see p176). With a trunk-like snout and a roar heard for a mile, males can be 21 feet long and weigh over 7000 pounds.

Federal laws protect marine mammals from harassment, so don't approach too closely—even if you see an "abandoned" seal pup on the beach. It's just resting while its mother hunts for food.

IN BOARDMAN STATE PARK (Hike #90) the Oregon Coast Trail passes North Island Viewpoint.

HARRIS BEACH State Recreation Area (see p223) has a campground with a secluded beach and scenic islands.

FACE ROCK, at Bandon (Hike #75), is the face of a headstrong Indian maiden, according to legend.

SALMONBERRY *(Rubus spectabilis)*. Hummingbirds rely on nectar from salmonberry's April flowers.

SALMONBERRY *(Rubus specta-bilis)*. This slightly stickery rainforest shrub has edible berries in July.

SALAL *(Gaultheria shallon)*. Salal covers coastal headlands with dense bushes. It has edible blue berries.

STAR-FLOWERED SOLOMONSEAL *(Maianthemum stellatum)*. These delicate stars decorate deep forests .

RHODODENDRON *(Rhododen-dron macrophyllum)* blooms in May and can grow 20 feet tall.

SOURGRASSS *(Oxalis oregana)*. The shamrock-shaped leaves carpet forests and taste tart when chewed.

FAIRY BELLS *(Disporum hookeri)*. This lily of moist woodlands later develops pairs of orange berries.

CANDYFLOWER *(Claytonia sibi-rica)*. Common by woodland creeks and trails, candyflower is edible.

BLEEDING HEART *(Dicentra formosa)*. Look near woodland creeks for these pink hearts.

COLUMBINE *(Aquilegia formosa)*. In wet woodlands, this bloom has nectar lobes for hummingbirds.

TRILLIUM *(Trillium ovatum)*. This spectacular woodland lily blooms in April, a herald of spring.

OREGON GRAPE *(Berberis aqui-folium)*. Oregon's state flower has holly-like leaves and blue berries.

BEACH PEA *(Lathyrus japonicus).* This native sweetpea loves dunes and coastal wetlands.

COW PARSNIP *(Heracleum lanatum).* This giant-leaved plant stands up to 8 feet tall in summer meadows.

WILD IRIS *(Iris tenax).* Also called an Oregon flag, this June bloom varies from blue to yellowish white.

PEARLY EVERLASTING *(Anaphalis margaritacea).* Try this roadside bloom in dried floral arrangements.

ASTER *(Aster spp.).* This daisy relative blooms in high meadows late in summer.

FOXGLOVE *(Digitalis purpurea).* Showy 5-foot foxglove stalks spangle sunny summer meadows.

PAINTBRUSH *(Castilleja spp.)* has showy red-orange sepals, but the actual flowers are green tubes.

WESTERN AZALEA *(Rhododendron occidentale)* blooms in May along the Southern Oregon Coast.

LUPINE *(Lupinus spp.)* has fragrant blooms in early summer and pea-pod-shaped fruit in fall.

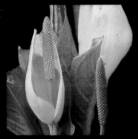

SKUNK CABBAGE *(Lysichiton americanum).* Pollinated by flies, this swamp bloom smells putrid.

SEA FIG *(Membryanthemum chilense).* The sea fig stores water in its fleshy leaves to survive in sand.

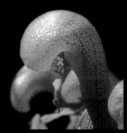

PITCHER PLANT *(Darlingtonia californica),* a bog-dweller, traps and dissolves insects for fertilizer.

STOUT GROVE in California's Jedediah Smith Redwoods
State Park (Hike #96) has an easy trail amid redwood giants.

Blossom Bar Rapids.

here. Book in advance at *www.paradise-lodge.com* or 888-667-6483 if you want a room. Rates include meals and run $165 for adults and $85 for kids. Paradise Lodge is a regular stop for Gold Beach jet boats from May through October. In winter, overnight guests can arrange to be ferried from Foster Bar at Illahe.

From Paradise Lodge, hike upriver 1.2 miles to Blossom Bar Creek, with camp-sites and a swimmable creek pool. Across a brushy lava flat to the right is the river's most treacherous rapids and the limit of jet boat traffic.

The trail climbs gradually for 1.4 miles to Inspiration Point, opposite Stair Creek's dramatic waterfall, and then traces the edge of Mule Creek Canyon, a gorge so narrow that boaters sometimes bridge sideways or spin helplessly in a cylindrical maelstrom called The Coffeepot. Half a mile beyond is the Marial trailhead. To shuttle a car here from Illahe, take Road 33 toward Powers for 15.6 miles, turn right on Road 3348, (following Glendale signs) for 22 miles to a 6-way junction, veer right at a Marial pointer for 18.3 miles to the Rogue River Ranch museum turnoff, and continue straight 1.8 rough miles to road's end.

If you're hiking onward past Marial, walk the road 1.8 miles and turn right into the Rogue River Ranch 200 yards, where the trail resumes. The final 23.2 miles to Grave Creek (not shown on map) have no jet boats, and the only lodges catering to hikers are at Marial (541-474-2057) and Black Bar ($135 per person, 541-479-6507 or *www.blackbarlodge.net*).

The path climbs along the canyon slope, seldom nearing the river itself. Measured from the Marial road, the trail's highlights are author Zane Grey's cabin at Winkle Bar (5.5 miles), the Kelsey Creek campsite (7.6 miles), Meadow Creek's campsite (9.4 miles), Black Bar (13.6 miles), the Russian Creek campsite (17.2 miles), Tyee Rapids (18.2 miles), Big Slide Camp (19.3 miles), the Whisky Creek Cabin museum (19.7 miles), Rainie Falls (21.2 miles), and Grave Creek (23.2 miles). To shuttle a car to Grave Creek, take Road 33 from the Illahe junction 2 miles west toward Gold Beach, turn left on paved Road 23 for 31 miles to Galice, and turn left for 8 miles.

86   Lower Rogue River 🏕️🗼🏕️⛺🚲🐎

Moderate (to Painted Rock Creek)
6.2 miles round-trip
500 feet elevation gain

Difficult (entire trail)
11.7 miles one way
900 feet elevation gain

Far less crowded than the famous wilderness portion of the Rogue River Trail (Hike #85), this path traces a milder portion of the rugged river canyon. The trail contours along a forested slope above the river, dipping to a gravelly beach at Big Eddy and climbing to a clifftop viewpoint at Copper Canyon. Along the way the path bridges a dozen side creeks and passes half a dozen private cabins.

The most interesting day hike begins at the trail's eastern end in Agness. To drive there from the Highway 101 bridge in Gold Beach, turn inland on Jerrys Flat Road for 32 miles. After crossing a river bridge, turn left at a sign for Agness. Follow paved Road 375 for 3 miles to the Old Agness Store and turn right on Cougar Lane for 0.2 mile. Immediately after a school, park on the right in the Agness Community Library's gravel lot. Then walk straight on the paved road (where there is no parking). Following trail signs, go straight on a gravel road after 200 yards. In another 200 yards, pass a mobile home, go through an open wooden gate, and follow the steep road up 150 yards to find the start of the actual trail on the right.

After this somewhat confusing start, the trail sets out through big Douglas firs and tanoaks with glimpses down to river riffles. Large gray squirrels shake their bushy silver tails at passing hikers. At the one-mile mark the trail forks. The larger, left-hand path descends to a large, clearly visible gravel bar beside Big Eddy, where the Rogue swirls at a tight bend. This is the trail's only convenient river access, so stop awhile. Then take the trail's right-hand fork half a mile through tanoak woods to a road. The path jogs 80 yards left on the road

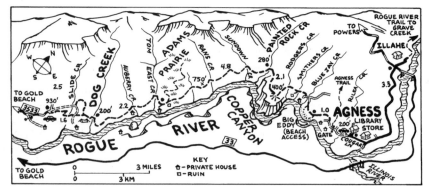

Copper Canyon from the Lower Rogue River Trail.   Opposite: Jet boat.

across Blue Jay Creek, turns right through a wooden gate, continues 0.4 mile to a footbridge over Smithers Creek, and then forks to the right for 0.2 mile to Morris Rodgers Creek. This lovely creek is, alas, on private land, so continue up the trail to the craggy viewpoint on the cliffs above Copper Canyon. A natural rock garden here includes tiny purple penstemon, red paintbrush, and blue, 6-petaled brodiaea lilies.

Day hikers could turn back here, but it's tempting to continue half a mile to the cool, mossy glen of cascading Painted Rock Creek. This is a place to dip your feet and stretch out on a shady rock before heading back. When you return to your car, check for ticks around your collar and cuffs. If you find any, unscrew them until they let go.

If you're backpacking or have arranged a car shuttle you can continue along the river trail 8.6 miles to the western trailhead. To find this trailhead by car, drive 11.3 miles east of Gold Beach on Jerrys Flat Road. Just beyond Lobster Campground, turn left on Road 3310 across a scenic one-lane bridge and then immediately turn right on gravel, one-lane, unmarked Road 3533. After 3.8 miles, cross Silver Creek and keep right. After another 1.1 mile fork uphill to the left to keep on Road 3533. Climb a mile on a rougher road to a parking pullout and signboard on the right. Park here (*GPS location N42° 29.75' W124° 125.35'*). The correct trail starts out faintly, paralleling the road ahead. Skirt the left-hand edge of a wire-fenced spring 200 feet to a registration box marking the trail.

87   Illinois River

Moderate (to Buzzards Roost)
5 miles round trip
900 feet elevation gain

Difficult (to Indian Flat)
8.8 miles round trip
1700 feet elevation gain

Very Difficult (to Silver Creek)
17.2 miles round trip
2900 feet elevation gain

The Illinois River is even wilder than its famous neighbor, the Rogue. In fact, the canyon here is so rugged that the 27-mile Illinois River Trail never actually reaches the riverbank. Instead the path traverses up to a viewpoint atop the cliffs of Buzzards Roost, dips deeply into the canyons of several side creeks, and finally climbs over 3747-foot Bald Mountain. Backpacking the entire 27 miles to the Briggs Creek Trailhead (not shown on map) is a serious adventure, but day hikers can get a good sample with trips to Buzzards Roost, Indian Flat, or Silver Creek. The route has recovered well from the 2002 Biscuit Fire, that mostly burned brush.

From the Highway 101 bridge in Gold Beach, take Jerrys Flat Road up the Rogue River 28 miles. On the far side of the Illinois River Bridge, turn right on Oak Flat Road for 3.1 miles to a gravel trailhead parking lot on left, just before pavement ends.

The trail starts at a register box and ambles through a forest of Douglas fir, tanoak, and canyon live oak. After 0.4 mile you enter the 2002 fire zone, but because fires here typically leave large trees intact, you'll hardly notice the change. Beware of poison oak bushes masquerading as tree seedlings. After crossing two creeks you'll climb to Buzzard Roost's saddle at the 2.5-mile mark. To get a panoramic view here you have to scramble (cautiously!) 100 feet up the crest of a precipitous ridge.

If you'd like a longer hike, continue on the main trail 1.7 miles downhill to a fork. To the left is Indian Flat's oasis-like meadow beside Indigo Creek. (The far end of the meadow is private property.) To the right, the main trail crosses Indigo

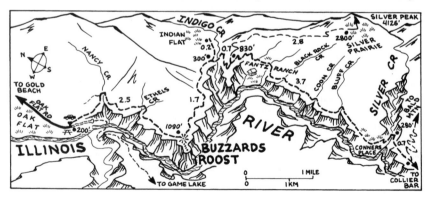

The Illinois River.   Opposite: Madrone branches.

Creek on a scenic footbridge, another possible turnaround point.

If you're headed for Silver Creek, cross the bridge and switchback up 0.7 mile to a ridgetop junction. Avoid the rarely used Silver Peak Trail to the left, which heads steeply up the ridge to distant bracken meadows. Instead continue on the main trail, descending to Fantz Ranch, a grassy bench with nice campsites beside a creek. Beyond Fantz Ranch the trail traverses a canyon slope 3 miles before dropping to Silver Creek's dramatic bedrock chasm. Camping is impossible in this gorge, but the creek makes a good turnaround point. After your hike, check for ticks around your collar and cuffs. If you find any, unscrew them until they let go.

Other Options

To backpack the remainder of the 27-mile Illinois River Trail, continue past Silver Creek 0.7 mile, fork left and switchback up 3200 feet in 4 grueling miles. The trail then ambles past small bracken meadows on the crest of Bald Mountain's ridge for 3.7 miles before gradually descending 10 miles to the Briggs Creek Trailhead at the end of Road 4103. This final portion is not shown on the map and should only be undertaken with the Forest Service's topographic Kalmiopsis Wilderness map. The difficult 94-mile car shuttle to the Briggs Creek Trailhead (via Galice, Grants Pass, and Selma) calls for a map of the Siskiyou National Forest.

Shrader Old Growth Trail.

88 Shrader Old Growth Trail

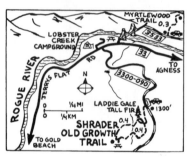

Easy (Shrader Old Growth Trail)
0.8-mile loop
100 feet elevation gain

Easy (Myrtlewood Trail)
0.6-mile round trip
300 feet elevation gain

This nature trail explores a stately glen of giant trees, including the 220-foot-tall, 10-foot-thick Laddie Gale Douglas fir. If the 0.8-mile loop seems short, add an encore — a nearby 0.3-mile path to the world's largest myrtlewood tree.

From the Highway 101 bridge in Gold Beach, turn toward Agness on Jerrys Flat Road for 11.2 miles. Just beyond the Lobster Creek Campground, turn right at a sign for the Frances Shrader Memorial Trail and follow steep, one-lane Road 3300-090 for 2.1 miles to a parking lot on the left. In June, 20-foot rhododendrons surround the lot with blooms.

The packed gravel path that begins across the road leads past benches and a picnic table beside the grove's mossy creek. A brochure available at the trailhead explains how the old-growth forest's complex ecosystem includes minute fungi, hollow snags, brushy streams, and blowdown openings. The Laddie Gale fir at loop's end is named for the basketball star who led the University of Oregon's legendary "Tall Firs" team to a national championship in 1939.

If you'd like to try the Myrtlewood Trail, drive back to Jerrys Flat Road 33 and turn right for 0.1 mile. Following Lower Rogue River Trail signs, turn left on Road 3310 across a scenic one-lane bridge and then immediately turn right on an unmarked road for 0.2 mile to a pullout on the right and a trail sign on the left. The steep, 0.3-mile trail that begins here switchbacks up to the massive myrtlewood tree, beside a picnic table and a lovely creek.

89   Cape Sebastian

Moderate (to cape)
1.2 miles round trip
200 feet elevation **loss**

Difficult (to Hunters Cove)
3.8 miles round trip
700 feet elevation **loss**

Moderate (to north beach)
3.2 miles round trip
700 feet elevation **loss**

An often-overlooked state park road leads to a spectacular viewpoint in the windswept meadows atop this huge coastal cliff. From there, a trail descends through spruce woods to one of Oregon's most-photographed beaches — a scene framed with craggy islands.

Drive Highway 101 south of Gold Beach 7 miles (or north of Brookings 22 miles) to milepost 335. Turn at a "Cape Sebastian Viewpoint" state park sign and keep left on a very steep paved road 0.5 mile to the viewpoint at the south parking turnaround. Strong winds here have mowed Sitka spruce trees to a waist-high mat. To the north, the shore stretches past Gold Beach to Humbug Mountain (Hike #80). To the south, grassy-topped Hunters Island and countless smaller sea stacks shelter the beach at Hunters Cove.

Take the paved path across the cape's meadow to an even better viewpoint. Then continue on an unpaved path along a ridge. At the 0.6-mile mark you'll reach a good turnaround point, where the trail begins switchbacking downhill.

If you choose to continue, you'll descend 0.8 mile to a rocky shore fringed with shore pine, evergreen huckleberry, and a few 3-leaved poison oak plants. Black, crook-necked cormorants dry their wings atop the wave-sculpted rocks here. Sea palms bend with the waves' spray. The trail levels for a scenic half-mile tour of the rocky shoreline. Then the trail dives steeply to the bouldery start of Hunters Cove's beach, a good goal for your hike. Sea otter hunters once sought refuge from storms here. By 1911, the hunters had driven their cute, fur-bearing prey to extinction in Oregon.

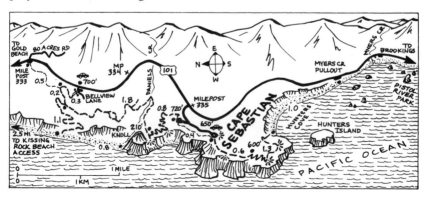

Beach north of Cape Sebastian. Below: South of Cape Sebastian.

If you like lonely beaches, you might try a new section of the Oregon Coast Trail that descends to the other side of Cape Sebastian. To find this trailhead, drive back to Highway 101 and head north 1.4 miles to Bellview Lane, between mileposts 333 and 334. After just 100 feet on Bellview Lane, park in a big gravel lot to the left. Then walk across Bellview Lane to find a locked, unmarked metal gate. Walk past this gate on the trail — an ancient roadbed that descends through alder woods.

Go straight at a junction after 0.3 mile. In another 0.2 mile you'll reach a major fork. Keep right to descend 1.1 mile to the beach, often a very windy place.

Other Options

If you're hiking the Oregon Coast Trail from Gold Beach, walk the sand 5 miles south. Just 0.8 mile before Cape Sebastian's cliff, turn left on a trail — an old road angling up a brushy slope into the woods. Keep right at junctions for 2.8 miles to a cliff-edge viewpoint in a small meadow beside a knoll. The trail turns left here, climbing steeply 0.8 mile to the cape's north parking lot. Cross the lot and climb over a low stone wall to find the 0.4-mile connector trail to the south lot. Then hike 1.9 miles down to Hunters Cove, take the beach 3 miles to Pistol River, and walk along Highway 101 for 6 miles to Boardman Park (Hike #90).

Highway 101 at the Pistol River, north of Brookings.

BROOKINGS

Known as Oregon's "banana belt," the Brookings coast has the state's balmiest climate, with average temperatures between 50° F and 70° F year-round. Boardman State Park preserves 13 miles of picturesque coves, capes, and islands along Highway 101. Inland, the 281-square-mile Kalmiopsis Wilderness drapes the rugged Klamath Mountains.

Brookings/ Harbor
Platted in 1908 as a lumber company town, Brookings has evolved into a major retirement destination. Attracted by the scenery and mild climate, retirees now account for over half the population. Across the Chetco River in the adjacent city of Harbor is the local port, with a large marina, docks, charter boats, a jetty, and a scenic beach.

Pistol River Scenic Viewpoint 禾
Hundreds of sea stacks and craggy islands shelter the beach at the mouth of the Pistol River, 23 miles north of Brookings. Parking areas along Highway 101 access the picturesque beach and grassy dunes (see Hike #89).

Samuel H. Boardman State Scenic Corridor
Plan to stop often when driving Highway 101 through this long, narrow coastal park. From north to south, top roadside attractions are Arch Rock Picnic Area (on a grassy bluff surrounded by views), Natural Bridges Cove (a viewpoint of churning sea caves), the 345-foot-tall Thomas Creek Bridge (Oregon's highest), Whaleshead Beach Picnic Area (a lovely beach with a whale-shaped island that sometimes spouts surf), Cape Ferrelo (a viewpoint on a grassy headland), and Lone Ranch Beach Picnic Area (at the foot of Cape Ferrelo). For maps and recommended trails, see Hikes #90 and #91.

Harris Beach State Recreation Area

This popular beachside park just north of Brookings overlooks Goat Island and offshore rocks that serve as habitat for seabirds and sea lions. The 149-site, year-round campground with 6 yurts accepts summer reservations at 800-452-5687. A 0.2-mile path from the camp fee booth climbs to a viewpoint atop Harris Butte.

Chetco Point

Ironically, the prettiest ocean views in the city of Brookings are hidden behind a sewage treatment plant. The 0.4-mile path out Chetco Point visits a picnic lawn, a hidden beach, and a bridge to a clifftop viewpoint of sea caves and birdlife. In downtown Brookings, where Highway 101 bends, turn west on Wharf Street for 0.4 mile. Park in a gravel lot to the left and walk along the sewage plant's fenceline.

Azalea Park

Wild western azaleas *(Rhododendron occidentale)* fill this park with fragrant white blooms in time for Brookings' Azalea Festival, held here each Memorial Day weekend. Follow signs from the north end of the Chetco River Bridge.

Chetco Valley Historical Museum

The state's largest Monterey cypress grows outside this restored 1857 stage-coach stop and trading post, just off Highway 101, south of Brookings 2 miles. The museum's collection of pioneer and Indian artifacts is open Friday to Sunday 1pm-4pm in summer. For information call 541-469-6651.

Alfred A. Loeb State Park

Along the Chetco River, surrounded by groves of huge myrtlewood trees and redwoods, this all-year park offers a 45-site campground, 3 cabins (for $39), and a picnic area beside a gravelly river bar. See Hike #93.

Chetco Point in Brookings.

90 Boardman Corridor North

Easy (four viewpoint walks)
2.8 miles round trip
600 feet elevation gain

Easy (Whaleshead Bch to Thomas Cr)
2.8 miles one way
500 feet elevation gain

Moderate (Thomas Cr to Arch Rock)
4.4 miles one way
700 feet elevation gain

   The coast along Boardman State Scenic Corridor is a spectacular parade of islands, coves, and capes. Both Highway 101 and the Oregon Coast Trail trace the 12.7-mile length of the narrow park. Because the two routes touch every mile or so, it's easy to divide the trail into smaller day hikes or to shuttle a car between trailheads for one-way hiking. Below are recommendations for the northern half of the park; Hike #91 describes the park's southern half.

If you only have time for a quick tour, the best bet is to stop at four different trailheads for short hikes to viewpoints. The northernmost of these stops is the Arch Rock Picnic Area, between mileposts 344 and 345. Park here and stroll the paved, 0.2-mile path around the rim of the picnic area's bluff. Waves crash against seabird-dotted islands on all sides of the cape.

Next drive south 1.2 miles to a pullout near milepost 346 marked "Natural Bridges Viewpoint." Trails leave from both the left- and right-hand edges of this parking area. First take the left-hand trail 100 feet to a viewpoint of the cove below, where

China Beach from North Island Viewpoint.   Above: China Beach.

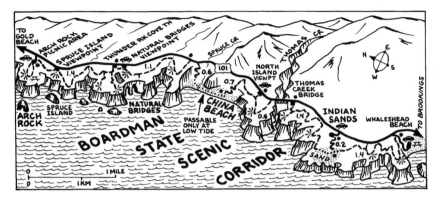

the sea boils through two archways into a collapsed former cave. Then return to the car and take the right-hand trail along the cove's rim 0.3 mile to discover another great viewpoint. This route crosses the Thunder Rock Cove Viewpoint pullout and continues into the woods. Then fork to the left and switchback downhill to a cliff-edge viewpoint before returning to your car.

For the third of the four short viewpoint hikes, drive south another 1.5 miles to a pullout with a guardrail and a small sign, "North Island Viewpoint." Take the trail to a junction in the woods and turn right. This path rounds a hill and descends 0.7 mile to beautiful, secluded China Beach.

After prowling China Beach, return to your car and drive Highway 101 south another mile to Indian Sands Viewpoint. From the left side of the parking lot's entrance, a 0.2-mile trail descends through forest to an unusual area of sand dunes perched above a rocky shore. It's a good place to explore or to let kids play in the sand before heading back.

If you'd prefer a longer, more connected hike, try the 2.8-mile trail between Whaleshead Beach and Thomas Creek Bridge. Drive Highway 101 to the Whaleshead Beach Picnic Area turnoff, south of milepost 349. Only drive 100 feet down the picnic area entrance road before parking beside a trail sign on the right.

The path begins at a Coast Trail post. After 0.2 mile, the trail forks to the right in a headland meadow with breathtaking views south to Cape Ferrelo. At the 0.5-mile mark, the path briefly parallels the highway guardrail before following posts across a meadow to the woods. After 1.4 miles you'll enter the trailless dunes of Indian Sands. Continue straight and slightly downhill, following posts along the forest edge 0.3 mile to the trail's continuation. After skirting four scenic coves (and briefly following the highway guardrail again), the trail ends at a big parking lot at the south end of Oregon's tallest bridge, the 345-foot-tall Highway 101 span across Thomas Creek's gorge.

The remaining 4.4-mile trail section between Thomas Creek and Arch Rock is also suitable as a day hike. The best place to park is 0.2 mile north of Thomas Creek Bridge at a pullout marked "North Island Viewpoint." Take the trail into the woods, turn right, descend 0.7 mile to China Beach, and turn right. Unless it's high tide, you'll be able to round a small headland on the sand. Beyond it, look for a Coast Trail post marking the steep trail back up to the highway. Then turn left along the highway shoulder 0.1 mile to find a trail post marking the path's continuation. The final 2.5 miles pass several viewpoints and three highway pullouts before reaching the Arch Rock Picnic Area's entrance road.

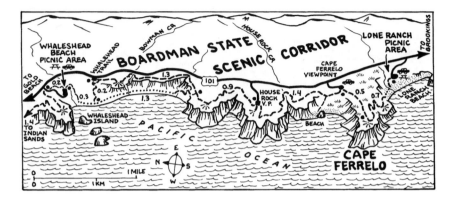

91 Boardman Corridor South

Easy (three viewpoint walks)
1.8 miles round trip
100 feet elevation gain

Easy (Lone Ranch to Cape Ferrelo)
2.4 miles round trip
300 feet elevation gain

Moderate (Lone Ranch to Whaleshead)
5.5 miles one way
600 feet elevation gain

Although it's possible to backpack the entire 12.7-mile length of Boardman State Scenic Corridor's spectacular coast, most hikers take advantage of the trail's frequent junctions with Highway 101 to plan shorter day trips. Below are suggestions for hikes in the park's southern half. (The northern half is described in Hike #90.)

Even if you're just passing through, squeeze in time for a collection of three short viewpoint walks. First turn off Highway 101 near milepost 352 at the Cape Ferrelo Viewpoint. From the parking area, walk 0.5 mile out through grassy wildflower meadows to the cape's panoramic tip. Then return to your car, drive 3 miles north, and take the Whaleshead Beach turnoff down a rough road to a picnic area beside a gorgeous, secluded beach.

Whaleshead Island won its name because waves send a spout-like plume of sea spray above its rocky "head" when the tide is just right. Explore the beach at the picnic area, then hop across Whaleshead Creek to a trail sign at the edge of the forest, and follow a 0.3-mile path up the creek to return to your car. Next drive 0.2 mile back uphill to the highway junction, and park by a trail sign on the left. Take this path 0.2 mile out along a meadowy cape to a breathtaking viewpoint overlooking Whaleshead Island.

If you have time for a more connected hike, climb Cape Ferrelo from Lone Ranch Beach. Start by driving to the Lone Ranch Beach Picnic Area, halfway between mileposts 352 and 353. Take the concrete path down to the beach, cross Lone

Ranch Creek on driftwood, and walk to the right until the beach's sand ends. Continue on boulders a few hundred feet to a trail post on a grassy bluff. The path that starts here makes three long switchbacks up through the wildflower meadows to the cape's tip. Continue inland 0.5 mile to the Cape Ferrelo Viewpoint parking area. For an easy hike, turn back here.

If you'd prefer a longer, 5.5-mile hike—and if you've had the foresight to shuttle a car ahead to the Whaleshead Beach Picnic Area—continue north on a trail that angles down from the Cape Ferrelo parking area. A left-hand spur of this path descends to a pocket beach. The main path climbs through woods, approaches the highway at House Rock Creek, crosses the parking lot at House Rock Viewpoint, and finally forks. Both routes take you to the Whaleshead Beach Picnic Area—but the left-hand path requires a mile of beach walking while the right-hand trail traces a scenic bluff-edge with views and a small waterfall before descending to the beach.

If you're trekking the entire Oregon Coast Trail, the official route from Lone Ranch Beach 11 miles south to the California border simply follows Highway 101.

Whaleshead Beach.   Opposite: Cape Ferrelo.

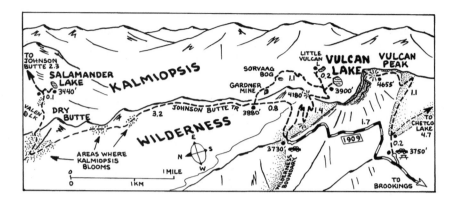

92 Vulcan Lake

Moderate (to Vulcan Peak)
2.6 miles round trip
900 feet elevation gain
Open May through November

Moderate (to Vulcan Lake)
3.7-mile loop
650 feet elevation gain

Difficult (to Salamander Lake)
8.2 miles round trip
1050 feet elevation gain

Stark red ridges, shimmering green lakes, and the strange plants of the Klamath Mountains highlight this remote but popular area. Pick up a Kalmiopsis Wilderness map at a Forest Service station, and remember that winter snows usually close the trails here until May. Although the 2002 Biscuit Fire overswept this entire region, here it mostly burned brush, leaving large trees intact.

From the Highway 101 bridge in Brookings, take North Bank Road 8 miles and continue straight on one-lane Road 1376 another 8 miles to a T-junction just beyond the South Fork Chetco Bridge. Then, following Kalmiopsis Wilderness signs, turn right on gravel Road 1909 for 13.4 miles (keeping right when in doubt) to a fork where signs point left for Vulcan Lake and right for Vulcan Peak. Here you face a decision.

If you have time for a side trip—or if your goal is a viewpoint—turn right and park at the Vulcan Peak trailhead. From here you can walk up the Chetco Divide Trail's abandoned roadbed 0.2 mile and fork left onto a well-graded path that climbs gradually 1.1 mile across an open, brushy slope to the rocky crest of Vulcan Peak. Anchor bolts and melted glass remain from the old lookout tower. A map-like view of the Kalmiopsis Wilderness spreads to the east, while the ocean glints to the west and the snowy Siskiyous rise to the south.

If your goal is Vulcan Lake, drive left at the road fork for 1.7 rough miles to a trailhead at road's end (*GPS location N42° 11.76' W123° 59.56'*). The road's final

1.7 miles may be closed from October to May. The path at this trailhead begins as an abandoned mining road, but after a few yards turn right on a trail that switchbacks up through snowbrush and wind-twisted Jeffrey pine. After a mile, reach a rocky pass with a view. The trail then angles down 0.4 mile to Vulcan Lake *(GPS location N42° 11.25' W123° 59.03')*, a magical place where red bedrock curves into deep green water. During the Ice Age this basin was a cirque — the birthplace of a glacier — and the immense weight of moving ice rounded and scratched the bedrock. If you're backpacking, bring a stove and build no campfire.

To find another lake nearby, backtrack 200 yards from Vulcan Lake to a rock cairn, turn right, and keep to the right on a faint downhill path. After 0.2 mile you'll reach Little Vulcan Lake's shore, ringed with carnivorous pitcher plants, the baseball-bat-shaped bog plants that trap insects for fertilizer.

Then walk back to the rock cairn near Vulcan Lake. The quickest way to your car is to return as you came, but if you'd like to try a loop route, walk 50 steps toward Little Vulcan Lake and turn left at a cairn in a wet spot. From here, a series of these rock piles marks a faint, level path. Follow this rocky trail 0.6 mile to Sorvaag Bog, a brushy pond. Walk to the right of the pond, cross its outlet creek, and continue straight to an old bulldozed road. Follow this track left for 0.5 mile — passing the Gardner Mine's tunnel entrance along the way — to a T-shaped junction with the Johnson Butte Trail. Your car is 0.8 mile to the left.

The difficult hike to Salamander Lake can either be added as a long side trip to the loop described above or as a separate trip. Hike this route in early June to see the pink blossoms of *Kalmiopsis leachiana,* an extremely rare, azalea-like shrub almost entirely confined to a few isolated patches within this wilderness.

Start at the Vulcan Lake Trailhead but keep left, following the Johnson Butte Trail's abandoned bulldozer road through sparse, brushy woods. The road peters out after 2.6 miles , and a view-packed trail continues along the crest of a rocky ridge. Look here for struggling *Kalmiopsis* shrubs, reduced to a mat by winter's snowstorms and summer's baking sun. In a saddle at the 4-mile mark, a side trail to the right leads 0.1 mile steeply down to Salamander Lake, a shallow, brush-rimmed lake full of yellow-blooming lilypads.

Vulcan Peak from Vulcan Lake.   Opposite: Vulcan Lake from Vulcan Peak.

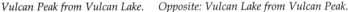

The Chetco River from the Riverview Trail at Loeb State Park.

93   Redwood Nature Trail

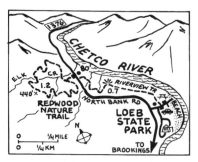

Easy
2.6-mile loop
400 feet elevation gain

Although redwoods are better known from California, 12-foot-thick *Sequoia sempervirens* giants also thrive along the Chetco River. A nature trail loop through this grove connects with the Riverview Trail through Loeb State Park.

From the Highway 101 bridge in Brookings, turn inland on North Bank Road for 7.3 miles and turn right into Loeb State Park to a trailhead parking area. The Riverview Trail starts on the left by a box with nature trail guides. Huge, gnarled myrtlewood trees form a canopy over a forest floor carpeted with shamrock-leaved oxalis and sword ferns. The parkland here was donated to the state for preservation in 1948 by a group called Save the Myrtlewoods.

The path crosses a picnic area and follows the bank of the broad, gravelly Chetco River. Foot-long moss fringes hang from bigleaf maple branches above the trail. Delicate, black-stalked maidenhair ferns wave beside the path. After 0.7 mile the path ends at the road. Cross to the Redwood Nature Trail parking area, follow the trail up along a creek, and turn left on the 1.2-mile loop route. The path climbs for 0.6 mile through ever grander redwoods. Then the trail descends and crosses a mossy, bouldery creek twice before completing the loop. Turn left and return along the Riverview Trail to your car.

94 Wheeler Ridge Bomb Site

Easy
1.6 miles round trip
100 feet elevation gain

Below: Trail sign showing WW II submarine-launched airplane.

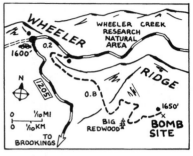

In the darkest hours of World War II, after Pearl Harbor and the retaliatory night bombing of Tokyo, a Japanese submarine surfaced off the southern Oregon Coast. Sailors rolled an airplane from a waterproof hangar on the wave-swept deck, attached a pair of wings, loaded two incendiary bombs, and launched the aircraft by catapult. With his family's 400-year-old samurai sword strapped to the seat to give him courage, pilot Nobuo Fujita flew inland, determined to undermine the U.S. war effort by starting a forest fire.

It was September 9, 1942. Fire lookouts spotted an unknown plane over Wheeler Ridge and scrambled through the dense redwood forest. They found a cluster of shattered trees and easily put out a few small, smoldering fires.

Fifty years later, Nobuo Fujita returned to the Wheeler Ridge bomb site, this time as an ambassador for peace. He had already presented his ancient samurai sword to the city of Brookings as a token of reconciliation. Now he hiked a short path across the ridge to plant a redwood seedling where his bomb had fallen.

To find the trail, turn off Highway 101 at the south end of Brookings' Chetco River bridge, take South Bank Road inland 5.2 miles to an "End Speed Zone" sign, fork right onto gravel Mt. Emily Road 1205 for 3.7 miles, and then fork left to stay on Road 1205 for another 8.2 twisty, uphill miles to the trailhead sign on the left.

Start by walking along the main road to the right 0.2 mile to the start of the actual trail. This path winds through a surprisingly varied forest where rhododendrons and tanoaks mingle with pines, 6-foot-thick Douglas firs, and redwoods up to 12 feet in diameter. The path ends at the bomb site's observation deck. Interpretive signs along the way tell Fujita's courageous story.

Hollow redwood snag on the Oregon Redwoods loop trail.

95   Oregon Redwoods

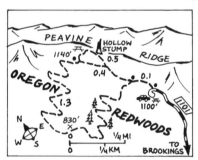

Easy
2-mile loop
320 feet elevation gain

California is famed for its redwoods, but this loop hike near the border proves that Oregon has some impressive groves too.

Drive Highway 101 south of Brookings 6 miles (or north of the California border 1 mile) and turn inland on paved Winchuck Road 896 for 1.6 miles. Then turn right across a narrow concrete bridge onto Peavine Ridge Road 1101 and climb this gravel road 4.2 miles to its end at a trailhead parking lot with an outhouse and a picnic table.

The trail starts near the entrance to the parking lot and soon forks. Keep right at junctions for the full loop. The redwoods at the start of the loop average just 2 to 6 feet in diameter, mixed with 3-foot Douglas firs, tanoaks, sword ferns, and a profusion of evergreen huckleberry bushes. Trilliums and oxalis provide white wildflowers in late spring.

After 0.4 mile you'll pass the hollow snag of a redwood 12 feet thick. Then the loop passes a picnic table on the ridgecrest, zigzags down a hillside, and climbs back to the car through a grove of stately 10-foot-diameter trees.

The Battery Point Lighthouse in Crescent City.

CRESCENT CITY

Behind the beaches of California's redwood coast, 15-foot-thick trunks vanish upward into the fog, like ancient pillars mooring the clouds to the rugged shore.

Redwood National Park

The area's most famous redwood preserve, Redwood National Park, hugs 50 miles of coastline south of Crescent City. Surprisingly, much of the park bears the scars of previous logging. The national park itself is only a few decades old, purchased from timber companies in a wave of national outrage over the clearcutting of the 1960s. The best redwood groves are tucked away in California state parks set aside in the 1920s. Today these preserves are surrounded by the long, narrow national park like Christmas presents stuffed in a tube sock. Visit the Redwood National and State Parks headquarters on 2nd Street in Crescent City (open daily 9-5, winter 9-4) for maps and information about all of the parks, or call 707-465-7335, or check *www.nps.gov/redw*.

Jedediah Smith Redwoods State Park

If you're arriving from Interstate 5 via Grants Pass, a good first stop in redwood country is the Hiouchi Information Center on Highway 199, east of Crescent City 9 miles. Open 9-5 in summer, this information center offers displays, books, and rangers with advice. The rangers usually advise that you visit the Stout Grove, a 44-acre stand of behemoth redwoods beside the Smith River (see Hike #96). From June through September (river levels permitting), a temporary plank footbridge spans the green Smith River to connect the grove with the park's popular, 86-site campground on Highway 199. A site costs $35 a night,

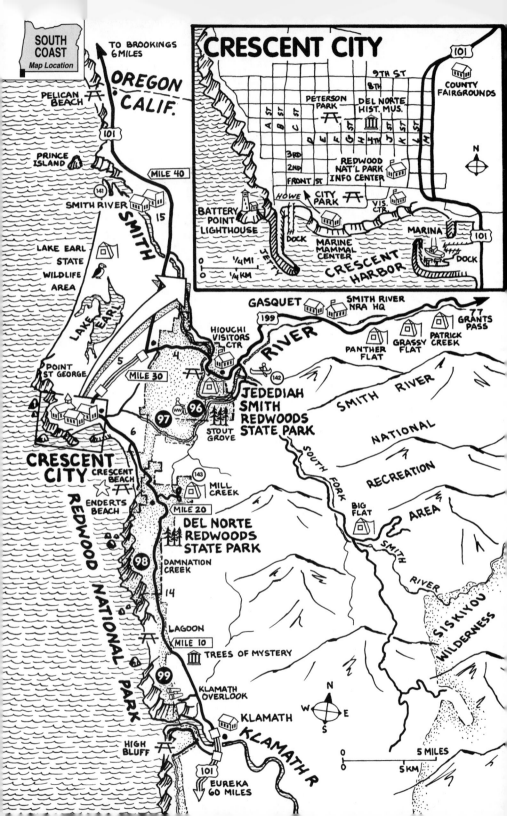

and reservations are strongly recommended between May 21 and September 5. Place them up to 8 weeks in advance at *www.reserveamerica.com* or 877-444-7275.

Del Norte Coast Redwoods State Park

This large state park covers the rugged, foggy coast south of Crescent City. The park's 145-site Mill Creek Campground is 3 miles inland in a second-growth redwood forest (reservations at 1-800-444-7275 or *www.reserveamerica.com*). In summer, you're likely to find unreserved sites available only if you arrive before noon.

Battery Point Lighthouse

Crescent City has been hit hard by the double whammy of logging cutbacks and declining fish runs, but this tenacious harbor town has been weathering hard times since the gold rush ebbed in the 1850s. To see a shining symbol of that tenacity, turn off Highway 101 at a "Visitors Info" pointer near the south end of town and drive the length of Front Street to a Battery Point Lighthouse viewpoint. When the tide is low you can walk out to the tower's island, a hundred yards offshore. Tide permitting, a museum there is open 10-4 daily April-Sept and 10-4 weekends Oct-March. Also at the end of Front Street are an explorable jetty and dock.

Del Norte County Historical Museum 𝕀𝕀𝕀𝕀

This Crescent City museum at 6th and H streets features a 5000-pound lighthouse lens and displays of pioneer, Tolowa, and Yurok artifacts. Open 10am-4pm Monday-Saturday from May through September (in winter, only Mondays and Saturdays).

Northcoast Marine Mammal Center

Volunteers nurse injured seals and seal lions back to health at this center on Crescent City's waterfront. Beside a city park on Front Street, the center is free and open to the public. Feeding times are most fun. Call (707) 465-6265 for hours or to report marine mammals in distress. The center warns visitors not to approach seal pups found on the beach, because they are most likely resting while mother hunts for food, and human contact could scare the mother away.

Crescent City harbor

Crescent City's waterfront, at the southern edge of town, was largely demolished by a 1964 tsunami, but has been rebuilt with a Citizens Dock, a boat ramp, and a commercial harbor full of fishing and pleasure boats.

Smith River National Recreation Area

California's largest undammed river churns through the forested canyonlands of this remote recreation area. A historic 1930s ranger station in Gasquet houses a visitor center. Kayaks, canoes, and rafts can run three of the wild river's forks. The most popular hiking trails climb to the alpine meadows of the Siskiyou Wilderness. The area's four campgrounds are less expensive, smaller, and less developed than those in the redwood parks to the west.

Crescent Beach

Two miles south of Crescent City on Enderts Beach Road, a picnic area flanks this popular beach. For the area's best tidepooling (and a quieter beach), drive another

2 miles to road's end, hike a scenic 0.6-mile section of the Coastal Trail south, and turn right through the walk-in Nickel Creek Campground to Enderts Beach.

California Coastal Trail

This ambitious trail, planned to extend the entire length of California's coast, includes a completed 44-mile segment through the redwood empire from Crescent Beach south to Orick. The Klamath River interrupts the trail, forcing long-distance hikers to detour inland on roads to the Highway 101 bridge. Elsewhere, much of the trail simply follows abandoned sections of Highway 101, and is used primarily by bicyclists. Hike #99 describes a scenic, unpaved portion of the path between Lagoon Picnic Area and the Klamath Overlook.

Trees of Mystery

Even if you skip the four themed nature trails and modern aerial tramway of this historic tourist trap, don't miss the astonishing and absolutely free museum of Native American artifacts at the back of the gift shop—among the best exhibits of its kind on the West Coast. Open 8:30am-6:30pm in summer and 9:30am-4:30pm in winter, it's on Highway 101, south of Crescent City 16 miles.

Klamath River

The Yurok Indian Reservation encompasses much of this wild river's lower canyon, but not the river mouth itself. Tribespeople keep alive the culture of the once powerful Yuroks, who built plank houses and carved huge sea-going canoes out of redwoods. The town of Klamath was swept away by a 1964 flood, but has been rebuilt with RV parks and a dock for jet boat tours upriver. For a sweeping view of the Klamath River's mouth, turn off Highway 101 north of the Klamath River bridge 3 miles and take Requa Road to the Klamath Overlook.

Enderts Beach just south of Crescent City.   Opposite: Footbridge near the Stout Grove.

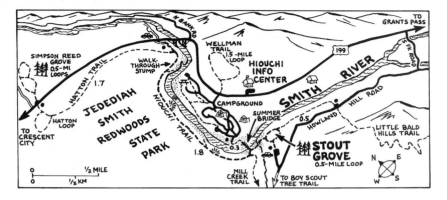

96   Stout Grove

Easy
0.5-mile loop
20 feet elevation gain

Moderate (via Hiouchi Trail)
4.1 miles round trip
100 feet elevation gain

    Towering above the green Smith River, the 44-acre Stout Grove was preserved by the Save-the-Redwoods League in 1929. Since then the grove has become the centerpiece of California's 9600-acre Jedediah Smith Redwoods State Park.

    Both the park and the river are named for Jedediah Strong Smith, the legendary mountain man who led the first party of white men overland from St. Louis to California in 1826. Because California's Mexican government did not welcome Americans, his crew of fur trappers trekked north through the redwood country to the mouth of Oregon's Umpqua River. Native Americans killed 15 of the group there, but Smith and three others escaped to Fort Vancouver. Three years later, at age 33, Smith was killed by Comanches while riding to Santa Fe. By then the tales and journals of his exploits had left his name emblazoned across the West.

    The redwoods here remain from Smith's day, but the trails are better. A good orientation point is the Hiouchi Information Center, open each summer on Highway 199, east of Crescent City 9 miles (or south of Grants Pass 77 miles). Dogs are not allowed on park trails.

    For the quickest route to the Stout Grove, drive Highway 199 east from the information center 2.1 miles, turn right on South Fork Road for 0.5 mile to a T-junction, and turn right on a one-lane road that becomes Howland Hill Road. After 1.5 miles you'll pass a pullout marked "Stout Grove Trail." The path that starts here follows the riverbank 0.5 mile before reaching the actual grove—a nice route, but most hikers skip it. Instead drive another 0.8 mile along Howland

Hill Road and turn right to a parking lot that's just a 150-yard walk from the Stout Grove's half-mile-long loop trail. Part way around the loop look for a fork that leads down 100 yards to a gravelly beach beside the Smith River. In summer, temporary plank footbridges cross Mill Creek and the river to the popular campground on the far shore.

For a more substantial hiking route to Stout Grove, try the Hiouchi Trail. To find it from the Hiouchi Visitors Center, drive Highway 199 west a mile to the far end of the Smith River Bridge, beside milepost 4.20. Park on the right (north), but the Hiouchi Trail itself heads left, following the Smith River bank upstream through a mixed forest of redwoods, Douglas fir, hemlock, and tanoak. Watch out for poison oak, growing both as a triple-leafletted bush and as a vine on tree trunks. The trail ducks through a 14-foot-thick redwood stump and passes viewpoints of river rapids. Just before reaching Mill Creek, take a left-hand spur to a river beach. Cross the beach's temporary footbridge across Mill Creek to the Stout Grove loop trail. When the bridge is removed in winter, cross Mill Creek at an easy, knee-deep ford.

Other Options

Jedediah Smith State Park has five other short loop trails through redwood groves. The most popular are the two connected half-mile loops through the Simpson Reed and Peterson groves, at milepost 2.9 of Highway 199. Across the road is the 0.2-mile Hatton Loop—a possible beginning point for a longer trek to Stout Grove. The 1.5-mile Wellman Trail loops over a ridge opposite the campground entrance. Finally, a 0.6-mile self-guided nature loop begins at the campground's picnic area.

97   Boy Scout Tree

Moderate (to Boy Scout Tree)
4.8 miles round trip
500 feet elevation gain

Moderate (to Fern Falls)
5.8 miles round trip
600 feet elevation gain

While crowds throng to the big redwoods in the Stout Grove (Hike #96), few hikers discover the even larger trees in this rainforest just a few miles away. A well-graded trail leads 2.4 miles to the 20-foot-thick Boy Scout Tree. An extra half mile walk takes you to lacy little Fern Falls. Dogs are not allowed.

Part of the fun of this trip is discovering the little road that meanders through giant groves to the trailhead. From Crescent City, drive Highway 101 half a mile south to a traffic light, turn left on Elk Valley Road for 1.1 mile, and turn right on Howland Hill Road. After 1.2 miles this road enters Jedediah Smith State Park and becomes a narrow, twisty track. Continue slowly another 2.5 miles to

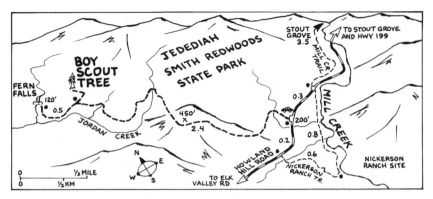

a long parking pullout on the left with a "Boy Scout Tree" trail sign. (To drive here from the Stout Grove, Hike #96, take Howland Hill Road 2.2 miles south.)

The path sets off through a great, ferny rainforest where redwoods tower above delicate white spring wildflowers: stalks of wild lily-of-the-valley, shamrock-leaved oxalis, and big, triple-leaved trillium.

After following the trail for two miles of gentle ups and downs you'll probably start wondering which of these giant redwoods is the Boy Scout colossus — and the trick is, it's not on the main trail. After crossing the third railed footbridge, continue 300 yards on the main trail. Then take a large scramble trail uphill to the right 60 feet to find the labeled Boy Scout Tree, two redwoods that grew together to create one behemoth trunk. If you continue on the main trail another half mile you'll traverse Jordan Creek's mossy jungle of alder, maple, and Sitka spruce to trail's end at the modest 20-foot fan of Fern Falls.

Redwoods in Jedediah Smith Park.   Opposite: The Boy Scout Tree.

Footbridge on the Damnation Creek Trail.

98   Damnation Creek   ☆🌲

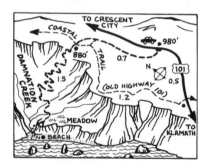

Difficult
4.4 miles round trip
1000 feet elevation **loss**

Massive redwoods line the trail down to the rocky beach at the mouth of Damnation Creek. The beach is in a wonderfully remote cove. Cliffs rise from the sea on either hand. Cormorants pose on white-stained rocks offshore. Green sea anemones line seaweedy tidepools. The only damnable part of the hike is that you have to gain a thousand feet of elevation to get back to your car. Dogs are banned.

To find the trailhead, drive 10 miles south of Crescent City into Del Norte Coast Redwoods State Park. Stop at a small pullout at the 16.0 mile marker of Highway 101. From the trailhead sign, take a wide path up to the right through a grand redwood forest. Among the big trees look for white trilliums in April, pink rhododendrons in May, and blue evergreen huckleberries in August.

After 0.7 mile the path crosses the Coastal Trail, an abandoned stretch of Highway 101 now used primarily as a paved bike route. This junction is a good turnaround point for hikers with children, because the Damnation Creek Trail promptly narrows and dives downhill in a series of switchbacks. Along the way the forest shifts from redwoods to Sitka spruce and Douglas fir, with thimbleberry bushes and maidenhair ferns. Finally the path crosses two side creeks on

Beach at the mouth of Damnation Creek. Below: Hidden Beach.

massive footbridges and enters a beachfront meadow. In summer this brushy garden blooms with big white cow parsnip, feathery white yarrow, purple iris, and a host of other coastal wildflowers.

If you continue straight, you'll cross an arch to a cliff-edge overlook of the beach. If you veer right in the meadow you'll find a scrambly path that descends across the driftwood of the creek's mouth to the beach itself. Normally the bouldery beach extends about 300 yards in either direction, but it disappears altogether at very high tides. Low tides reveal pools with sea anemones and black turban snails. On the horizon to the north are Sister Rocks and the cliffs of Midway Point. To the south are the onshore Footsteps Rocks and distant False Klamath Rock.

99   Hidden Beach

Easy (to Hidden Beach)
2.4-mile loop
100 feet elevation gain

Easy (to Klamath Overlook)
1 mile round trip
350 feet elevation gain

Moderate (entire trail, with shuttle)
4.1 miles one way
700 feet elevation gain

The prettiest part of the Redwood Coast's portion of the California Coastal Trail has no redwoods at all. Instead it traverses headland meadows and windswept Sitka spruce forests overlooking a dramatic, island-dotted shore. One short walk along this route leads to a viewpoint of the Klamath River's mouth. A different short walk visits Hidden Beach, a sandy cove with a ship-sized rock anchored in the surf. For a longer hike, shuttle a car and do the entire trail one way. Dogs are not allowed on these trails.

Start by driving Highway 101 south of Crescent City 14 miles (or 1 mile north of the Trees of Mystery) to the Lagoon Creek Picnic Area. Park at the far right-hand end of the picnic area. The trail that begins here skirts a lagoon full of yellow pond lilies. This slough is actually an old Klamath River channel, abandoned when the river found a shortcut through the sea cliffs 4 miles to the south. False Klamath Rock, a landmark island offshore, won its name because early sailors were sometimes fooled by this old, silted-up river entrance.

After 100 yards turn left on the Coastal Trail and cross a footbridge to the start of the Yurok Loop trail. The Yurok tribe still flourishes along the lower Klamath River. Historically, the Yuroks used the trunks of fallen redwoods to build plank houses and to carve huge sea-going canoes. They sailed to offshore rocks to gather mussels and hunt sea lions. In Yurok, False Klamath Rock is called *olrgr* ("digging place") because of the edible brodiaea wildflower bulbs there. A smaller rock near shore is *prgris-o-tsiguk,* "where bald eagle rests."

Following Coastal Trail pointers, traverse a meadow with views up and down the coast. Small white yarrow, big white cow parsnip, and daisy-like wild chrysanthemum bloom amongst the bracken ferns. After 0.6 mile the trail forks. To the left is the return route for the Yurok Loop, but don't take it yet. Instead veer right for another 0.6 mile on the Coastal Trail and take a right-hand spur to Hidden Beach. This secluded, sandy, quarter-mile-long cove is perfect for a picnic. If you've brought kids, they'll find plenty of driftwood and boulders to climb around on. Low tide exposes marine life among the rocks.

If you're not yet ready to return to your car, you can continue south on the Coastal Trail past Hidden Beach. This route climbs along bluffs above the rocky shore, passing increasingly dramatic viewpoints. The best view of all is at Klamath Overlook, near trail's end.

Even if you don't have a second car to shuttle to the Klamath Overlook trailhead for a one-way hike, consider driving here anyway, just so you can take the half-mile path down to the viewpoint. Wear long pants because the narrow path is bordered with blackberries and poison oak. Also bring binoculars. Bald eagles are common, and in summer you can watch brown pelicans dive into the river's mouth, scooping up fish to feed crowds of pelican babies on nearby islands.

To find this trailhead, drive Highway 101 south of Lagoon Creek Picnic Area 3.7 miles to a Klamath Overlook pointer and turn right on Requa Road for 2.4 miles to a parking area. The trail begins on the left, beside the parking lot's entrance.

Opposite: The Klamath River's mouth from Klamath Overlook.

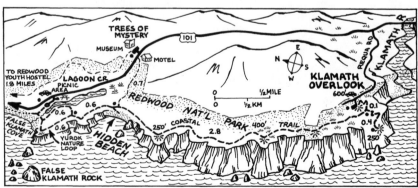

Roosevelt elk at Gold Bluffs Beach in Prairie Creek Redwoods State Park.

REDWOODS

Some of the world's tallest trees grow in this portion of the redwood coast. A network of trails and roads helps visitors explore the parklands. Elk and bear are common.

Redwood National Park
Discovery of the world's tallest trees in a bend of Redwood Creek in the 1960s led to the creation of this national park. By that time, nearly all old-growth redwoods outside of state parks had already been logged. To protect the remaining tall trees, the lower third of Redwood Creek's valley was added to the park and logging roads are being painstakingly removed. Note that pets are not allowed on national or state park trails in this region.

Kuchel (Redwood) Information Center
If you're coming from the south, make this visitor center on Highway 101 near Orick your first stop. In addition to maps, exhibits, and advice, the center features a nature trail boardwalk through coastal wetlands.

Tall Trees Grove
Only hikers can visit this grove with many of the world's tallest trees and the broken-topped former champion. The moderate 2-mile trail starts at the end of a 7-mile gravel spur off paved Bald Hills Road. A free permit, available at any of the park information centers, is required to take a private car on the trailhead road. Only 50 permits are available each day, starting at 9am. The only time it may be hard to get a permit is on a weekend afternoon in summer.

Redwood Creek Trail
A longer hiking route to the Tall Trees Grove follows the 8.2-mile Redwood Creek Trail, an old roadbed. In summer, two temporary footbridges across Redwood Creek make the trip an easy backpack (tenters with permits are allowed on gravel bars), but in winter the route is all but blocked by dangerous creek fords.

Lady Bird Johnson Grove
The paved Bald Hills Road from Orick climbs to this ridgetop grove of big redwoods, with a picnic area and a 1.3-mile loop trail. Lady Bird Johnson used

her position as first lady to support creation of Redwood National Park. President Nixon dedicated the park here in 1969.

Prairie Creek Redwoods State Park

Surrounded by the national park and bypassed by Highway 101's new freeway, this state park has the best redwood forests, the most hiking trails, and the only developed public campgrounds in the area. When driving north from Orick (or south from Klamath), be sure to take the Drury Scenic Parkway, a lovely portion of old Highway 101 through the park's redwoods. The parkway crosses Elk Prairie, a meadow that often really does have a herd of Roosevelt elk. Pullouts north of Elk Prairie allow travelers to see the Corkscrew Tree and Big Tree, a 304-foot giant circled by easy walking paths.

Elk Prairie Campground

In Prairie Creek Redwoods State Park 6 miles north of Orick, this mile-long meadow is bordered by a visitor center, a picnic area, and a 75-site campground. Campsite reservations, critical in summer, can be placed up to 7 months in advance by calling 800-444-7275. Stop at the visitor center here to see the displays, get free advice, and pick up a $1 map to the park's trails—many of which begin at the center's front door (see map below).

Coastal Drive

Redwoods, viewpoints, and a World War II radar station camouflaged as a farmhouse highlight this 8-mile loop road from the northern end of the Drury Parkway to Highway 101 at the Klamath River. Portions are unpaved, narrow, and closed to trailers or RVs.

Gold Bluffs Beach

Prospectors flocked to this remote beach in 1850 when grains of gold were discovered in the sand. Today, elk, redwoods, and the quiet beach are the big draws. Prairie Creek Redwoods State Park provides a 26-site campground in the beachside grass here, strictly on a first-come-first-served basis. Drive 3 miles north of Orick on Highway 101 and turn left on Davison Road (trailers and vehicles over 24 feet prohibited). Beyond the campground, the road ends at Fern Canyon Picnic Area, beside a misty grotto where Home Creek winds between green cliffs (see Hike #100 and map below).

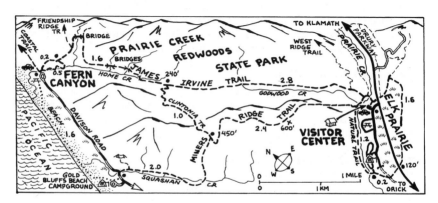

100   Fern Canyon

Easy (Fern Canyon)
0.7-mile loop
150 feet elevation gain

Moderate (to Clintonia Trail)
6.7-mile loop
500 feet elevation gain

Above: Fern Canyon.
Right: Redwood on Miners Ridge Trail.

Ferns cling to the sheer walls of this jungly grotto at Gold Bluffs Beach in Prairie Creek Redwoods State Park. A quick 0.7-mile loop through the canyon is fine if you're bringing the kids. But if you have time for a 6.7-mile loop, continue onward through groves of giant redwoods and return along the beach. Dogs and bicycles are not allowed. Expect to pay a small parking fee.

Drive Highway 101 south of Crescent City 38 miles (or north of Orick 3 miles) to a Gold Bluffs sign and turn west onto Davison Road. After just 0.4 mile this becomes a one-lane gravel road closed to trailers and motorhomes over 24 feet long. Drive slowly for 3.4 twisty miles down to a fee booth and then continue another 3.5 miles, splashing across a shallow ford or two, to road's end at a parking turnaround beside Home Creek.

Five wandering prospectors discovered gold here at the mouth of Fern Canyon in the spring of 1850. Within months a boomtown tent city sprang up. The bonanza faded when the miners realized the gold dust was so small it could only be separated from the beach sand with expensive processing.

To hike into Fern Canyon simply follow Home Creek upstream. In summer, planks are laid across the trail's half-dozen creek crossings. In winter, expect to wade. After half a mile the path climbs to a junction with the James Irvine Trail.

For the quick loop turn left to return to your car. For a longer loop through the redwoods, however, turn right. Hundreds of men stormed over this route in the spring of 1851 on their way to the gold strike. The modern trail crosses four footbridges in 1.6 miles. Then turn right on the Clintonia Trail for 1 mile and turn right again on the Miners Ridge Trail for 2 miles to descend to the Davison Road near the Gold Bluffs Beach Campground. Turn right and follow either the road or the beach 1.6 miles back to your car.

Barrier-Free Trails of the Oregon Coast & Coast Range

People with limited physical abilities need not miss the fun of exploring new trails. Here are dozens of paths accessible to everyone. To find the trails listed below, look for wheelchair symbols on the 18 Travel Guide overview maps throughout this book. Many campgrounds also have accessible campsites, restrooms, and yurts. To check site availability and to place reservations at state parks call 800-452-5687 or go to *www.oregonstateparks.org*.

LONG BEACH (map on page 16)

A. Discovery Trail. All of Hike #2 in the Long Beach area is barrier-free.

B. North Head Lighthouse. A gravel 0.3-mile path leads to the lighthouse (Hike #3).

C. Lewis & Clark Interpretive Center. Explore an artillery bunker along the 300-yard trail to this accessible museum and coastal vista (Hike #4).

ASTORIA (map on page 28)

D. Astoria. The entire 2.8-mile riverfront promenade is paved or planked, and the Columbia River Maritime Museum is also accessible (see Hike #9).

E. Warrenton Waterfront. A 4.5-mile trail along a dike and railroad grade starts at Skipanon River Park at 3rd St. in downtown Warrenton (map at *warrentontrails.org*) and follows the bird-rich Columbia riverbank to Seafarers Park.

F. Fort Stevens Park. The entire bicycle path network described in Hike #7 is barrier-free. So are several campsites and a 100-yard trail to a birdwatching blind from Clatsop Spit's parking lot D (Hike #6).

G. Fort Clatsop. The museum here is barrier-free, and so are many trails—to the fort replica, 1.2 miles to Netul Landing, 1.5 miles of gravel to Clatsop Overlook, and 0.3 mile to Sunset Beach's viewpoint (Hike #8).

SEASIDE (map on page 38)

H. Seaside Promenade. This concrete, 1.6-mile beachfront promenade (Hike #10) ends at a barrier-free restroom at 12th Street.

I. Ecola Park. From Ecola Point a paved 0.1-mile path leads to a viewpoint platform. From Indian Beach the gravel 1.2-mile trail to the backpacking shelters is demanding but barrier free (Hike #11).

J. Banks-Vernonia Railroad. This entire 20-mile trail is barrier free, as are many campsites and most cabins in Stewart Park (see Hike #15).

K. Manzanita. The city of Manzanita (see page 39) loans free, fat-tired wheelchairs to use on the beach. Reservations are required: *info@manzanitabikesandboards.com*.

L. Nehalem Bay Park. Traverse woods, grassy dunes, and bayshore on this park's paved, 1.5-mi bike path loop. A boat dock and three campsites are also barrier-free (see Hike #18).

TILLAMOOK (map on page 54)

M. Cape Meares Lighthouse. A paved 0.4-mile loop passes dramatic viewpoints of ocean cliffs and lighthouse (see Hike #21).

N. Wilson River. The Tillamook Forest Center and suspension footbridge are all-accessible, but trails on the far shore are not (Hike #22).

O. Hagg Lake. A 260-foot fishing pier at Boat Ramp C is barrier-free, and a lakeshore trail from Boat Ramp A is paved for 100 yards to a viewpoint (Hike #25).

PACIFIC CITY (map on page 78)

P. Cape Lookout Park. Go south from the day-use parking area on a 0.4-mi Nature Trail loop, or go north on a 0.2-mi loop through a wooded picnic area beside the beach. Two barrier-free campsites are nearby (Hike #26).

Q. Hebo Lake. The gravel and boardwalk 0.5-mile loop around this shallow lake passes four fishing docks and a barrier-free campsite (see Hike #28).

LINCOLN CITY (map on page 94)

R. Drift Creek Falls. The packed gravel trail is open to all for 1.3 miles, to the far end of the bridge overlooking the waterfall (Hike #36).

NEWPORT (map on page 102)

S. Oregon Coast Aquarium. This completely acces- *South Beach State Park.*
sible Newport museum has trails through outdoor
bird, seal, otter exhibits (see page 105).

T. Yaquina Bay Estuary. Signs describe estuarine ecology along an 0.7-mile paved bayfront path from the Hatfield Marine Science Center (Hike #40).

U. South Beach State Park. Take a paved path from campsite B-1 for 0.3 mile to a beach viewpoint, or take the paved South Jetty Trail a mile from the Day Use Area to the South Jetty (Hike #40).

WALDPORT (map on page 112)

V. Ona Beach Park. A paved 0.3-mile loop circles picnic lawns and forest to a 180-foot footbridge (see Hike #41).

W. Kings Valley. Gravel paths lead up Plunkett Creek 0.9 mile at Beazell Forest, and the fort site 0.5 mile at Fort Hoskins (Hike #46).

X. Jackson-Frazier Wetland. The Bob Frenkell boardwalk loops 0.8 mi to birdwatching benches at Corvallis' NE city limits. Drive Hwy 99 to N edge of town, turn R on Conifer Blvd 0.4 mi, turn L on Lancaster St 0.3 mi.

Y. Marys Peak. Park at Observation Pt and go around a gate to reach the graveled 0.6-mile trail to the summit (Hike #45). The nearby 6-site campground is also accessible.

Z. Finley Wildlife Refuge. Take the gravel 1.2-mile Woodpecker Loop to a viewpoint platform on an oak knoll. It's open all year, but the 2.9-mile Mill Hill Loop is accessible only in dry weather (Hike #48).

YACHATS (map on page 130)

AA. Yachats. The dramatic gravel path along a scenic lava shore from Smelt Sands Wayside is accessible for 0.7 mile, almost to the beach (Hike #50).

BB. Cape Perpetua. From the visitor center, take a 1-mi gravel path to the Giant Spruce or a paved 0.8-mile loop to tidepools and Cooks Chasm (Hike #51).

FLORENCE (map on page 140)

CC. Holman Vista. A 200-foot path from this picnic area to a viewpoint deck overlooks Sutton Creek and the coastal dunes (see Hike #55).

DD. Darlingtonia State Natural Site. A 100-yard boardwalk from a forested picnic area leads to a bog with insect-eating pitcher plants (see page 142).

EE. Coast Horse Trails. The trail network in Cape Mountain's forest is designed to let disabled equestrians park, mount, and ride. Wheelchairs can't use the trails, but the Horse Creek Trailhead has accessible campsites (Hike #56).

FF Sweet Creek Falls. Packed gravel makes the first 200 yards of Hike #59 accessible—a woodsy route from Homestead Trailhead to Split Falls.

GG. North Fork Smith River. At the lower trailhead for Hike #60, a graveled 0.7-mile loop tours a rainforest with old-growth Douglas fir 8 feet in diameter. 🌲

HH. Honeyman Park. From the campground's Loop B you can take a paved path across the highway 0.6 mile to Woahink Lake. From the Sand Dunes Picnic Area, you can take a 0.4-mi paved loop around Lily Lake (partly on a road), or take a paved path along Cleawox Lake's shore 0.6 mile (see Hike #61). 🚲

REEDSPORT (map on page 156)

II. Taylor Lake Dunes. A packed gravel trail amid rhodies and woods leads 0.1 mile to a lakeside deck, then climbs 0.4 mile to a dunes overlook platform (Hike #64).

JJ. Oregon Dunes. Take a 50-yard boardwalk ramp to a viewpoint of coastal dunes (see Hike #65). A naturalist is on hand daily from 10am to 3pm in summer.

KK. Tahkenitch Creek. The first 200 yards of Hike #66 is an accessible, packed gravel trail to a scenic 80-foot bridge over this lazy coastal creek.

LL. Umpqua Discovery Center. A barrier-free interpretive center features a 200-yard boardwalk along Reedsport's riverfront docks (see page 157).

MM. Lake Marie. Park at Umpqua Lighthouse Park's picnic beach and take a paved trail to the left along the shore 0.3 mile. The rest of the 1-mile lake loop is challenging (Hike #68).

COOS BAY (map on page 172)

NN. Empire Lakes. Topits Park off Newmark Street in Coos Bay has 4 miles of paved paths along forested lakeshores (map, page 172). 🚲

OO. Shore Acres Park. Paved trails follow oceanfront cliffs 0.3 mile from the observation building. Nearby, gravel paths tour the formal gardens (Hike #71).

PP. South Slough Estuary. Stop at this nature reserve's interesting interpretive center, get a key to the gate, drive 0.6 mile to the disabled parking, and take a woodsy 1.3-mile loop trail to the shore of Coos Bay's estuary (see Hike #72).

BANDON (map on page 180)

QQ. Bullards Beach Park. A 1.3-mile paved bike path from the campground fee booth crosses picnic areas, forest, to parking area at beach's foredune (Hike #74). The park has two barrier-free campsites nearby. 🚲

GOLD BEACH (map on page 196)

RR. Humbug Mountain Park. An old section of Hwy 101 forms a 2.6-mile segment of the Oregon Coast Trail from the campground fee booth through coastal woods to ocean viewpoints (see Hike #80 map). Nearby are two accessible campsites. 🚲

SS. Cape Sebastian. The first 300 yards of Hike #89 are paved, leading across a meadow to a dramatic ocean viewpoint.

BROOKINGS (map on page 222)

TT. Boardman Park. Stop at Arch Cape for an 0.2-mile paved viewpoint trail around the picnic area. Drive south 1.2 mile to Natural Bridges Cove Viewpoint for a 100-foot trail to an overlook of sea caves (see Hike #90).

UU. Oregon Redwoods. The upper trail to the hollow snag and picnic table is barrier free for 0.5 mile (Hike #95). 🌲

VV. Azalea Park. Wild azaleas bloom in May along the paved pathways of this forested Brookings park (see page 222).

CRESCENT CITY (map on page 234)

WW. Stout Grove. An unpaved but well-packed 0.5-mile loop tours Jedediah Smith State Park's grandest redwood grove (Hike #96). 🌲

REDWOODS (map on page 244)

XX. Elk Meadow. A paved bike path leads 0.4 mile from the Elk Meadow picnic area to a bridge with an elk viewing platform (see map for Hike #100).

More Hikes of the
Oregon Coast & Coast Range

Adventurous hikers can explore lots of additional paths in Oregon's coastal country. Many of the trails themselves are rough, and descriptions are brief, so be sure to bring appropriate maps. Unless noted, mileages given are one way, not round trip. For more information, check with the trail's administrative agency, abbreviated (C) — City of Corvallis, (CF) — Central Coast Ranger District / Florence, (CS) — California State Parks, (CW) — Central Coast Ranger District / Waldport, (F) — Finley Wildlife Refuge, (G) — Gold Beach Ranger District, (OF) — Oregon Dept of Forestry, (OD) — Oregon Dunes Nat'l Rec Area, (OS) — Oregon State Parks, (OSU) — OSU Research Forest, (P) — Powers Ranger District, (R) — Redwood Nat'l Park, (WR) — Willapa Wildlife Refuge. Phone numbers for agencies are on page 13.

LONG BEACH (map on page 16)

101. Long Island Cedar Grove. An 0.8-mi loop tours old-growth cedars on a Willapa Bay island (map, p 14). From Willapa Refuge HQ (12 mi N of Ilwaco on Hwy 101) paddle a boat to island, walk rd 2.5 mi to tr. (WR)

102. Columbian White-Tailed Deer Refuge. Once thought extinct, this deer species survives on Columbia riverbank fields. Drive 2 mi W of Cathlamet, Washington (or 29 mi W of Longview) on Hwy 4, turn L on Steamboat Slough Rd 0.3 mi, park on R just beyond refuge HQ. Walk gated Center Rd 2.8 mi (expect swans, geese, ducks), turn L for 3.3 mi on Steamboat Slough Rd along Columbia R dike to return to car. (WR)

ASTORIA (map on page 28)

103. Gnat Creek. Hike 3.5 mi from a small campground up a woodsy creek, or sample just half a mile from a fish hatchery to a small falls. Drive Hwy 30 E of Astoria 20 mi (or W or Rainier 31 mi). Near milepost 78, park at either the hatchery or the campground, where the 4 walk-in sites run $5 a night.(OF)

104. Cathedral Tree. Popular 0.8-mi trail in Astoria starts on Irving Ave at 28th St, climbs to Cathedral Tree (giant spruce), continues to Astoria Column on Coxcomb Hill, gaining 400 ft. (Astoria Parks, 800-875-6807)

TILLAMOOK (map on page 54)

105. Cedar Butte. Climb 21 switchbacks in 0.7 mi to this rocky knoll overlooking the Tillamook State Forest. Drive 18 mi E of Tillamook on Hwy 6. Near milepost 18, turn L on Cedar Bu Rd for 5.6 miles of steep, rough, narrow gravel to trailhead *(GPS: N45° 34.97' W123° 38.76')*. (OF)

106. University Falls. This 100-ft cascade can be reached either by a 0.5-mile path (drive south from summit of Hwy 6 and follow signs) or by a 8.4-mi loop from Rogers Camp Trailhead, although the longer route crosses many logging roads and motorcycle trails. See map, p 64. (OF)

PACIFIC CITY (map on page 78)

107. Hebo Plantation Trail. An 0.7-mi loop tours Douglas fir woods replanted in 1912. Drive as to Mt. Hebo (Hike #28), but stop at hiker-symbol sign 0.9 mi before Hebo L. (Hebo Ranger District)

WALDPORT / CORVALLIS (map on page 112)

108. Little Luckiamute River. Follow a Coast Range river amid mossy maples and Doug firs for 1 easy mile and an additional 1.5 faint miles to a brushy clearcut. From Falls City, drive Black Rock Rd 0.4 mi, fork L for 3.3 mi on gravel, park at gate, walk across bridge 200 yd to trail on L. (Salem BLM)

109. Calloway Creek. This nature trail near Corvallis loops 3.3 mi through experimental Doug fir plantations, crosses creek (see Hike #46 map). Drive into Peavy Arboretum, keep R for 0.2 mi to "Additional Parking" lot. Start on Intensive Management Trail, keep L. (OSU)

110. McDonald Forest Old Growth. Drive 4 mi N of Corvallis on Hwy 99W, turn L on Lewisburg Ave 1.5 mi, turn R on Sulphur Spgs Rd 1.5 mi to Lewisburg Saddle. Hike gated Rd 580 on right for 0.3 mi, turn L onto 0.5-mi Old Growth Tr loop, turn R on Rd 580 for 0.8 mi to return to car. (OSU)

111. McCullough Peak. Hike 4.2 mi on mtn bike trails, gated rds through McDonald Forest to vista. Drive 5 mi W of Corvallis on Harrison Blvd (which becomes Oak Cr Dr) to gate blocking the rd. Hike L on Homestead Tr 0.4 mi, keep R on log rds 0.7 mi, jog L 100 ft on Rd 6020, continue uphill on Extendo Tr 1 mi, turn left on Rd 680, and keep left at all rd jcts (except avoid Rd 770) for 2.1 mi to find summit viewpoint at end of Rd 1790. (OSU)

112. Alsea River Run. Rough 1-mi riverbank trail through maples, blackberries. Drive Hwy 34 E of Waldport 17 mi (or W of Corvallis 47 mi), cross river at Mike Bauer boat ramp, keep L for 1.5 mi to parking lot at switchback. (CW)

113. Bald Hill. A 284-acre Corvallis city park on Oak Cr Rd by the Benton Co Fairgrounds offers a 3-mi loop that gains 400 ft up this oak-dotted butte. From the same trailhd, the Mulkey Cr Tr ambles 1.2 mi to a creek bridge, then climbs 0.8 mi to a viewpoint on Benton Co land. (CC)

114. Cabell Marsh. Just E of Finley Wildlife Refuge HQ (Hike #48) walk gated rd 0.8 mi along diked marsh. Turn left along 0.8-mi Muddy Cr Tr for return loop. Or turn right for 2.1 mi to Pigeon Butte. Only open 4/1 to 10/31. (F)

115. Pigeon Butte. Grassy oak knoll with Willamette Valley views is 1.7 mi up gated old rds. Drive Hwy 99W to milepost 96 (S of Corvallis 13 mi), turn W on Bruce Rd 1 mi to hiker-symbol sign. Only open 4/1 to 10/31. (F)

YACHATS (map on page 130)

116. Cummins Ridge. A car shuttle is recommended when hiking this 6-mi trail down a viewless, forested Wilderness ridge, losing 1200 ft of elevation. Drive Hwy 101 to MP 169 (4 mi S of Yachats) and take gravel Rd 1051 2.2 mi to the lower trailhead. For the upper trailhead, drive Hwy 101 south for 2.5 mi, turn left on Tenmile Cr Rd for 2mi, fork left on Rd 5694 for 8.2 mi, and turn left on Rd 515 for 0.3 mi to its end. See map on p 130. (CW)

117. Rock Creek. A rough trail follows the left bank of this coastal creek into a Wilderness rainforest, but peters out after 0.2 mile. Start at the far end of the Rock Cr Campground, 16 mi N of Florence off Hwy 101 (map, p 130). (CW)

FLORENCE (map on page 140)

118. Alder Lake. 0.5-mi tr circles forest lake at N end of Alder Dune CG (see Hike #55). At S end of CG, sand slide descends into Dune Lake. (CF)

119. Enchanted Valley. Elk roam this abandoned dairy farm. Hike 1.6 mi path to upper end of mdw. Drive 5 mi N of Florence on Hwy 101, turn R on Mercer Lk Rd 3.7 mi, fork L on Twin Fawn Dr 0.3 mi to rd's end. (CF)

REEDSPORT (map on page 156)

120. Threemile Lake South. Woodsy 0.6-mi tr leads to fork: go left 0.2 mi to open dunes and campsite (0.5 mi from ocean), or go right 0.2 mi to beach at tip of long lake. Drive 4 mi N of Reedsport on Hwy 101, turn left on Spar-

Easy · Moderate · Difficult

row Park Rd 3.4 mi to a small sign on the right (see map on page 167). (OD)

121. Umpqua Spit. Circle this sand peninsula on a 13.1-mi loop. Drive 4 mi N of Reedsport on Hwy 101, turn L on Sparrow Park Rd 4 mi to its end, walk 100 yds to beach (vehicles allowed on beach), hike left 5.7 mi to Umpqua R jetty, continue L through grassy dunes along river 4.8 mi, cut L across spit 1.3 mi on dune buggy track, turn R along beach 1.3 mi to car. (OD)

122. Reedsport Dike. Walk dike (built after 1964 flood to protect Reedsport) along scenic slough 1 mi from Hwy 101 to riverfront district. Park at Scholfield Market on Hwy 101 at 16th St. 📖

123. Tenmile Creek Dunes. Secluded, scenic portion of Oregon Dunes (no vehicles), ideal for birdwatching. Park at Spinreel CG picnic area, N of Coos Bay 11 mi (see map p 168), wade across cr, follow cr 2.6 mi through dunes to beach. Avoid snowy plover habitat in driftwood zone. (OD) 📖

COOS BAY (map on page 172)

124. Bluebill Lake. Forested 1-mi loop around lakeless meadow (good birding in spring) passes Bluebill CG, crosses boardwalks. Drive 1 mi N of Coos Bay's Hwy 101 bridge, turn L toward Horsfall Bch 2.7 mi. (OD) 📖

125. Oregon's Largest Douglas Fir. The 0.5-mi trail to this 329-foot behemoth is easy, but the drive is long and hard. Take Interstate 5 south of Roseburg 3 mi to exit 119, drive 3 mi to Winston, turn R on Hwy 42 for 9 mi, turn R on Reston Rd 4.5 mi, turn L on Coos Bay Wagon Rd 1.5 mi, turn R on Burnt Mtn Rd 7.3 mi, fork L for 4.6 mi, and turn L on gravel Rd 27-9-21.0 for 4.3 mi to the Doerner Fir pullout on the L. (Coos Bay BLM, 541-756-0100) 🐾🥾

126. Millicoma Marsh. Look for birds on a 1-mile loop or a 0.5-mi path, both along Coos Bay slough. From Hwy 101 at S end of Coos Bay, follow "Allegany" sign E to bridge, turn L on 6th Ave 0.5 mi, turn L on D St 2 blocks, turn R on 4th Ave to school field. Trails begin at right-hand end of track. 📖

127. Wasson Creek. Two 0.7-mi loops explore mdw, breached dikes, lazy creek of former farm in South Slough Reserve. Drive as to Hike #72, but continue 1 mi S on 7 Devils Rd, turn L on Hinch Rd 1 mi. (S Slough Res) 📖

GOLD BEACH (map on page 196)

128. Barklow Mountain. Hike 0.6 mi through woods to a viewpoint at a former lookout site, then take a 0.4-mi spur to a collapsed shelter. From Powers, drive 11.5 mi S on Rd 33, turn R on gravel Rd 3353 for 11 mi. (P) 🐾

129. Sucker Creek Trail. Yellow iris, 7-ft-thick Doug fir line this trail above Sucker Cr. From Powers, drive 11.5 mi S on Rd 33, turn R for 3.1 mi on Rd 3353, turn L on Rd 5591 for 1.4 mi. Trail promptly crosses creek (slippery 20-ft wade), then gains 1200 ft in 2.4 mi to end at spur 260 of Rd 3353. (P) 🏕🥾

130. Azalea Lake. Wild azaleas bloom in May at brush-rimmed lake. Tr gains 640 ft in 0.8 mi, then circles lake 0.4 mi. Drive Rd 33 south of Powers 34.1 mi (or N of Agness bridge 15.3 mi), turn W on Rd 3347 past Rock Cr CG 1 mi. (P)

131. Grassy Knob. A half-mile trail climbs an old roadbed to this lookout site, targeted by a Japanese bomber in World War II. Take Highway 101 north of Port Orford 4 miles and turn right on Grassy Knob Road for 7.7 miles to its end. (P)

132. Game Lake. From a primitive CG at this remote lake, the steep, rough Pupp's Camp Trail 1174 descends 3500 ft in 6 mi to a treacherous Illinois R ford at Collier Bar (see Hike #87), and the faint Lawson Butte Trail 1173 descends 13 mi to the Illinois R mouth. Drive 1 mi S of Gold Beach, turn L for 27.4 mi on Hunter Cr Rd (which becomes Rd 3680), veer R on Rd 400 for 5.5 mi. (G) ❄

BROOKINGS (map on page 222)

133. Windy Valley. Expect knobcone pines, insect-eating pitcher plants, Port

Orford cedars, and wild azaleas on the 2-mi trail to this lovely mountain meadow. The route gains 500 ft and is open May-Nov. From the Hwy 101 bridge in Brookings, take N Bank Rd for 8 mi and go straight on Rd 1376 another 8 mi to a bridge. Turn L to stay on gravel Rd 1376 for 13 mi to signed trailhead on the left *(GPS N42° 18.70' W124° 08.22')*. (G)　❄ ❀ ⚲ 🏠 🚲

134. Snow Camp Mountain. Walk 0.1 mile to a viewpoint atop this Klamath peak—and a fire lookout tower you can rent for $40 a night between June 17 and Sept 30 (*www.recreation.gov*). Then hike steeply downhill 2.1 mi to Snow Camp Mdw or 2.5 mi to Windy Valley. Drive as to Windy Valley (#133) but continue 4 mi farther on Rd 1376. (G)　❄

135. Chetco Gorge. Wade Chetco R (only possible in summer) to access easy 1.7-mi riverbank tr. From Brookings, take N Bank Rd (#1376) 16 mi to T-jct. Turn L for 0.6 mi, then turn L on Rd 170 to trailhd. (G)　❄

136. Tincup Trail. Prospector's trail gains 1450 ft in 3.6 mi along canyon slope to remote Chetco R bar at edge of Kalmiopsis Wilderness. From Bookings take N Bank Rd (#1376) 16 mi to T-jct, turn L to continue on Rd 1376 another 10 mi to milepost 18, turn R on Rd 360 for 3 rough mi to road's end. (G)❄

137. Upper Chetco River. Tr #1102 crosses Kalmiopsis Wilderness 17.5 mi, scales rocky ridges, meets Chetco River 3 times. From Brookings take N Bank Rd (#1376) 16 mi to T-jct, follow signs 10 mi to Quail Prairie Lookout, continue 0.3 mi to tr. (G)　❄ ⚲

138. Chetco Divide. Park as for Vulcan Pk (Hike #92), follow rocky Tr #1210 along ridge 4.7 mi to brushy Chetco L, continue 2.3 mi to lookout site. Gains 1300 ft, loses 500. (G)　❄

139. South Fork Chetco River. Start on Chetco Divide Tr (Hike #138) for 1.5 mi, turn R on Tr #1105 and descend either 2400 ft in 2.5 mi to Cottonwood Camp or 2700 ft in 3.2 mi to Navy Monument (1944 plane crash site). Both forks reach campsites near remote river. (G)　❄ ⚲

140. Sourdough Trail. Pitcher plants, odd Klamath flora line 3.9-mi tr from Packsaddle Mtn to bridgeless N Fk Smith River. Loses 1300 ft elevation. From Brookings, drive S for 5 mi on Hwy 101, turn L on Winchuck Rd 8 mi, turn R on gravel Rd 1107 for 10 mi, turn R on Rd 220 for 1 mi. (G)

CRESCENT CITY (map on page 234)

141. Yontocket. Explore Smith R Spit, remote beach, site of Indian village along closed roads through grassy dunes in Lake Earl State Wildlife Area. Drive Hwy 101 N of Crescent City 6 mi, turn L on Elk Valley Rd 1 mi, turn R on Lk Earl Dr 2 mi, turn L on Lower Lk Rd 6 mi, turn L on Pala Rd 1 mi to gate. Walk past gate 1 mi to village site. Turn R on old rds to Smith R (0.6 mi) and beach (0.8 mi). Mouth of Smith R is 2.5 mi beyond. (CS)　𝆕

142. Craigs Creek. Tr along S Fk Smith R leads 7.4 mi to mouth of Craigs Cr. Drive Hwy 199 E of Hiouchi 2 mi (or E of Crescent City 11 mi), turn R on S Fk Rd 0.4 mi. (Smith River Nat'l Rec Area, 707- 457-3131)　🌲

143. Mill Creek Campground. In Del Norte Redwoods SP, hike 2 mi around CG on loop trail through young redwoods, along creek. The connecting Hobbs Wall Tr climbs 2 mi from CG toward Hwy 101. (CS)　🌲 🐾

REDWOODS (map on page 244)

144. South Fork Loop. Expect big redwoods on 3.2-mi loop from pullout at milepost 129 of Drury Scenic Parkwy. Hike S Fk Tr 0.8 mi (gains 600 ft), turn L on Rhododendron Tr 1.2 mi, turn L on Brown Cr Tr for 1.2 mi to car. (CS)🌲

145. Trillium Falls. This moderate 2.5-mile loop begins at a meadow full of grazing elk and weaves through old redwood groves to a ferny grotto with a small, tumbling brook. From Orick drive Hwy 101 north 3 mi, turn L on Davison Rd for 0.4 mi, and turn L to the Elk Mdw Day Use Area. (R) 🌲 🐾

Index

Victorian home in Astoria.

About the Author

William L. Sullivan is the author of eighteen books and numerous articles about Oregon, including an "Oregon Trails" column for the Eugene *Register-Guard* and the Salem *Statesman-Journal*. A fifth-generation Oregonian, Sullivan began hiking at the age of five and has been exploring new trails ever since. After receiving an English degree from Cornell University and studying at Germany's Heidelberg University, he completed an M.A. in German at the University of Oregon.

In 1985 Sullivan set out to investigate Oregon's wilderness on a 1,361-mile solo backpacking trek from the state's westernmost shore at Cape Blanco to Oregon's easternmost point in Hells Canyon. His journal of that two-month adventure, published as *Listening for Coyote*, was chosen by the Oregon Cultural Heritage Commission as one of Oregon's "100 Books."

Information about Sullivan's speaking schedule, his books, and his favorite adventures is available online at *www.oregonhiking.com*.

He and his wife Janell live in Eugene, but spend summers at the log cabin they built by hand on a remote, roadless tract in Oregon's Coast Range. Sullivan's memoir, *Cabin Fever*, chronicles the adventure of building that cabin retreat.